CONTENTS

S0-BAQ-066

FINNISH:
AN ESSENTIAL
GRAMMAR

Fred Karlsson

London and New York

First published 1983 as *Finnish Grammar*
by WSOY, Helsinki

New edition published 1999
by Routledge
11 New Fetter Lane, London EC4P 4EE

Simultaneously published in the USA and Canada
by Routledge
29 West 35th Street, New York, NY 10001

Reprinted 2001, 2002

Routledge is an imprint of the Taylor & Francis Group

© 1983; 1999 Fred Karlsson
Translated by Andrew Chesterman

Typeset in Times by The Florence Production, Stoodleigh, Devon
Printed and bound in Great Britain by MPG Books Ltd, Bodmin

British Library Cataloguing in Publication Data
A catalogue record for this book is available from the British Library

Library of Congress Cataloguing in Publication Data
Karlsson, Fred,
    [Finsk grammatik. English]
    Finnish: an essential grammar / Fred Karlsson; [translated by
Andrew Chesterman].
    p. cm. – (Routledge grammars)
    Revised and updated version of: Finnish grammar. Helsinki : WSOY
[Werner Söderström Osakeyhtiö], 1983. Finnish grammar is a translation of
Suomen peruskielioppi, 1982, a translation of: Finsk grammatik. Originally
published: Helsinki : Finnish Literature Society (Suomalaisen Kirjallisuuden
Seura), 1978.
    Includes bibliographical references and index.
    1. Finnish language – Grammar. 2. Finnish language – Textbooks for
foreign speakers – English. I. Chesterman, Andrew. II. Title. III. Series.
PH135.K35 1999
494′.5415–dc21   98–55439
                                             CIP

ISBN 0–415–20705–3 (pbk)
ISBN 0–415–20704–5 (hbk)

PREFACE

Finnish: An Essential Grammar is a slightly modified version of the book *Finnish Grammar* published by WSOY in Helsinki in 1983. The second edition went out of print in 1995. *Finnish Grammar* was a translation of the Finnish book *Suomen peruskielioppi* published in 1982. The original Swedish edition *Finsk grammatik* appeared in 1978. These versions were published by the Finnish Literature Society (Suomalaisen Kirjallisuuden Seura), Helsinki.

Finnish: An Essential Grammar is primarily intended for those wanting to learn the basics of the language. The book covers the grammatical core; rare forms and constructions have not been included. I have tried to formulate the grammatical rules as precisely as possible using reasonable terminology. At the same time, all essentials should be easy to find in the numerous examples.

The book relies on some basic insights of modern linguistics and might therefore serve as an introduction to the structure of Finnish for professional linguists as well. Chapters 3 and 7 contain surveys of the word and clause structure, respectively, and for those readers unfamiliar with the basics it is recommended that these are read first.

In this edition, compared to the previous versions, I have changed the typography of the grammatical rules, written more on Finnish pronunciation, and updated many examples.

My sincere thanks are due to Professor Andrew Chesterman, who skilfully and critically made the translation, to the anonymous referee of Routledge who suggested several improvements, and to the Finnish Ministry of Education for financially supporting the original translation in 1982. Last but not least: thank you, Sylvi, as well as Max, Linn and Maj for continuous support!

Fred Karlsson
Helsinki, November 1998

Some twenty-five amendments and corrections have been made to this first reprint, mainly inspired by reviews by Hannele Branch (*Scandinavica* 39:1, 2000), and John Dingley (to be published in the journal *Scandinavian-Canadian Studies*).

Fred Karlsson
Helsinki, June 2000

ABBREVIATIONS

-V-	a vowel which is the same as the nearest preceding vowel
+	resulting weak grade in consonant gradation
=	internal word boundary
~	sound alternation
:	relation between different stems of a word, e.g. **käsi** 'hand' : **käde/ssä** 'in the hand'
/	boundary between stem and ending, or between endings, e.g. **käde/ssä/ni** 'in my hand'
§	section
ablat.	ablative
adess.	adessive
allat.	allative
cf.	compare
cond.	conditional
elat.	elative
emph.	emphatic
ess.	essive
gen.	genitive
illat.	illative
imp.	imperative
indic.	indicative
iness.	inessive
inf.	infinitive
intrans.	intransitive
lit.	literally
masc.	masculine
nom.	nominative
p.	person
part.	partitive
pass.	passive
pl.	plural
pot.	potential
pres.	present
sing.	singular
sth.	something
trans.	transitive
transl.	translative

1 INTRODUCTION

- *The relation of Finnish to other languages*
- *Finnish past and present*
- *The basic characteristics of Finnish*
- *What are the special difficulties?*

§1 THE RELATION OF FINNISH TO OTHER LANGUAGES

The Finnish language is a member of the Finno-Ugric language family. This is quite different from the Indo-European family, to which languages such as Swedish, English, French, German, Russian, Persian and Hindi belong. Only four of the major Finno-Ugric languages are spoken outside Russia: Finnish, Estonian, Hungarian and the Sámi ('Lappish') languages in the north of Finland, Norway, Sweden and the far north-west of Russia. The term 'Lappish' is derogatory.

The languages most closely related to Finnish are Estonian, Karelian, Vepsian, Ludian, Votian and Livonian, which are all spoken around the south and east of the Gulf of Finland. Of these Finnic languages Finnish and Estonian are spoken most widely. These two are so similar in grammar and vocabulary, so closely related, that after a little practice Finns and Estonians can understand each other's languages fairly well. If we group together the other Finno-Ugric languages according to their relations to each other and to Finnish, we have the following traditional picture:

The Finno-Ugric languages

Finnish	Estonian	Sámi (Lapp)	Mordvin	Komi (Zyryan)	Hanti (Ostyak)
	Karelian		Mari (Cheremis)	Udmurt (Votyak)	Mansi (Vogul)
	Vepsian				Hungarian
	Ludian				
	Votian				
	Livonian				

→ → → → → → increasing distance from Finnish → → → → → →

Finnish and Hungarian are thus quite distant from each other, and the relation between these two languages can really only be established on historical linguistic grounds. Roughly speaking, Finnish is as far from Hungarian as English or German is from Persian.

Samoyed languages are spoken by a few small groups of people in the north of Russia, especially in western Siberia. The Finno-Ugric languages and the Samoyed languages constitute the Uralic language family. The number of speakers of Uralic languages varies considerably. Six Uralic languages have more than 500,000 speakers: Hungarian (14 million), Finnish (5 million), Estonian (1 million), Mordvin (Erzya and Moksha, 750,000), Mari (550,000), and Udmurt (500,000). Several Uralic languages have very few speakers and their future is gravely endangered. This is true of all four remaining Samoyed languages, and of Hanti (13,000), Mansi (3,000), the ten Sámi languages (30,000), Livonian (30), Votian (50), Ludian (5,000), and Vepsian (6,000).[1]

§2   FINNISH PAST AND PRESENT

The size of the population of Finland on 31 December 1997 was 5,147,349 persons. The distribution of language speakers, according to first (native) language, is given in the table below (source: Statistics Finland, Internet address **http://www.stat.fi/tk/tilsivu.html**).

Population of Finland by first language

	1900	1950	1980	1995	1996	1997	1997
Language	%	%	%	%	%	%	Number
Finnish	86.75	91.10	93.50	92.92	92.86	92.74	4,773,576
Swedish	12.89	8.64	6.28	5.76	5.73	5.71	293,691
Sámi	0.06	0.06	0.03	0.03	0.03	0.03	1,716
Russian	0.29	0.12	0.03	0.31	0.35	0.40	20,398
Other	0.01	0.08	0.16	0.98	1.03	1.13	57,968
Sum							5,147,349

Finnish is the native language of 92.7 per cent of Finland's population of 5.15 million people. The population also includes a minority group of about 294,000 Swedish-speaking Finns, the Finland Swedes, who are guaranteed the same basic rights as the Finnish-speaking majority by the country's constitution, about 2,000 Sámi-speaking people, 6,000 gypsies (the number of Romany speakers is not known), about 5,000 deaf people, whose first language is Finnish sign language, and about a thousand Tatars. Since the collapse of the Soviet Union, more than 10,000 people belonging mostly to Finno-Ugric minorities in the west of Russia (especially Ingrians)

1 Up-to-date information in English on the Uralic languages is provided on the Internet pages **http://www.helsinki.fi/hum/sugl/fgrlang.html** and **http://www.helsinki.fi/~tasalmin/fu.html**.

have emigrated to Finland. The overall proportion of foreigners resident in Finland is much smaller than in continental European countries.

Finland is officially a bilingual country, whose national languages are Finnish and Swedish. Waves of emigration have resulted in large Finnish-speaking minorities particularly in North America (both the USA and Canada) and in Sweden. In Sweden today there are approximately 300,000 Finns, i.e. about the same number as there are Swedish-speaking Finns in Finland.

The earliest archaeological remains unearthed in Finland are from 7,500 BC, but it has not been possible to determine the cultural and language background of the first inhabitants. There were Finno-Ugric settlements in Finland as long ago as 4,000 BC. This population incorporated Baltic elements around 2,000 BC and Germanic elements as early as c. 1,500 BC. The original population thus formed then absorbed the Baltic Finns from across the Gulf of Finland about 2,000 years ago. Politically, Finland was a part of Sweden until 1809, and an autonomous Grand Duchy within Tsarist Russia from 1809 to 1917. Finland has been an independent republic since 1917.

During the Swedish period Finnish was very much a secondary language in official contexts. Its basic public use was in church services and to some extent in law enforcement. The language of the administration and the intelligentsia was Swedish. It was not until 1863 that Finnish was decreed to have equal status with Swedish 'in all matters directly concerning the Finnish-speaking population of the country', to be implemented within a 20-year period of transition.

The earliest actual texts in Finnish date from the 1540s. The father of written Finnish is considered to be Mikael Agricola (1510?–1557), the Bishop of Turku (Åbo), who started the Finnish translation of parts of the Bible during the Reformation. Some 5,350 of the words used by Agricola are still used in contemporary Finnish.

Finnish was greatly influenced by Swedish for a long time, especially as regards its vocabulary, which was quite natural considering that the authorities were generally Swedish-speaking. Since Turku (Åbo) was the capital city until 1827, it is understandable that standard Finnish developed primarily out of south-western dialects. In the nineteenth century there was increasing influence from eastern Finland, mostly owing to the national epic *Kalevala*, the first edition of which was published in 1835. The *Kalevala* is based on the folk poetry of eastern Finland and Karelia, as collected and compiled by Elias Lönnrot and others. The *Kalevala* was an important source of inspiration for the nineteenth century nationalist movement, whose central figure was Johan Vilhelm Snellman.

The nationalist movement also had a variety of linguistic effects. Many language scholars wanted to 'finnicize' Finnish by getting rid of Swedish loan words and a number of grammatical structures borrowed directly from Swedish.

Language is not a uniform system: it varies in different ways, for example in regional dialects. The main dialect areas of Finnish are shown on the following map.

FINLAND'S DIALECT AREAS

regional dialects

1. South-western dialects
2. South-western transition dialects
3. Häme dialects
4. Southern Ostrobothnian dialects
5. Central and northern Ostrobothnian dialects
6. Northern dialects
7. Savo dialects
8. South-eastern dialects
▨ Swedish-speaking areas

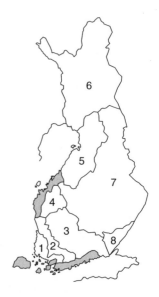

In the latter half of the twentieth century this traditional picture of dialect areas has been radically levelled by urbanization, mass education, improved means of communication and transport, and other societal processes. However, this book does not deal with regional dialects and their differences. Instead, we shall be concerned with the official norm of the language, Standard Finnish, one important variant of which is normal written prose. But even the standard language is not completely uniform. Its grammatical structures and also (in spoken Standard Finnish) its pronunciation both vary slightly depending on the speech situation and a number of other factors. The standard language spoken in official or formal situations is grammatically close to the written norm; but colloquial spoken Finnish differs in many ways from more formal usage in both pronunciation and grammar. The differences between everyday and more formal Finnish are discussed in more detail in Chapter 22.

§3   THE BASIC CHARACTERISTICS OF FINNISH

The basic principle of word formation in Finnish is the addition of endings (bound morphemes, suffixes) to stems. For example, by attaching the endings **-i** 'plural', **-ssa** 'in', **-si** 'your', and **-kin** 'too, also' to the stem **auto** 'car' in different ways, the following words can be formed.

auto/ssa	in the car	(car/in)
auto/i/ssa	in the cars	(car/s/in)
auto/ssa/si	in your car	(car/in/your)
auto/si	your car	(car/your)
auto/kin	the car too	(car/too)
auto/si/kin	your car too	(car/your/too)
auto/ssa/kin	in the car too	(car/in/too)
auto/i/ssa/kin	in the cars too	(car/s/in/too)
auto/i/ssa/si/kin	in your cars too	(car/s/in/your/too)

Finnish verb forms are built up in the same way. Using the verb stem **sano-** 'say', and the endings **-n** 'I', **-i** 'past tense', and **-han** 'emphasis', we can form these examples:

sano/n	I say	(say/I)
sano/n/han	I do say	(say/I/emphasis)
sano/i/n	I said	(say/past/I)
sano/i/n/han	I did say	(say/past/I/emphasis)

The adding of endings to a stem is a morphological feature of many European languages, but Finnish is nevertheless different from most others in two respects.

In the first place Finnish has more case endings than is usual in European languages. Finnish case endings normally correspond to prepositions or postpositions in other languages: cf. Finnish **auto/ssa**, **auto/sta**, **auto/on**, **auto/lla** and English '*in* the car', '*out of* the car', '*into* the car', '*by* car'. Finnish has about 15 cases; English nouns have only one 'morphologically marked' case.

The second difference is that Finnish sometimes uses endings where Indo-European languages generally have independent words. This is also true of the Finnish possessive suffixes, which correspond to possessive pronouns, e.g. **-ni** 'my', **-si** 'your', **-mme** 'our', cf. **kirja/ni** 'my book', **kirja/mme** 'our book'.

Another set of endings particular to Finnish is that of the enclitic particles, which always occur in the final position after all other endings. It is not easy to say exactly what these particles mean; their function is often emphasis of some kind, similar to that of intonation in some other languages. The particles include **-kin** 'too, also', **-han** 'emphasis' (often in the sense 'you know, don't you?'), and **-ko** 'interrogative', cf. **kirja/ssa/kin** 'in the book too', and **On/ko tuo kirja?** 'Is that a book?'.

Another characteristic feature of Finnish is the wide-ranging use made of endings in the formation of new independent words. Compare the basic word **kirja** 'book' with the derived forms **kirj/e** 'letter', **kirja/sto** 'library', **kirja/llinen** 'literary', **kirja/llis/uus** 'literature', **kirjo/itta(a)** '(to) write', and **kirjo/itta/ja** 'writer'. Derivational morphemes (derived words) can also be followed by other endings, for nouns such as case endings, possessive suffixes and particles. We can then form such words as:

kirja/sto/ssa	in the library
kirjo/ita/n/ko	shall I write?
kirjo/itta/ja/n/kin	of the writer, too
kirja/sto/sta/mme	out of our library

Learning the endings is not as difficult as is often thought. Since the endings are often piled up one behind the other rather mechanically, Finnish word forms are usually easy to analyse if one knows the endings.

Finnish nouns differ from those of many Indo-European languages in that there is no grammatical gender. In German there is the 'der – die – das' difference, French has 'le – la', Swedish 'en – ett', and so on, but these distinctions do not occur in Finnish.

Finnish does not have articles, either (cf. '*a* car – *the* car'). The semantic function of articles is often expressed by word order in Finnish:

Kadulla on auto.	There is a car in the street.
Auto on kadulla.	The car is in the street.

When adjectives occur as attributes they agree in number and case with the headword, i.e. they take the same endings.

iso auto	the big car
iso/ssa auto/ssa	in the big car
iso/n auto/n	of the big car
iso/t auto/t	the big cars
iso/i/ssa auto/i/ssa	in the big cars

There are 21 phonemes (basic sounds) in Finnish: eight vowels and 13 consonants. The number is noticeably smaller than in most European languages. The main stress always falls on the first syllable of a word. The writing system is regular in that a given phoneme is always written with the same letter. The converse is also true: a given letter always corresponds to the same phoneme.

§4   WHAT ARE THE SPECIAL DIFFICULTIES?

It is worth mentioning the areas of Finnish grammar which can cause most learning difficulty. Since Finnish is not an Indo-European language the basic vocabulary differs from Indo-European. The 15 most frequent words in Finnish are the following:

1 **olla**	(to) be		4 **ei**	no	
2 **ja**	and		5 **joka**	which	
3 **se**	it		6 **hän**	he, she	

7 **että**	that	12 **niin**	so
8 **tämä**	this	13 **kuin**	than
9 **mutta**	but	14 **tulla**	(to) come
10 **saada**	(to) get	15 **minä**	I
11 **kun**	when		

It is immediately clear that learning Finnish words requires an effort. The burden is lightened, however, by the fact that Finnish has hundreds of direct loan words (mostly from Swedish) and a great many translation loans, expressions that have been translated into Finnish equivalents.

Examples of direct loans are the following (both Swedish and English equivalents are given):

ankka	anka, duck	**kahvi**	kaffe, coffee	**kakku**	kaka, cake
kallo	skalle, skull	**keppi**	käpp, cane	**kirkko**	kyrka, church
kruunu	krona, crown	**pankki**	bank	**penkki**	bänk, bench
posti	post, mail	**sokki**	chock	**rokki**	rock, rock and roll
sohva	soffa, sofa	**tulli**	tull, customs	**viini**	vin, wine

Compound words which are translated loans include: **kirja/kauppa** '*bokhandel*, bookshop'; **olut/pullo** '*ölflaska*, bottle of beer'; **rauta/tie/asema** '*järnvägsstation*, railway station'.

In §3 it was said that the inflection of Finnish words is easy in that the endings are often attached 'mechanically' to the stem. However, this is not always true. The form of the basic stem (root, lexical form) often alters when certain endings are added to it, i.e. a lexical word may be represented by different stems depending upon which endings it is followed by. Compare for example the inflection of the noun **käsi** 'hand' in different cases.

kä<u>si</u>	hand	(hand)
kä<u>de</u>/ssä	in the hand	(hand/in)
kä<u>te</u>/en	into the hand	(hand/into)
kä<u>t</u>/tä	hand	(hand/partitive case)
kä<u>s</u>/i/ssä	in the hands	(hand/s/in)
kä<u>si</u>/kin	the hand, too	(hand/too)
kä<u>te</u>/ni	my hand	(hand/my)

The basic form **käsi** takes different forms according to the following ending and its sound structure. These sound alternations are governed by rules that can sometimes be extremely complex. Here are a few more example pairs:

tun<u>te</u>/a	(to) know	~	**tun<u>ne</u>/n**	I know
hyp<u>pää</u>/n	I jump	~	**hyp<u>ä</u>/tä**	(to) jump
mat<u>to</u>	mat	~	**ma<u>to</u>/lla**	on the mat

m<u>aa</u>	country	~	**m<u>a</u>/i/ssa**	in countries
t<u>ie</u>	road	~	**t<u>e</u>/i/llä**	on the roads
tiet<u>ä</u>/ä	(to) know	~	**tie<u>s</u>/i**	(he) knew

Case endings are usually added to nouns, adjectives and other nominals, but they may also be added to verbs.

| **Minä lähden Jyväskylä/än.** | I'm going to Jyväskylä. |
| **Minä lähden kävele/mä/än.** | I'm going 'walking' (= for a walk). |

The verb form **kävelemään** literally means 'into walking', just as **Jyväskylään** means 'into (the town of) Jyväskylä'. Both forms contain the case ending **-än** meaning 'into'.

The object in Finnish is marked by a case ending. In the two following sentences the ending **-n** indicates 'this word is the object of the sentence'. The rules governing the use of this ending and the other possible object endings are fairly complex.

| **Minä ostan kirja/n.** | I (shall) buy the book. |
| **Kalle näki auto/n.** | Kalle saw the car. |

The most difficult feature of the pronunciation of Finnish is the length (duration) of the sounds: differences of length serve very frequently to distinguish separate words. Compare pairs such as:

kansa	people	–	**kanssa**	with
tuli	fire	–	**tulli**	customs
muta	mud	–	**mutta**	but
muta	mud	–	**muuta**	other
muta	mud	–	**mutaa**	mud (partitive case)
tuulee	it is windy	–	**tuullee**	it is probably windy

2 PRONUNCIATION AND SOUND STRUCTURE

- *Letters and sounds*
- *Vowels and consonants*
- *Short and long sounds*
- *Diphthongs*
- *Syllables*
- *Stress and intonation*
- *Vowel harmony*

§5 LETTERS AND SOUNDS

Disregarding words of foreign origin, Finnish has eight letters for vowels and 13 for consonants: **i e ä y ö u o a** and **p t k d g s h v j l r m n**. With few exceptions the following important correspondence holds between letters and phonemes in carefully pronounced Standard Finnish (phonemes are sounds thought of as types, irrespective of slight variations in the speech of the same person or between different people).

> Each letter corresponds to one and the same phoneme, and each phoneme corresponds to one and the same letter.

Note the following pronunciation details:

- The vowel corresponding to the letter **ä** is an open unrounded front vowel (cf. the short vowels in British English 'shall, rat', and the long vowel in Swedish *bär* 'berry').
- The vowel corresponding to the letter **y** is a close rounded front vowel (cf. German *Führer*).
- The vowel corresponding to the letter **ö** is a half-close rounded front vowel (cf. German *Göring*).
- The combination of letters **ng** is pronounced as a long [ŋŋ] sound as in **rengas** 'ring' [reŋŋas].
- The letter **n** before a **k** is pronounced as a fairly long [ŋ] sound as in **Helsinki** [helsiŋki] (cf. English 'drink').
- When length is used to differentiate meanings, short phonemes are

written with one letter and long phonemes with two, as in **tuli** 'fire' – **tuuli** 'wind' – **tulli** 'customs'; **kansa** 'people' – **kanssa** 'with'; **muta** 'mud' (nominative case) – **mutaa** 'mud' (partitive case).

- Words of foreign origin may contain other letters than those mentioned above, for example **b c f w x z**. Names of Swedish origin may contain the letter **å** (**Å**) as in **Åbo**, **Åke**, **Svartå**.
- The alphabetical order of letters is **a b c d e f g h i j k l m n o p q r s t u v w x y z å ä ö**.
- The pronunciation of the everyday spoken language differs in several respects from that of the standard spoken norm (see Chapter 22). The strict correspondence between letters and phonemes does not hold in everyday spoken language.

§6   VOWELS AND CONSONANTS

Finnish (apart from words of foreign origin) has eight vowel and 13 consonant phonemes: **i e ä y ö u o a** and **p t k d s h v j l r m n ŋ**. All vowels and almost all consonants can occur as either short or long sounds. The phonetic definitions of the Finnish vowels and consonants are as follows (with examples of near-equivalent British English sounds):

i	close front unrounded	*sleep*
e	half-close front unrounded	*bed*
ä	open front unrounded	*bank*
y	close front rounded	
ö	half-close front rounded	
u	close back rounded	*book*
o	half-close back rounded	*dock*
a	open back unrounded	*but*
p	unvoiced unaspirated bilabial stop	*drop*
t	unvoiced unaspirated alveolar stop	*bit*
k	unvoiced unaspirated velar stop	*rock*
d	voiced lax alveolar stop	*down*
s	unvoiced alveolar sibilant	*sound*
h	glottal fricative or glide	*honey*
v	voiced labiodental fricative or glide	*voice*
j	voiced palatal glide	*young*
l	voiced alveolar lateral	*London*
r	voiced alveolar trill	*round*
m	voiced bilabial nasal	*music*
n	voiced alveolar nasal	*noise*
ŋ	voiced velar nasal	*ring*

Special attention should be paid to the following details.

- There is no difference in quality between the corresponding long and short vowels **ii** – **i**, **ee** – **e**, **ää** – **ä**, **yy** – **y**, **öö** – **ö**, **uu** – **u**, **oo** – **o**, **aa** – **a**.

- All long vowels are pronounced as pure long vowels, not as if they were diphthongs or as if they ended in **-j** or **-w**.

- The vowel **y** [y] is articulated with strongly protruded lips and a small opening between them.

- The quality of the long vowel **öö** is [ø:] and that of the short **ö** is [ø], cf. **sinäkö** 'you?', **pöllö** 'owl', **mörkö** 'goblin', **Närpiöön** 'to Närpiö'. The lips are protruded and half-closed.

- The vowels **ee** and **e**, and also **ää** and **ä**, are differentiated in all positions in a word, including before **r** and in unstressed syllables. Cf. **te** 'you' – **tee** 'tea', **meille** 'to us' – **meillä** '"at" us' (= at our house), **teellä** 'with tea' – **täällä** 'here', **piste** 'point' – **pistä** 'sting!', **veneen** 'of the boat' – **nenään** 'into the nose', **lehti** 'leaf' – **lähti** '(he) left', **veri** 'blood' – **väri** 'colour', **perkele** 'devil', **merkki** 'mark', **Eero** (masculine name), **väärä** 'wrong'.

- The consonants **p t k** are pronounced without aspiration, i.e. without a breathy 'h' sound after them.

- The consonant **s** is often pronounced as a rather dark, thick sound that can be close to **š**, especially in the environment of **u**. Cf. **pussi** 'bag', **luussa** 'in the bone', **sumu** 'fog', **myös** 'also'.

- The consonant **h** may occur between vowels and is then pronounced weakly. It can also co-occur with consonants, and is then a stronger sound, particularly if the following consonant is **t** or **k**. Cf. **huono** 'bad', **miehen** 'of the man', **paha** 'evil', **ihminen** 'person', **varhain** 'early', **vanha** 'old', **vihko** 'notebook', **vihta** 'bunch of birch twigs', **sähkö** 'electricity', **tuhka** 'ash'.

- The consonant **l** is pronounced as a rather thick sound when it occurs between the vowels **u** and **o**. Cf. **pullo** 'bottle', **hullu** 'mad', **kulta** 'gold', **pala** 'bit', **villi** 'wild'.

- The consonant **r** is always trilled with the tip of the tongue, e.g. **pyörä** 'wheel', **Pori** (town), **Turku** (town), **virrassa** 'in the stream', **kierrän** 'I turn'.

- *After* certain grammatical forms the initial consonant of the following word or particle *lengthens*. These forms are mainly nominals ending in **-e** like **perhe** 'family' (§19), the present indicative negative e.g. **en tule** 'I am not coming' (§29), the second person singular imperative e.g. **tule!** 'come!' (§66), and the first infinitive e.g. **tulla** '(to) come' (§74).

Examples:

Imperative second p. sing.	**mene pois**	**[meneppois]**	go away
	ole hiljaa	**[olehhiljaa]**	be quiet
	tule tänne	**[tulettänne]**	come here
Nominative in **-e**	**vene tuli**	**[venettuli]**	the boat came
	venekin	**[venekkin]**	the boat, too
	liikemies	**[liikemmies]**	businessman

Pres. indic. negative	**en tule Turkuun**	**[entuletturkuun]**
		I'm not coming to Turku
	emme tulekaan	**[emmetulekkaan]**
		We're not coming after all
	en ole sairas	**[enolessairas]**
		I am not ill

First infinitive	**haluan olla täällä**	**[haluanollattäällä]**
		I want to be here
	haluan lähteä pois	**[haluanlähteäppois]**
		I want to go away

§7   SHORT AND LONG SOUNDS

The difference between short and long sounds is used very widely in Finnish to distinguish different words. Long sounds can occur in almost any position in a word, and there are few restrictions on permissible combinations of long and short sounds. This is clear from the following examples.

Tule tänne.	*Come* here.
Ulkona ei *tuule*.	Outside *it is not windy*.
Ulkona ei *tuulle*.	Outside *it is probably not windy*.
Ulkona *tuulee*.	Outside *it is windy*.
Pekka *tulee*.	Pekka *comes*.
Pekka *tullee*.	Pekka *will probably come*.
Ulkona *tuullee*.	Outside *it is probably windy*.

Almost all the possible combinations of short and long sounds occur: short-short-short, short-long-short, long-short-long, long-long-short, short-long-long, long-long-long, etc. Note in particular the following three points:

There is a difference between a short and a long vowel before a short and a long consonant.

Examples:

tili	account	– **tiili**	brick	– **tilli**	dill	
tuli	fire	– **tuuli**	wind	– **tulli**	customs	
mutta	but	– **muuttaa**	change	– **muuta**	other *(partitive case)*	
muna	egg	– **muuna**	other *(essive case)* –	**muunna**	transform!	

The following six words are all pronounced differently and have distinct meanings:

takka	fireplace
taakka	burden
takkaa	fireplace *(partitive case)*
taakkaa	burden *(partitive case)*
taka	back
takaa	from behind

> There is a distinction between a short and a long **p**, **t**, **k** or **s** when they occur after **l**, **r**, **m**, **n** or **ŋ**. Before a short **p**, **t**, **k** or **s** the consonants **l**, **r**, **m**, **n** and **ŋ** are fairly long.

Examples:

karta	avoid!	–	**kartta**	map
korpi	wilderness	–	**korppi**	raven
arki	weekday	–	**arkki**	ark
kansa	people	–	**kanssa**	together with
pelko	fear	–	**palkki**	beam
lampi	pond	–	**lamppu**	lamp
valta	power	–	**valtti**	trump
sanka	spectacle frame	–	**sankka**	dense

Thus, **kanssa** 'together with' is pronounced [kansːa] while **kansa** 'people' is pronounced either [kanːsa] or [kansa].

The main stress is always on the first syllable of the word (§10). Long vowels elsewhere than in the first syllable are pronounced without main stress, cf. **táloon** 'into the house', **hýppään** 'I jump', **káappiin** 'into the cupboard', **rávintolaan** 'into the restaurant', **tálossaan** 'in his house'.

§8   DIPHTHONGS

Finnish has 16 common diphthongs, i.e. combinations of two vowels occurring in the same syllable. Diphthongs can be divided into four groups according to the final vowel.

(1) **ei**   **ei**   no   **leipä**   bread   **Veikko**   (masculine name)

    äi   **äiti**   mother   **päivä**   day   **väittää** (to) claim

    ui   **uin**   I swim   **puissa**   in the trees   **kuin**   than

    ai   **kaikki** all   **aika**   time   **vaikka**   although

    oi   **poika**   boy   **voin**   I can   **toinen**   other

    öi   **söin**   I ate   **töissä**   in the works

    yi   **hyi**   ugh!   **lyijy**   lead

(2) **au**   **taulu**   picture   **kaula**   neck   **sauna**   sauna

    ou   **koulu**   school   **noudan**   I fetch   **krouvi**   tavern

    eu   **reuna**   edge   **Keuruu**   (place name)   **seutu**   region

    iu   **viulu**   violin   **kiusaan**   I tease   **hius**   hair

(3) **äy**   **täynnä** full   **käyn**   I go   **näytän**   I show

    öy   **köyhä**   poor   **löydän**   I find   **löyly**   steam

(4) **ie**   **tie**   road   **vien**   I take   **mies**   man

    yö   **yö**   night   **työ**   work   **syön**   I eat

    uo   **tuo**   that   **Puola**   Poland   **juon**   I drink

Note particularly the differences between the pairs **ei – äi**, **öi – öy**, **äy – öy**, **ei – eu** and **äy – eu**. Finnish also has other kinds of vowel combinations, but these others do not form diphthongs.

Between the vowels there is almost always a syllable boundary. Examples:

sanoa	(to) say	**rupean**	I begin
ainoa	only	**tapahtua**	(to) happen
vaikea	difficult	**kireä**	tense
sallia	(to) allow	**etsiä**	(to) look for

§9   SYLLABLES

Syllabification in Finnish is in most cases determined by the following basic rule.

> There is a syllable boundary before every sequence of a single consonant followed by a vowel.

In the following examples the syllable boundary is indicated by a dash (-):

ka-la	fish	**jo-kai-nen**	every
kui-ten-kin	however	**sit-ten**	then
päi-vä	day	**al-kaa**	(to) begin
pur-kis-sa	in the jar	**purk-kiin**	into the jar
An-tin	of Antti	**An-til-le**	to Antti
Hel-sin-kiin	to Helsinki	**Hel-sin-gis-sä-kin**	in Helsinki, too

There is also a syllable boundary between vowels that do not form a diphthong (§8) in words such as:

no-pe-a	fast
ai-no-a	only
hert-tu-an	of the duke
sal-li-a	(to) allow

§10 STRESS AND INTONATION

Finnish word stress follows this important rule:

> The main stress is always on the first syllable of the word.

Vowels elsewhere than in the first syllable therefore do not receive main stress. The main stress also falls on the first syllable in loan words which may have been stressed differently in the original language. Examples:

Hélsinkiin	to Helsinki	**vápaa**	free	**vóida**	(to) be able
jókainen	every	**máalaan**	I paint	**áatteellisuus**	idealism
élefantti	elephant	**límonaati**	lemonade	**psýkologi**	psychologist
psýkologia	psychology	**búlevardi**	boulevard		

Finnish sentence intonation is generally falling, but the first syllable of the final word of a sentence can nevertheless be pronounced with a rising intonation without the word being given a strong stress. In the following examples the intonation contour is shown above the sentence.

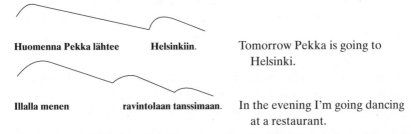

Huomenna Pekka lähtee   Helsinkiin.   Tomorrow Pekka is going to
                                             Helsinki.

Illalla menen   ravintolaan tanssimaan.   In the evening I'm going dancing
                                                at a restaurant.

Urho　Kekkonen　oli　Suomen presidentti　　Urho Kekkonen was the
　　　　　　　　　　　　　　　　　　　　　　President of Finland.

When a word needs to be given particularly strong emphasis this is done
by means of intonation. In addition, such a word is often moved to the
beginning of the sentence.

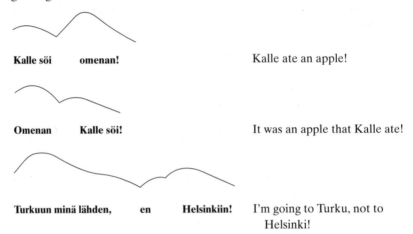

Kalle söi　　omenan!　　　　　　Kalle ate an apple!

Omenan　　Kalle söi!　　　　　　It was an apple that Kalle ate!

Turkuun minä lähden,　　en　　Helsinkiin!　I'm going to Turku, not to
　　　　　　　　　　　　　　　　　　　　Helsinki!

§11　VOWEL HARMONY

Many endings occur in two forms with alternative vowels, e.g. **-ssa ~ -ssä** 'in',
-ko ~ -kö (interrogative), **-nut ~ -nyt** (past participle). These vowel alternations form three pairs; each pair has one back vowel and one front vowel.

Back vowel	*Front vowel*	*Example*
a	ä	**-ssa ~ -ssä**
o	ö	**-kö ~ -kö**
u	y	**-nut ~ -nyt**

If a given ending contains one of these six vowels, there will also exist a
parallel ending with the other vowel of the pair. If we have the ending
-han 'emphasis', there will also be **-hän**; if **-koon** (third p. sing. imp.), then
also **-köön**, etc. The vowels of the stem determine which ending of the
pair is to be chosen.

If the stem contains one or more of the vowels **u, o, a**, the ending
also has to have a back vowel (**u, o, a**). If the stem has no back
vowels, the ending has to have a front vowel (**y, ö, ä**).

Ending with back vowel		*Ending with front vowel*	
talo/ssa	in the house	**kylä/ssä**	in the village
Turu/ssa	in Turku	**käde/ssä**	in the hand
Pori/ssa	in Pori	**venee/ssä**	in the boat
Porvoo/ssa	in Porvoo	**Helsingi/ssä**	in Helsinki
poja/lla	boy	**äidi/llä**	mother
auto/lla	by car	**tä/llä**	with this
kato/lla	on the roof	**miehe/llä**	man
naise/lta	from the woman	**Ville/ltä**	from Ville
Kekkose/lta	from Kekkonen	**tytö/ltä**	from the girl
sisare/lta	from the sister	**velje/ltä**	from the brother
he tule/vat	they come	**he syö/vät**	they eat
he sano/vat	they say	**he mene/vät**	they go
on luke/nut	has read	**on pitä/nyt**	has kept
tuo/ko?	that?	**tämä/kö?**	this?
tuo/ssa/ko?	in that?	**tä/ssä/kö?**	in this?
kirja/han	book (+ emphasis)	**kynä/hän**	pen (+ emphasis)
kirja/ssa/han	in the book (+ emphasis)	**kynä/llä/hän**	with a pen (+ emphasis)
Turu/sta/ko?	from Turku?	**Kemi/stä/kö?**	from Kemi?
kahvi/la/ssa/han	in the café (+ emphasis)	**kylpy/lä/ssä/ hän**	at the bathing resort (+ emph.)

Some recent words of foreign origin which contain conflicting combinations of harmony vowels fluctuate in ending selection, e.g. **amatööri** 'amateur' : **amatööri/na** (recommended usage) 'as an amateur' ~ **amatööri/nä**.

If the stem contains only the so-called neutral vowels **i**, **e** some derivational endings contain a back vowel, e.g. **men/o** 'the going' (c.f. **men/nä** 'to go' = first infinitive).

3 A SURVEY OF WORD STRUCTURE

- *Nominals and their endings*
- *Finite verb forms and their endings*
- *Non-finite verb forms and their endings*

§12 NOMINALS AND THEIR ENDINGS

Nominals are nouns, adjectives, pronouns and numerals, i.e. words like the following:

Nouns		Adjectives		Pronouns		Numerals	
auto	car	**iso**	big	**minä**	I	**yksi**	one
katu	street	**kallis**	expensive	**he**	they	**kymmenen**	ten
nainen	woman	**pitkä**	long	**tämä**	this	**toinen**	second
hinta	price	**vanha**	old	**se**	it	**seitsemäs**	seventh

These four word classes take the same endings, they are inflected in the same way. In addition to derivational suffixes, Finnish nominals can take four kinds of endings: number and case endings, possessive suffixes, and enclitic particles. The main features of all these will be introduced here, and they will be discussed in more detail in later chapters. For the purpose of understanding how Finnish words are made up, it is important to get a grasp of their maximal structure and see how the endings follow one another in a fixed sequence. Occasionally, there may be even four or five endings occurring one after another in the same word.

The Finnish number system has two terms: singular and plural. The singular is never marked by an ending. The plural has two endings: **-t** in the nominative or basic form, and **-i-** in all other cases. The ending **-i-** sometimes takes the shape **-j-**.

Singular		Plural	
auto	car	**auto/t**	cars
auto/ssa	in the car	**auto/i/ssa**	in the cars
auto/sta	from the car	**auto/i/sta**	from the cars
auto/on	into the car	**auto/i/hin**	into the cars
auto/lla	by (the) car	**auto/i/lla**	by (the) cars
pullo	bottle	**pullo/t**	bottles
pullo/sta	out of the bottle	**pullo/i/sta**	out of the bottles
pullo/lla	with a bottle	**pullo/i/lla**	with the bottles
pullo/a	bottle (*partitive*)	**pullo/j/a**	some bottles

Finnish has some 15 cases. The table below shows the grammatical names of the cases, their endings and basic meanings or functions. The principle of vowel harmony (§11) determines whether the ending variant contains a front or a back vowel.

System of cases

Case	Endings	Function	Example	Translation[1]
Nominative	– (pl. **-t**)	(basic form)	**auto**	car
Genitive	**-n**; **-den**, **-tten**	possession	**auto/n**	of the car
Accusative	**-n, -t,** –	object ending	**häne/t**	him, her
Partitive	**-a ~ -ä**;	indefinite	**maito/a**	(some) milk
	-ta ~ -tä;	quantity	**vet/tä**	(some) water
	-tta ~ -ttä		**perhe/ttä**	(some) family
Inessive	**-ssa ~ -ssä**	inside	**auto/ssa**	in the car
Elative	**-sta ~ -stä**	out of	**auto/sta**	out of the car
Illative	**-Vn, -hVn**,[2]	into	**auto/on**	into the car
	-seen, -siin		**maa/han**	into the country
			Porvoo/seen	to Porvoo
Adessive	**-lla ~ -llä**	on; instrument	**pöydä/llä**	on the table
Ablative	**-lta ~ -ltä**	off	**pöydä/ltä**	off the table
Allative	**-lle**	onto	**pöydä/lle**	onto the table
Essive	**-na ~ -nä**	state	**opettaja/na**	as a teacher
Translative	**-ksi**	change of state	**opettaja/ksi**	(become) a teacher
Comitative	**-ine-**	accompanying	**vaimo/ine/ni**	with my wife
Instructive	**-n**	(*idiomatic*)	**jala/n**	on foot

Listed below are the possessive suffixes; with the exception of the third person, the endings are different for each person.

---

1 *Translator's note*: With the adessive and translative cases there is often no straightforward equivalent in English that can be used to gloss examples of isolated words. The meanings of these cases are explained in the relevant chapters below, but in the tables and short examples of the book the conventions adopted are as follows. The adessive ending is glossed 'on' where this could make sense ('on the table'), 'with' where an instrument interpretation would be more natural ('with a hammer'), 'at' or 'in' for places, and '"at"' for people, etc. since in these latter contexts the adessive case commonly marks the possessor (**minulla on** 'I have', glossed literally as '"at" me is'). The translative is glossed 'to (become) + nominal' in order to indicate how it would be usually understood in context; thus e.g. **punaiseksi** would be glossed 'to (become) red', since the form would typically occur in such contexts as 'it became/turned/changed to red'. The essive is usually glossed 'as', although this might not be natural in all contexts. And the partitive is simply marked 'partitive', since it often corresponds to 'no article' in English.

2 The sign **-V-** indicates a vowel which is the same as the nearest preceding vowel, e.g. **Turku/un** 'to Turku', **Helsinki/in** 'to Helsinki', **maa/han** 'into the country', **tie/hen** 'to the road'.

Singular
First person   **(minun) kirja/<u>ni</u>**   my book
Second person   **(sinun) kirja/<u>si</u>**   your book
Third person   **hänen kirja/<u>nsa</u>**   his/her book

Plural
First person   **(meidän) kirja/<u>mme</u>**   our book
Second person   **(teidän) kirja/<u>nne</u>**   your book
Third person   **heidän kirja/<u>nsa</u>**   their book

The fourth group of suffixes is that of the enclitic particles; these occur also with finite and non-finite verb forms. The most common particles are **-kin** 'also', **-kaan ~ -kään** '(not . . .) either', **-ko ~ -kö** 'interrogative', **-han ~ -hän** 'emphasis', and **-pa ~ -pä** 'emphasis'.[3] Examples:

Sinä/<u>kö</u> tulit?   Was it you who came?
Kekkonen/<u>ko</u> lähti Moskovaan?   Was it Kekkonen who went to
                                              Moscow?
Sinä/<u>hän</u> tulit.   It was you who came.
Sinä/<u>kin</u> tulit.   You came too.
Kekkonen/<u>kin</u> tuli.   Kekkonen came too.
Sinä/<u>kään</u> et tullut.   You did not come either.
Kekkonen/<u>kaan</u> ei tullut.   Kekkonen did not come either.
Kekkonen/<u>ko</u>/<u>han</u> lähti   Was it really Kekkonen who went
  Moskovaan?   to Moscow?
Vo/isi/tte/<u>ko</u> tulla?   Could you (*plural*) come?
Vo/isi/tte/<u>ko</u>/<u>han</u> tulla?   Could you (*plural*) come, please?

A Finnish nominal can have endings from all of the above four groups, but the order in which the endings occur is fixed:

More examples are given in the diagram on the next page. Each column of endings also shows how many endings there are of that type. Root here means the basic form of the word, without any ending. Some roots have different stems depending upon which ending immediately follows. For example, the root **käsi** 'hand' has the stem **käde-** if certain case endings

---

3 *Translator's note*: Both **-han** and **-pa** are glossed 'emphasis' since an idiomatic translation in English would usually have to be structurally rather different. However, the two particles are not synonymous. The particle **-han** often has the sense 'I assume you know' (**Mutta sehän on kallis** 'But it's expensive, isn't it?'), while **-pa** is closer to surprise or pure emphasis (**Onpa kallis!** 'That *is* expensive!'). Furthermore, **-han** often functions as a politeness marker and corresponds to the English word 'please'.

follow, as in the word **käde/ssä** 'in the hand' (inessive case). Note that if a word contains derivational suffixes these occur between the root and the number ending.

					Structure of nominals	
Root	*Number*	*Case*	*Poss*	*Particle*	*Whole*	*Meaning*
	(2)	(15)	(6)	(6)	*example*	
pullo					**pullo**	bottle
pullo	t				**pullot**	bottles
pullo		ssa			**pullossa**	in the bottle
pullo			ni		**pulloni**	my bottle
pullo				kin	**pullokin**	the bottle too
pullo	i	sta			**pulloista**	out of the bottles
pullo		sta	ni		**pullostani**	out of my bottle
pullo		ssa		han	**pullossahan**	in the bottle (+ emphasis)
pullo	t			kin	**pullotkin**	the bottles too
pullo		ssa	si	ko	**pullossasiko**	in your bottle?
pullo	i	ssa	mme		**pulloissamme**	in our bottles
pullo	i	sta		kaan	**pulloistakaan**	(not) out of the bottles, either
pullo	i	ssa	nne	kin	**pulloissannekin**	in your bottles too
hylly		ssä			**hyllyssä**	in the shelf
hylly		llä			**hyllyllä**	on the shelf
hylly			si		**hyllysi**	your shelf
hylly		lle	si		**hyllyllesi**	onto your shelf
hylly		ltä		kö	**hyllyltäkö**	off the shelf?
hylly	t			kö	**hyllytkö**	shelves?
hylly		n		hän	**hyllynhän**	of the shelf (+ emphasis)
talo		on			**taloon**	into the house
(heidän) talo			nsa	ko	**heidän talonsako**	their house?
(hänen) hylly			nsä		**hänen hyllynsä**	his/her shelf
hylly	i	llä	mme		**hyllyillämme**	on our shelves

§13 FINITE VERB FORMS AND THEIR ENDINGS

A finite verb form means a form with a personal ending, e.g. (**minä**) **tule/n** 'I come', **sinä tule/t** 'you come', **Maija tule/e** 'Maija comes'. In addition to person, Finnish finite verb forms also inflect for tense, mood and the passive. The passive forms contain two endings: that of the passive itself, and also a personal ending **-Vn**. The enclitic particles can also be attached to finite verb forms.

There are six personal endings, one for each grammatical person. The personal pronouns occurring before the verbs in the first and second person singular and plural are frequently omitted.

Singular

First person	(minä) puhu/**n**	I speak
Second person	(sinä) puhu/**t**	you (sing.) speak
Third person	hän puhu/**u**	he/she speaks

Plural

First person	(me) puhu/**mme**	we speak
Second person	(te) puhu/**tte**	you (pl.) speak
Third person	he puhu/**vat**	.they speak

Finnish has two simple tenses: present, which indicates non-past time, and past, which indicates past time. There is no separate ending for the present, and the ending for the past tense is **-i-**. The personal endings occur after the tense ending.

Present		*Past*	
minä puhu/n	I speak	**minä puhu/i/n**	I spoke
me sano/mme	we say	**me sano/i/mme**	we said
he sano/vat	they say	**he sano/i/vat**	they said
te seiso/tte	you (pl.) stand	**te seiso/i/tte**	you (pl.) stood

Finnish has four moods, which express for example the speaker's attitude to the content of the message.

Mood	*Form*
Indicative	Ø
Conditional	**-isi-**
Potential	**-ne-** (*and other variants*)
Imperative	*see below*

The indicative is the most common of the moods; it has no ending, and represents an action as a fact or as something that has happened. The conditional mood is mainly used in conditional clauses; cf. English 'would'. The potential is a rare mood, presenting an action as possible or likely.

The personal ending is attached after the tense ending. The fourth mood, the imperative, is different in that its own ending either merges with the personal ending so that the two become indistinguishable (second person plural), or is followed by personal endings that are specific to this mood (third person singular and plural).

	Singular		*Plural*	
First person	–		sano/**kaa**/**mme**	let us say
Second person	**sano**	say!	sano/**kaa**	say!
Third person	sano/**ko**/**on**	may he say	sano/**ko**/**ot**	may they say

The most common form is the second person singular, which has no ending. Because of vowel harmony the endings for the other persons also have front-vowel variants: **vie/köön** 'may he take', **vie/käämme** 'let us take', **vie/kää** 'take!', **vie/kööt** 'may they take'. The third person imperatives express a wish rather than a command, and these forms are rare.

The passive forms indicate that the performer of the action is an indefinite, unspecified person, cf. English 'one (can say that . . .)'.[4] The endings for the passive itself are **-tta** ~ **-ttä** and **-ta** ~ **-tä** depending on the structure of the preceding stem. Sometimes the final vowels **a** or **ä** disappear.

These endings are attached directly to the root form of the verb (or the derived stem). Possible tense and mood endings come after the passive ending, and after them comes the passive personal ending **-Vn**, where **V** again stands for a vowel which is the same as the nearest preceding vowel.

Active		*Passive*	
sano/n	I say	**sano/ta/an**	one says, it is said
sano/isi/n	I would say	**sano/tta/isi/in**	one would say
sano/i/n	I said	**sano/tt/i/in**	one said

To conclude this section, the table on the next page shows the order in which these endings occur. The tense and mood endings are in the same column, since they are mutually exclusive (the same word form may not contain both tense and mood endings). Some of the imperative endings are between those for mood and person, since they have become merged. In final position there may be an enclitic particle.

4 *Translator's note*: the passive will usually be glossed with the impersonal 'one' in order to show the sense of the Finnish, but a corresponding English passive form will often sound more natural in context ('one says' – 'it is said').

Structure of finite verb forms

Root	Passive ending	Tense, mood ending	Person ending	Particle	Whole example	Meaning
puhu			n		**puhun**	I speak
puhu			mme		**puhumme**	we speak
puhu		i	tte		**puhuitte**	you spoke
(he) puhu		isi	vat		**(he) puhuisivat**	they would speak
puhu			t	han	**puhuthan**	you will speak!
sano		i	n	ko	**sanoinko?**	did I say?
sano		isi	mme	ko	**sanoisimmeko?**	should we say?
sano	ta		an		**sanotaan**	one says, it is said
sano	tta	isi	in		**sanottaisiin**	one would say
sano	tt	i	in	han	**sanottiinhan**	one did say!
sano	tta	ne	en		**sanottaneen**	one may say
sano		kaa			**sanokaa**	say (*imperative*)
sano		kaa		pa	**sanokaapa**	say (*impera-tive + emphasis*)
sano		kaa	mme		**sanokaamme**	let us say
sano		ko	ot		**sanokoot**	may they say
sano	tta	ko	on		**sanottakoon**	may, let one say
saa			n	ko	**saanko**	do I get?
sa		isi	n	ko	**saisinko**	might I get?
sa		i	t	han	**saithan**	you did get
syö	t	i	in		**syötiin**	one ate
syö	tä	isi	in		**syötäisiin**	one would eat
syö	tä	isi	in	kö	**syötäisiinkö**	might one eat?
syö	t	i	in	kin	**syötiinkin**	one also ate

§14   NON-FINITE VERB FORMS AND THEIR ENDINGS

Non-finite verb forms are those which, unlike finite verbs, do not contain personal endings. There are two kinds of non-finite forms: infinitives and participles. As regards the way they are used, infinitives can be compared to nouns and participles to adjectives.

Characteristic of non-finite verb forms is a function ending which does not usually carry any real meaning but simply indicates that 'this is a non-finite form'. Some non-finite forms are inflected in the passive like finite verbs (participles, and the inessive case of the second infinitive). Unlike finite verbs, but like nouns, non-finite forms often take a case ending and a possessive suffix. Participles are also inflected for number. Enclitic particles can be attached to all non-finite forms.

Finnish has three important infinitives. The main one is the first infinitive, which is the dictionary form of a verb. Each infinitive has its own function ending indicating which infinitive it is. Case inflection in the infinitives is very defective. The first infinitive occurs in only two cases (nominative and translative), the second also in only two (inessive and instructive), and the third in six (inessive, elative, illative, adessive, abessive and instructive). Infinitives do not appear in the plural. With some cases infinitives may also take a possessive suffix.

Infinitives

	Function ending	Example	Meaning
First	-a ~ -ä	sano/<u>a</u>	(to) say
	-da ~ -dä	syö/<u>dä</u>	(to) eat
	-ta ~ -tä	juos/<u>ta</u>	(to) run
Second	-e-	sano/<u>e</u>/ssa/ni	while I say
	-de-	syö/<u>de</u>/ssä/mme	while we eat
	-te-	juos/<u>te</u>/n	running
Third	-ma- ~ -mä-	syö/<u>mä</u>/llä	by eating
		sano/<u>ma</u>/tta	without saying
		sano/<u>ma</u>/an	(in order) to say

Finnish has two participles, the present and the past, which have almost the same function as ordinary adjectives; they also occur in the compound forms of verbs. Participles also have passive forms. Being similar to adjectives, participles take all cases and are also inflected for number. They can sometimes take possessive suffixes. The active participles are given below.

Active participles

	Function ending	Example	Meaning
Present	-va ~ -vä	juo/<u>va</u>	drinking
		syö/<u>vä</u>	eating
Past	-nut ~ -nyt	juo/<u>nut</u>	drunk
		syö/<u>nyt</u>	eaten

The following table shows the structure of the non-finite verb forms, and the order in which the endings occur.

Structure of non-finite verb forms

Root	Passive ending	Non-finite ending	Number ending	Case ending	Poss. ending	Particle ending	Whole example	Meaning
puhu		a					**puhua**	(to) speak
puhu		a		kse	si		**puhuaksesi**	in order for you to speak
puhu		ma		lla			**puhumalla**	by speaking
syö		dä					**syödä**	(to) eat
syö		dä		kse	mme		**syödäksemme**	in order for us to eat
puhu		va				kin	**puhuvakin**	(the) speaking (one) too
puhu		va		ssa		kin	**puhuvassakin**	in the speaking (one) too
puhu		v	i	ssa		kin	**puhuvissakin**	in the speaking (ones) too
puhu		va	t				**puhuvat**	(the) speaking (ones)
(on) puhu		nut					**puhunut**	(has) spoken
(ovat) puhu		nee	t				**puhuneet**	(have) spoken
syö		mä		än			**syömään**	(in order) to eat
juo		ma		an			**juomaan**	(in order) to drink
juo		ma		an		ko	**juomaanko**	(in order) to drink?
syö		mä		ttä			**syömättä**	without eating
juo		ma		tta		han	**juomattahan**	without drinking (+ *emphasis*)
juo	ta	va					**juotava**	that can be drunk
(on) sano	ttu						**sanottu**	(one has) said
sano	tu			sta			**sanotusta**	out of the said (thing)
sano	tta	va					**sanottava**	(the) to-be-said (thing)
sano	tta	va		lla			**sanottavalla**	by the to-be-said (thing)
sano	tta	v	i	lla			**sanottavilla**	by the to-be-said (things)
sano	tta	v	i	ssa		ko	**sanottavissako**	in the to-be-said (things)?
syö	tä	e		ssä			**syötäessä**	while one eats

Root	Passive ending	Non-finite ending	Number ending	Case ending	Poss. ending	Particle ending	Whole example	Meaning
vetä		mä		llä		hän	**vetämällähän**	by pulling (+ *emphasis*)
vetä		e		ssä	si		**vetäessäsi**	while you pull
vetä		e		ssä	ni		**vetäessäni**	while I pull
syö	ty	ä			mme		**syötyämme**	we having eaten
(**Kallen**) syö		vä		n			**syövän**	(Kalle) eating
syö		de		ssä	än		**syödessään**	while he/she eats

4 TWO IMPORTANT SOUND ALTERNATIONS

- *Consonant gradation (p, t, k)*
- *Vowel changes before -i- endings*

§15 CONSONANT GRADATION (p, t, k)

It would be easy to form Finnish words if all the endings were attached mechanically one after the other according to the patterns given above for nominals and finite and non-finite verb forms. But the adding of endings is in fact a more complex matter, since endings are often accompanied by sound alternations (changes) in the stem (to the left of the ending).

The most important of these alternations is that known as consonant gradation, which affects the long and short stops **p**, **t** and **k**. Section 15.1 below outlines the various types of alternation. Section 15.2 deals with the conditions determining the changes, and also presents some important rules. Sections 15.3–5 contain a great many examples to show how the rules are applied, and section 15.6 gives some special cases. The form to which the rules of consonant gradation are applied is called the 'strong grade', and the resulting alternative form is called the 'weak grade' (occasionally indicated by a '+' prefixed to the word).

§15.1 THE TYPES OF CONSONANT GRADATION

The long consonants **pp**, **tt**, **kk** alternate with the corresponding short consonants **p**, **t**, **k**. This is called quantitative consonant gradation.

(1) **pp**	~ **p**	**kaappi**	cupboard	**kaapi/ssa**	in the cupboard
(2) **tt**	~ **t**	**matto**	mat	**mato/lla**	on the mat
(3) **kk**	~ **k**	**kukka**	flower	**kuka/n**	of the flower

The short consonants generally alternate with other consonants; however, **k** may sometimes be dropped altogether. These alternations are called qualitative consonant gradation (types (4)–(16)).

(4) **p**	~ **v**	**tupa**	hut	**tuva/ssa**	in the hut
(5) **Vt**	~ **Vd**	**katu**	street	**kadull/a**	on the street
(6) **ht**	~ **hd**	**lähte-**	leave	**lähde/n**	I leave
(7) **k**	~ **ø**	**jalka**	foot	**jala/n**	of the foot

The consonant **t** changes to **d** both after a vowel, **V** (= a vowel which is the same as the nearest preceding vowel), and after **h**. A different type of alternation takes place in the following five cases, where either **p**, **t**, **k** occur after a nasal consonant (**m**, **n**, **ŋ**), or **t** occurs after **l** or **r**.

(8) **mp**	~ **mm**	**ampu-**	shoot	**ammu/mme**	we shoot
(9) **nt**	~ **nn**	**ranta**	shore	**ranna/lla**	on the shore
(10) **nk**	~ **ng [ŋŋ]**	**kenkä**	shoe	**kengä/n**	of the shoe
(11) **lt**	~ **ll**	**kulta**	gold	**kulla/n**	of the gold
(12) **rt**	~ **rr**	**parta**	beard	**parra/ssa**	in the beard

Alternations (4)–(7) operate when the stops are not preceded by a nasal consonant or **l** or **r**: in such cases alternations (8)–(12) apply. In addition to these there are also four fairly rare alternations applying to **k**.

(13) **lke** ~ **lje**	**polke-**	trample	**polje/n**	I trample
(14) **rke** ~ **rje**	**särke-**	break	**särje/n**	I break
(15) **hke** ~ **hje**	**rohkene/t**	you dare	**rohjet/a**	(to) dare
(16) **k** ~ **v**	**puku**	dress	**puvu/n**	of the dress

Alternations (13)–(15) are very similar: in each of these **k** changes to **j** before **e**. Type (16) is rare, and occurs only in a few nominals, when **k** is preceded and followed by **u/y**.

§15.2   THE RULES OF CONSONANT GRADATION

All the alternations (1)–(16) are determined by the same set of conditions. Stops change in the stem of words with two or more syllables when certain endings are added. The change is determined partly by the vowels between the stop and the ending (alternation occurs only if the vowels are short; there is no alternation if this position is taken by a long vowel or a consonant), and partly by the following ending (alternation is caused only by certain types of case and personal ending). The following rule A applies to all words, nominals as well as verbs.

Rule A

In polysyllabic stems long and short **p**, **t**, **k** are subject to consonant gradation if they are followed by an ending which:

A(a) consists of only one consonant or
A(b) begins with two consonants,
and also on condition that
A(c) between **p**, **t**, **k** and the ending there is only a short vowel or
        a diphthong (not consonants or a syllable boundary)
A(d) the ending causing consonant gradation is usually the case
        ending in nominals and the personal ending in verbs

Cont . . .

A(e) between this ending and the consonants **p**, **t**, **k** there can be
an **-i-** ending (plural or past tense)
A(f) alternation never occurs before a long vowel
A(g) there is no alternation in monosyllabic stems

In addition to the basic rule A there is a second rule B, which governs consonant gradation in verbs only.

Rule B
In verbs, **p**, **t**, **k**, are always subject to consonant gradation before a short vowel if they occur

B(a) before the passive ending (e.g. **-tta-** ~ **-ttä-**, **-ta-** ~ **-tä-**)
B(b) in the second person singular imperative
B(c) in the present indicative negative

Cases B(b) and B(c) are in fact equivalent, since these verb forms are always the same, e.g. **kerro!** 'tell!' ~ **en kerro** 'I do not tell'; **anna!** 'give' ~ **en anna** 'I do not give'.

The examples below illustrate the way in which the basic rule A is applied to the noun **katto** 'roof', where there is alternation between **tt** and **t**. It is the structure of the following case ending that primarily determines whether the alternation occurs or not; the reason is given on the right.

katto	roof	NO	no ending
kato/n	of the roof	YES	ending consists of one consonant
kato/lla	on the roof	YES	ending begins with two consonants
katto/na	as a roof	NO	ending does not consist of one consonant or begin with two
kato/lta	from the roof	YES	ending begins with two consonants
katto/on	into the roof	NO	no alternation before a long vowel
kato/lle	onto the roof	YES	ending begins with two consonants
kato/t	roofs	YES	ending consists of one consonant
kato/i/lla	on the roofs	YES	ending begins with two consonants; in between there can be an ending consisting of **-i-**
katto/i/na	as roofs	NO	see **katto/na**
kato/ksi	to (become) a roof	YES	ending begins with two consonants

ka_tt_o/mme	our roof	NO	no alternation before a possessive suffix
ka_tt_o/kin	a roof, too	NO	ending does not consist of one consonant or begin with two
ka_t_o/i/_ll_e	onto the roofs	YES	ending begins with two consonants; in between there can be an ending consisting of **-i-**
ka_tt_o/i/hin	into the roofs	NO	ending does not consist of one consonant or begin with two
ka_t_o/i/_lt_a	from the roofs	YES	ending begins with two consonants; in between there can be an ending consisting of **-i-**
ka_tt_o/nne	your roof	NO	no alternation before a possessive suffix
ka_tt_o/a	roof (*partitive*)	NO	ending does not consist of one consonant or begin with two
ka_tt_o/j/en	of the roofs	NO	same as above; **j** = the plural **i**

The two following sections contain further examples of the application of rules A and B, in both nominals and verbs.

§15.3   APPLYING THE BASIC RULE TO NOMINALS

The table on page 33 shows how consonant gradation applies to the word **katu** 'street', where the alternation is of type (5); **t** changes to **d**. The examples are given in the familiar way; the actual word form is written on the right, followed by the reason for the occurrence or non-occurrence of the alternation.

The nominative plural ending **-t** also causes consonant gradation. This form shows both number and case. In accordance with the basic rule, alternation occurs only before short vowels. The vowels of diphthongs are short, and therefore there is usually alternation before a diphthong: **ka_t_o/_ll_a** 'on the roof' ~ **ka_t_o/i/_ll_a** 'on the roofs'. The latter form has the diphthong **-oi**, before which consonant gradation occurs. (However, the type **renka/i/ssa** 'in the rings' is an exception to this diphthong rule: see below.)

Before long vowels the rules of consonant gradation do not apply, even if the case ending does consist of one consonant or begin with two. Nominals with an inflectional stem ending in a long vowel (§19, §20.3) are unaffected by consonant gradation in almost all singular and plural case forms, including those where the otherwise long stem vowel shortens before the plural ending **-i** (§16). The examples below illustrate what happens in the inflection of **rengas : renkaa-** 'ring'.

Singular		*Plural*	
renkaa/n	of the ring	renkaa/t	rings
renkaa/ssa	in the ring	renka/i/ssa	in the rings
renkaa/sta	out of the ring	renka/i/sta	out of the rings
renkaa/lla	with the ring	renka/i/lla	with the rings
renkaa/na	as a ring	renka/i/na	as rings
renkaa/seen	into the ring	renka/i/siin	into the rings
renkaa/lta	from the ring	renka/i/lta	from the rings

In these words the vowel preceding the plural **i** counts as long because it is long in almost all the corresponding singular forms.

In words of the **rengas : renkaa-** type consonant gradation does apply, however, in two case forms: the nominative singular, which ends either in a short vowel + **s** (§20.3) or in **-e** (§19), and the partitive singular; occasionally also the genitive plural. Cf. **rengas** 'ring' (nom. sing.), **rengas/ta** (part. sing.), **rengas/ten** (gen. pl.). Further examples of this type (the basic form is the nominative singular):

	Alternation		*Stem*	*Basic form*	*Meaning*
(1)	pp	~ p	saappaa-	saapas	boot
(2)	tt	~ t	rattaa-	ratas	wheel
(3)	kk	~ k	rakkaa-	rakas	dear
(4)	p	~ v	varpaa-	varvas	toe
(5)	t	~ d	hitaa-	hidas	slow
(6)	ht	~ hd	tehtaa-	tehdas	factory
(7)	k	~ Ø	kokee-	koe	experiment
(8)	mp	~ mm	lampaa-	lammas	lamb
(9)	nt	~ nn	kintaa-	kinnas	mitten
(10)	nk	~ ng	kuninkaa-	kuningas	king
(11)	lt	~ ll	altaa-	allas	basin
(12)	rt	~ rr	portaa-	porras	step
(13)	lke	~ lje	hylkee-	hylje	seal
(15)	hke	~ hje	pohkee-	pohje	calf (of leg)

We thus have **saapas** 'boot' (nom. sing.) and **saapas/ta** (part. sing.) but **saappaa/n** (gen. sing.), **saappaa/na** (ess. sing.), **saappaa/t** (nom. pl.), **saappa/i/ssa** (iness. pl.), etc.

In three-syllable nominals like **keittiö** 'kitchen', **lapio** 'spade', **herttua** 'duke', where there is a syllable boundary between the two final vowels in the basic form (§9), there is no consonant gradation A(c). They are thus inflected **keittiö/n** (gen. sing.), **keittiö/ssä** (iness. sing.), **keittiö/tä** (part. sing.), **keittiö/i/ssä** (iness. pl.), etc.

Root (base)	Number	Case	Poss.	Particle	Whole example	Meaning	Cons. grad.?	Reason
katu		n			kadun	of the street	YES	case ending of one consonant
katu			nne		katunne	your street	NO	no case ending
katu				kin	katukin	the street, too	NO	no case ending
katu		lla			kadulla	on the street	YES	case ending begins with two consonants
katu		na			katuna	as a street	NO	case ending is one consonant + vowel
katu		lle			kadulle	onto the street	YES	case ending begins with two consonants
katu		a			katua	street (partitive)	NO	case ending is vowel
katu	i	lla			kaduilla	on the streets	YES	case ending begins with two consonants
katu			mme	ko	katummeko	our street?	NO	no case ending
katu	t				kadut	streets	YES	case ending of one consonant
katu				han	katuhan	street (+ emphasis)	NO	no case ending
katu	j	a			katuja	streets (partitive)	NO	case ending is vowel
katu	i	ssa			kaduissa	in the streets	YES	case ending begins with two consonants
katu		n		pa	kadunpa	of the street (+ emphasis)	YES	case ending of one consonant
katu		lta	nne		kadultanne	from your street	YES	case ending begins with two consonants
katu	i	na			katuina	as streets	NO	case ending is one consonant + vowel
katu		t	han		kaduthan	streets (+ emphasis)	YES	case ending of one consonant
katu		un			katuun	into the street	NO	long vowel

§15.4 APPLYING THE RULES TO VERBS

In verbs the personal ending generally determines whether or not consonant gradation occurs (A(d)). In addition to the basic rule verbs are also governed by rule B: the rules of consonant gradation are always applied before the passive ending, and also in the second person singular imperative and the present indicative negative.

Let us take the verb **kerto-** '(to) tell' as an example: **rt** alternates with **rr** (alternation type (12)). On the right of the table (page 35) there is an indication of whether or not consonant gradation has occurred, and a brief explanation.

Note condition A(e): there may be the past tense ending **-i-** between an alternating **p**, **t** or **k** and the personal ending. But the rules of consonant gradation cannot be applied if this mid-position contains the conditional **-isi** or the potential **-ne** ending. We therefore have **kerro/i/n** 'I told' but **kerto/isi/n** 'I would tell' and **kerto/ne/n** 'I may tell' (this potential mood form is very rare).

As with nominals, consonant gradation does not occur before long vowels in verbs either (A(c)). In the following important class of verbs, known as contracted verbs (§23.2), there is thus no consonant gradation in the present tense, nor in the past tense although the vowel is shortened (§60).

Present		*Past*	
hyppää/n	I jump	**hyppä/si/n**	I jumped
hyppää/t	you (sing.) jump	**hyppä/si/t**	you (sing.) jumped
(**hän**) **hyppää**	he/she jumps	(**hän**) **hyppä/si**	he/she jumped
hyppää/mme	we jump	**hyppä/si/mme**	we jumped
hyppää/tte	you (pl.) jump	**hyppä/si/tte**	you (pl.) jumped
(**he**) **hyppää/vät**	they jump	(**he**) **hyppä/si/vät**	they jumped

In addition, contracted verbs are not affected by consonant gradation in the second person singular imperative, nor in the present indicative negative: **hyppää!** 'jump' ~ **en hyppää** 'I do not jump'. But these verbs do have a few inflected forms where the otherwise long stem vowel is shortened, the second vowel being replaced by a linking consonant **t** comparable to the case and personal endings that do cause consonant gradation (A(a)), e.g. **hyppää/n** 'I jump': **hypät/ä** '(to) jump'. The following forms are based on a stem containing the linking consonant, and consonant gradation therefore applies.

First infinitive	**hypät/ä**	(to) jump
Second infinitive	**hypät/e/n**	jumping
Passive	**hypät/t/i/in**	one jumped
Imperative	**hypät/kää**	jump! (plural; not second person sing.)
Past participle	**hypän/nyt**	jumped (*note*: **t** has changed to **n**)

How consonant gradation is triggered in certain types of finite verb forms

Root (base)	Passive	Tense, mood	Person	Particle	Whole example	Meaning	Cons. grad.?	Reason
kerto			**n**		**kerron**	I tell	YES	pers. ending of one cons.
kerto			**mme**		**kerromme**	we tell	YES	pers. ending begins with two cons.
kerto		**isi**	**mme**		**kertoisimme**	we would tell	NO	conditional mood **-isi-**
kerto	**ta**		**an**		**kerrotaan**	one tells	YES	passive
kerto		**i**	**tte**		**kerroitte**	you (pl.) told	YES	pers. ending begins with two cons.
kerto			**vat**		**kertovat**	they tell	NO	pers. ending begins cons. + vowel
kerto		**i**	**vat**		**kertoivat**	they told	NO	pers. ending begins cons. + vowel
kerto					**kerro**	tell (sing.)!	YES	imperative second person singular
kerto	**tt**	**i**	**in**		**kerrottiin**	one told	YES	passive
kerto			**o**		**kertoo**	tells	NO	personal ending of a vowel
(en) kerto					**(en) kerro**	(I don't) tell	YES	negative form
kerto		**kaa**			**kertokaa**	tell (pl.)!	NO	ending of consonant + vowel
kerto			**t**		**kerrot**	you (sing.) tell	YES	pers. ending of one cons.
kerto		**i**	**t**		**kerroit**	you (sing.) told	YES	pers. ending of one cons.
kerto		**ne**	**tte**		**kertonette**	you (pl.) may tell	NO	potential mood **-ne-**
kerto				**pa**	**kerropa**	tell (sing.)! + emph.	YES	second pers. sing. imp.
kerto			**tte**	**han**	**kerrottehan**	you (pl.) tell + emph.	YES	pers. ending begins with two cons.
kerto			**t**	**ko**	**kerrotko**	do you (sing.) tell?	YES	pers. ending of one cons.
kerto		**isi**	**vat**	**ko**	**kertoisivatko**	would they tell?	NO	conditional mood **-isi-**

Almost all types of consonant gradation may occur with contracted verbs:

	Alternation		Long vowel stem	Basic form	Meaning
(1)	pp	~ p	sieppaa-	siepat/a	snatch
(2)	tt	~ t	konttaa-	kontat/a	crawl
(3)	kk	~ k	hakkaa-	hakat/a	hew
(4)	p	~ v	kelpaa-	kelvat/a	be good enough
(5)	Vt	~ Vd	hautaa-	haudat/a	bury
(6)	ht	~ hd	rahtaa-	rahdat/a	freight
(7)	k	~ Ø	makaa-	maat/a	lie
(8)	mp	~ mm	kampaa-	kammat/a	comb
(9)	nt	~ nn	ryntää-	rynnät/ä	rush
(10)	nk	~ ng	hankaa-	hangat/a	rub
(11)	lt	~ ll	valtaa-	vallat/a	conquer
(12)	rt	~ rr	virtaa-	virrat/a	flow

§15.5 MORE EXAMPLES OF TYPES OF CONSONANT GRADATION

Quantitative gradation

(1)	pp	~ p	kauppa	shop	kaupassa	in the shop
			lamppu	lamp	lamput	lamps
			tappa-	kill	tapan	I kill
(2)	tt	~ t	katto	roof	katolla	on the roof
			käyttä-	use	käytämme	we use
			otta-	take	otan	I take
(3)	kk	~ k	takki	coat	takissani	in my coat
			kaikke-	everything	kaikessa	in everything
			nukku-	sleep	nukuimme	we slept

Qualitative gradation

(4)	p	~ v	kylpe-	bathe	kylven	I bathe
			kipu	pain	kivussa	in pain
			tarpee-	need	tarve	need
(5)	t	~ d	tietä-	know	tiedätkö?	do you know?
			vetä-	pull	vedä!	pull!
			äiti	mother	äidille	to mother
(6)	ht	~ hd	vihta	whisk	vihdalla	with a whisk
			vaihta-	change	vaihdatteko?	do you change?
			lehte-	newspaper	lehdessä	in the newspaper
(7)	k	~ Ø	joke-	river	joesta	out of the river
			jaka-	divide	jaamme	we divide
			poika	boy	pojalle	to the boy
			aika	time	ajassa	in time

(8)	mp	~	mm	ampu-	shoot	ammutaan	one shoots
				kampa	comb	kammalla	with a comb
(9)	nt	~	nn	tunte-	feel	ei tunne	does not feel
				anta-	give	annamme	we give
				ranta	shore	rannalla	on the shore
(10)	nk	~	ng	kenkä	shoe	kengästä	out of the shoe
				tunke-	shove	älä tunge!	don't shove!
				tinki-	bargain	tingitkö?	do you bargain?
(11)	lt	~	ll	ilta	evening	illalla	in the evening
				kulta	gold	kullaksi	to (become) gold
				viheltä-	whistle	vihellän	I whistle
(12)	rt	~	rr	kiertä-	turn	kierrä!	turn!
				kerta	time	kerran	once
				kerto-	tell	kerronko?	do I tell?
(13)	lke	~	lje	sulke-	close	suljemme	we close
				jälke-	trace	jäljet	traces
				kulke-	go	kuljet	you go
(14)	rke	~	rje	särke-	break	särjetkö?	do you break?
				arke-	everyday	arjen	of everyday
(15)	hke	~	hje	rohkene-	dare	rohjeta	(to) dare
(16)	k	~	v	suku	family	suvussa	in the family
				puku	dress	puvut	dresses
				luku	number	luvun	of a number

Note the exceptional words **poika** 'boy' and **aika** 'time' (type (7)) where the loss of **k** makes **i** change to **j** in the weak grade. Type (13) and particularly types (14)–(16) are rare.

§15.6 ADDITIONAL COMMENTS

Besides the case and personal endings dealt with above there are also certain other (derivational) endings which cause consonant gradation, in particular the ending **-sti** on adjectives (which forms adverbs from them), the comparative ending **-mpi** (§85), and the superlative ending **-in** (§86). Note also the semantically negative derivational ending **-ton ~ -tön: koti** 'home' : **kodi/ton** 'homeless'; **palkka** 'salary' : **palka/ton** 'unsalaried'. (Cf. §93 for more examples of derivational endings that trigger consonant gradation.)

Basic form	Adverbs	Comparative	Superlative
kiltti	**kilti/sti**	**kilti/mpi**	**kilte/in**
nice	nicely	nicer	nicest
tarkka	**tarka/sti**	**tarke/mpi**	**tark/in**
accurate	accurately	more accurate	most accurate
helppo	**helpo/sti**	**helpo/mpi**	**helpo/in**
easy	easily	easier	easiest

The derivational endings undergo consonant gradation themselves when they are inflected, for example the comparative **-mpi**: **helpo/mma/ssa** 'in the easier (one)'.

The stop consonants **p**, **t**, **k** do not undergo consonant gradation when they occur next to **s** or **t**. The consonant **k** in the combination **hk** alternates occasionally.

sk	tasku	pocket	taskusta	out of the pocket
sp	piispa	bishop	piispat	bishops
st	piste	point	pisteet	points
tk	matka	journey	matkalla	on the journey
hk	keuhko	lung	keuhkot	lungs
Note:	vihko	notebook	vihot	notebooks
Note:	nahka	leather	nahasta	out of leather

Many loan words and proper names do not have consonant gradation. This is particularly true of alternation types (4)–(16).

auto	car	autolla	by car
Malta	Malta	Maltan	of Malta
Kauko	(masc. name)	Kaukolle	to Kauko
Arto	(masc. name)	Artolta	from Arto

§16   VOWEL CHANGES BEFORE -i- ENDINGS

The second important group of sound alternations is the set of vowel changes which often occur before certain endings beginning with **-i**. These endings are:

In nominals	*In verbs*
the plural **-i-**	the past tense **-i-**
(sometimes **-j-**: see §26)	
the superlative **-in**	the conditional mood **-isi-**
(of adjectives)	

The vowel changes are often the same for all these endings, but there are also some differences. Eight rules are given below. (Consonant gradation is indicated by a prefixed '+'.)

---

(1) The short vowels **-o**, **-ö**, **-u**, **-y** (i.e. rounded vowels) do not change before **-i-** endings.

Basic form	Plural		Basic form	Superlative	
talo	taloissa	in the houses	helppo	helpoin	easiest
pöllö	pöllöille	to the owls	jörö	jöröin	crossest
katu	+ kaduilla	on the streets	hullu	hulluin	craziest
hylly	hyllyissä	in the shelves	pidetty	+ pidetyin	most liked

Basic form	Past		Conditional	
sano-	sanoi	said	sanoisi	would say
löhö-	löhöi	lounged	löhöisi	would lounge
puhu-	puhui	spoke	puhuisi	would speak
pysähty-	pysähtyi	stopped	pysähtyisi	would stop

---

(2) A long vowel shortens.

Basic form	Plural		Basic form	Superlative	
puu	puita	trees (part.)	vapaa	vapain	most free
maa	maissa	in the countries	vakaa	vakain	firmest
syy	syiden	of the reasons	tervee-	tervein	healthiest
venee-	veneistä	out of the boats			
perhee-	perheissä	in the families			

Basic form	Past		Conditional	
saa-	sai	got	saisi	would get
jää-	jäi	remained	jäisi	would remain
avaa-	avasi	opened	avaisi	would open
makaa-	makasi	lay (cf. §60)	makaisi	would lie

---

(3) The first vowel of the diphthongs **ie**, **uo**, **yö** is dropped.

Basic form	Plural		
tie	teillä	on the roads	(there are no adjectives)
tuo	noissa	in those	
yö	öitä	nights (part.)	
suo	soista	out of the marshes	
työ	töiden	of the works	

Basic form	Past		Conditional	
vie-	vei	took	veisi	would take
juo-	joi	drank	joisi	would drink
syö-	söi	ate	söisi	would eat
tuo-	toi	brought	toisi	would bring
lyö-	löi	hit	löisi	would hit

---

(4) **i** is dropped in diphthongs ending in **-i**.

Basic form	*Plural*
hai	**ha/i/ssa** in the sharks (there are no adjectives)
koi	**ko/i/ta** moths (part.)
täi	**tä/i/den** of the lice

Basic form	*Past*		*Conditional*
voi-	**vo/i**	could	**vo/isi**	would be able
ui-	**u/i**	swam	**u/isi**	would swim
nai-	**na/i**	married	**na/isi**	would marry

---

(5) Short **e** is always dropped.

Basic form | *Plural* | | *Basic form* | *Superlative* |
:--|:--|:--|:--|:--|:--
tuule- | **tuulia** | winds (part.) | **nuore-** | **nuorin** | youngest
tule- | **tulia** | fires (part.) | **suure-** | **suurin** | greatest
lapse- | **lapsilla** | 'at' the children | **uute-** | **uusin** | newest
kiele- | **kielinä** | as languages
naise- | **naisille** | to the women

Basic form	*Past*		*Conditional*
tule-	**tuli**	came	**tulisi**	would come
mene-	**meni**	went	**menisi**	would go
ole-	**oli**	was	**olisi**	would be
hymyile-	**hymyili**	smiled	**hymyilisi**	would smile
teke-	**teki**	did	**tekisi**	would do
näke-	**näki**	saw	**näkisi**	would see

---

(6) Short **i** changes to **e** before the plural and the superlative, but is dropped before the past tense and the conditional.

Basic form | *Plural* | | *Basic form* | *Superlative* |
:--|:--|:--|:--|:--|:--
lasi | **laseissa** | in the glasses | **kiltti** | + **kiltein** | nicest
tuoli | **tuoleilla** | on the chairs | **nätti** | + **nätein** | prettiest
väri | **väreinä** | as colours
tunti | + **tunneilla** | in the lessons

Basic form	Past		Conditional	
salli-	sall/i	allowed	sall/isi	would allow
etsi-	ets/i	looked for	ets/isi	would look for
oppi-	opp/i	learned	opp/isi	would learn
vaati-	vaat/i	demanded	vaat/isi	would demand

---

(7) The vowel **ä** is dropped except in the conditional.

Basic form	Plural		Basic form	Superlative	
päivä	**päiviä**	days (part.)	**syvä**	**syvin**	deepest
ystävä	**ystävillä**	'at' the friends	**ikävä**	**ikävin**	dullest
seinä	**seinien**	of the walls	**kylmä**	**kylmin**	coldest
kylä	**kyliin**	into the villages	**märkä**	**+ märin**	wettest
hedelmä	**hedelmiä**	fruit (part.)	**hämärä**	**hämärin**	dimmest

Basic form	Past		Conditional	
vetä-	**veti**	pulled	**vetäisi**	would pull
kestä-	**kesti**	lasted	**kestäisi**	would last
kiittä-	**kiitti**	thanked	**kiittäisi**	would thank
viettä-	**vietti**	spent	**viettäisi**	would spend
tietä-	**tiesi**	knew	**tietäisi**	would know

Contrary to this rule, in some three-syllable nouns **-ä** changes in the plural to **-ö**, e.g. when the only vowel of the preceding syllable is **i** or **y**: **kynttilä**, **kynttilö/i/tä** 'candles (part.)'; **tekijä**, **tekijö/i/tä** 'makers (part.)'; **päärynä**, **päärynö/i/ssä** 'in the pears'.

---

(8) The vowel **a** remains unchanged in the conditional and is dropped in the superlative. In the plural and past tense of two-syllable words **a** changes to **o** if the first vowel is **a**, **e** or **i**, but is dropped if the first vowel is **u** or **o**.

Basic form	Conditional	
anta-	**antaisi**	would give
otta-	**ottaisi**	would take
sata-	**sataisi**	would rain
muista-	**muistaisi**	would remember
alka-	**alkaisi**	would begin

Basic form	Superlative	
kova	kovin	hardest
vahva	vahvin	strongest
tarkka	+ tarkin	most accurate
vanha	vanhin	oldest
matala	matalin	lowest

Basic form	Plural		Basic form	Past	
matka	matkoilla	on the journeys	alka-	alkoi	began
kirja	kirjoissa	in the books	anta-	antoi	gave
sana	sanoilla	with words	sata-	satoi	rained
piha	pihoilla	in the yards	kaata-	kaatoi	fell
herra	herrojen	of the masters	raata-	raatoi	toiled

Basic form	Plural		Basic form	Past	
koira	koirien	of the dogs	otta-	otti	took
poika	poikien	of the boys	muista-	muisti	remembered
muna	munia	eggs (part.)	osta-	osti	bought
kuuma	kuumissa	in the hot	huuta-	huusi	shouted

In nouns with three or more syllables -a either changes to -o or is dropped; sometimes both changes may be possible. The change to -o occurs in particular when (a) the only vowel of the preceding syllable is i; (b) -a is preceded by a short l, n or r; or (c) -a is preceded by two consonants.

(a)	lukija	lukijoiden	of the readers
	apina	apinoilla	'at' the monkeys
	pakina	pakinoissa	in the columns
	vakoilija	vakoilijoille	to the spies
(b)	omena	omenoita	apples (part.)
	ikkuna	ikkunoissa	in the windows
	tavara	tavaroita	things (part.)
	kampela	kampeloita	flounders (part.)
(c)	kirsikka	+ kirsikoihin	into the cherries
	vasikka	+ vasikoille	to the calves
	sanonta	sanontojen	of the expressions
	jalusta	jalustoilla	on the pedestals

In the plural forms of other nouns of three or more syllables, and of nearly all adjectives, and also in the past tense of verbs with three or more syllables, -a is dropped.

kanava	kanavissa	in the canals
korkea	korkeiden	of the high
sanoma	sanomia	messages (part.)
ainoa	ainoissa	in the only
vaikea	vaikeita	difficult (part.)

ihana	**ihania**	lovely (part.)
kamala	**kamalia**	frightful (part.)
matkusta-	**matkusti**	travelled
pohjusta-	**pohjusti**	founded

5 THE DECLENSION OF NOMINALS

- *General*
- *Nominals with a basic form in -i*
- *Nominals with a basic form in -e*
- *Nominals with a basic form ending in a consonant*

§17 GENERAL

Both nominals and verb forms are built up by the addition of endings to stems. For nominals, in general the basic form itself functions as the stem, and in many declension types the basic form remains unchanged when endings are added: e.g. **auto/n**, **auto/ssa**, **auto/on**, **auto/ni**, **auto/kin**. However, sound alternations may sometimes occur with certain endings; **p**, **t** and **k** in the stem are subject to consonant gradation (§15), and the final vowel may change or disappear when an **-i-** ending is added (§16).

A word may sometimes have different stems according to what kind of ending follows. The different stems are formed via sound alternations. Often the basic form (nominative singular), or the basic form and the partitive singular have their own stems, and all other case, number and possessive endings are attached to a second or third stem. This is called the inflectional stem.

Nominals where the basic form differs from the inflectional stem can be divided into three groups. The first consists of nominals with a basic form ending in **-i** and a corresponding inflectional stem in **-e**, e.g. **kieli** 'language' : **kiele/n**. The second group comprises nominals with a basic form ending in **-e** and an inflectional stem in **-ee**, e.g. **perhe** 'family' : **perhee/n**. Finally, in the third group the basic form ends in a consonant which alternates with other sounds in the inflectional stem, e.g. **kysymys** 'question' : **kysymykse/n**.

In the following sections these groups are presented in turn. The inflectional stem is represented by the genitive form, e.g. **kiele/n**, **perhee/n**, **kysymykse/n**. Almost all the other forms can be made by replacing the genitive ending **-n** by other endings, e.g. **kiele/n**, **kiele/ssä**, **kiele/stä**, **kiele/llä**, **kiele/ni**, **kiele/mme**, etc. The following rule is therefore an important one:

All case, number and possessive forms are made from the inflectional stem (although the partitive sometimes has a separate stem).

The rules of consonant gradation and vowel change affect both basic form stems and inflectional stems.

Consonant gradation (§15) and vowel changes before **-i-** endings (§16) also affect inflectional stems.

Some examples now follow of how the inflectional stem **kiele-** is combined with various nominal endings marking case, number and possession.

Basic form		*Inflectional stem + case*	
kieli̱	language	**kiele̱/n**	of the language
		kiele̱/t	languages
		kiele̱/ssä	in the language
		kiele̱/stä	out of the language
		kiele̱/en	into the language
		kiele̱/llä	with the language
		kiele̱/lle	to the language
		kiele̱/nä	as the language
		kiel/tä	language (part.)

Inflectional stem + plural		*Inflectional stem + possessive*	
kiel/i/ssä	in languages	**kiele̱/ni**	my language
kiel/i/stä	out of languages	**kiele̱/si**	your language
kiel/i/in	into languages	**kiele̱/nsä**	his/her/their language
kiel/i/llä	with languages	**kiele̱/mme**	our language
kiel/i/nä	as languages	**kiele̱/nne**	your language
kiel/i/lle	to languages		

Enclitic particles are attached directly to the inflected or uninflected form.

kieli/k̲i̲n̲	the language too
kiele/n/h̲ä̲n̲	of the language + emph.
kiele/ssä/h̲ä̲n̲	in the language + emph.
kiel/tä/k̲ö̲?	language? (part.)
kiel/i/ssä/h̲ä̲n̲	in languages + emph.
kiele/ni/p̲ä̲	my language + emph.

§18   NOMINALS WITH A BASIC FORM IN -i

§18.1   TUNTI NOMINALS

Most nominals with a basic form ending in -i do not have a separate inflectional stem, but endings are attached directly to the basic form itself (and consonant gradation and vowel change rules consequently apply, §15, §16). These nominals of the type **tunti** 'hour, lesson' include the following. The + symbol indicates that the form has undergone consonant gradation.

		Inflectional stem followed by:		
Basic form		*Case*	*Plural*	*Poss. suffix*
tunti	hour	+ **tunni/n**	+ **tunne/i/ssa**	**tunti/mme**
merkki	mark	+ **merki/n**	+ **merke/i/ssä**	**merkki/mme**
väri	colour	**väri/n**	**väre/i/ssä**	**väri/mme**
laki	law	+ **lai/n**	+ **lae/i/ssa**	**laki/mme**
risti	cross	**risti/n**	**riste/i/ssä**	**risti/mme**
sali	hall	**sali/n**	**sale/i/ssa**	**sali/mme**

§18.2   KIVI NOMINALS

There are three kinds of nominals with a basic form ending in -i, all with an inflectional stem in -e. The first group, words like **kivi** 'stone', also form the partitive singular from this inflectional stem.

		Inflectional stem followed by:		
Basic form		*Case*	*Plural*	*Poss. suffix*
kivi	stone	**kive/n**	**kiv/i/ssä**	**kive/mme**
Suomi	Finland	**Suome/n**	–	**Suome/mme**
kaikki	all	+ **kaike/n**	+ **kaik/i/ssa**	**kaikke/mme**
lehti	newspaper	+ **lehde/n**	+ **lehd/i/ssä**	**lehte/mme**
hetki	moment	**hetke/n**	**hetk/i/ssä**	**hetke/mme**
talvi	winter	**talve/n**	**talv/i/ssa**	**talve/mme**
järvi	lake	**järve/n**	**järv/i/ssä**	**järve/mme**
lahti	bay	+ **lahde/n**	+ **lahd/i/ssa**	**lahte/mme**
jälki	trace	+ **jälje/n**	+ **jälj/i/ssä**	**jälke/mme**
joki	river	+ **joe/n**	+ **jo/i/ssa**	**joke/mme**
nimi	name	**nime/n**	**nim/i/ssä**	**nime/mme**
ovi	door	**ove/n**	**ov/i/ssa**	**ove/mme**

Words like **kivi** thus form their partitive singular from an inflectional stem in **-e**, and differ in precisely this respect from words of the **kieli** type (§18.3) and the **vesi** type (§18.4).

Basic form		Inflectional stem followed by partitive
kaikk<u>i</u>	all	kaikk<u>e</u>/a
Suom<u>i</u>	Finland	Suom<u>e</u>/a
kiv<u>i</u>	stone	kiv<u>e</u>/ä
leht<u>i</u>	newspaper	leht<u>e</u>/ä
hetk<u>i</u>	moment	hetk<u>e</u>/ä
ov<u>i</u>	door	ov<u>e</u>/a

A comparison of the **tunti** and **kivi** types shows that it is not possible to derive a rule from the basic form which would determine which nominals have an inflectional stem in **-e** and which do not. However, it is possible to state a rule operating in the opposite direction.

> Nominals with an inflectional stem ending in short **-e** have a basic form ending in short **-i**.

This rule always allows us to derive the basic form from the inflectional stem. The rule does not cover nominals with an inflectional stem in long **-ee**, such as **perhe** 'family', **perhee/n** (§19). There are a few exceptions: **kolme** 'three', **kolme/n**; **itse** 'self', **itse/n**; **nalle** 'teddy', **nalle/n**; **nukke** 'doll', + **nuke/n**.

§18.3 KIELI NOMINALS

Kieli type nominals only differ from the **kivi** type in the partitive singular, where the **-e-** of the inflectional stem is dropped. Compare §18.2 and note the partitive singular.

		Inflectional stem followed by:		
Basic form		Case	Plural	Poss. suffix
kiel<u>i</u>	language	kiel<u>e</u>/n	kiel/i/ssä	kiel<u>e</u>/ni
ver<u>i</u>	blood	ver<u>e</u>/n	ver/i/ssä	ver<u>e</u>/ni
mer<u>i</u>	sea	mer<u>e</u>/n	mer/i/ssä	mer<u>e</u>/ni
tul<u>i</u>	fire	tul<u>e</u>/n	tul/i/ssa	tul<u>e</u>/ni
tuul<u>i</u>	wind	tuul<u>e</u>/n	tuul/i/ssa	tuul<u>e</u>/ni
ään<u>i</u>	sound	ään<u>e</u>/n	ään/i/ssä	ään<u>e</u>/ni
lum<u>i</u>	snow	lum<u>e</u>/n	lum/i/ssa	lum<u>e</u>/ni
un<u>i</u>	dream	un<u>e</u>/n	un/i/ssa	un<u>e</u>/ni
nuor<u>i</u>	young	nuor<u>e</u>/n	nuor/i/ssa	–
suur<u>i</u>	great	suur<u>e</u>/n	suur/i/ssa	–
pien<u>i</u>	small	pien<u>e</u>/n	pien/i/ssä	–
laps<u>i</u>	child	laps<u>e</u>/n	laps/i/ssa	laps<u>e</u>/ni

		Inflectional stem followed by:		
Basic form		*Case (except partitive)*	*Partitive*	
kieli	language	**kiele/n**	**kiel/tä**	
veri	blood	**vere/n**	**ver/ta**	(*Note*: -ta)
meri	sea	**mere/n**	**mer/ta**	(*Note*: -ta)
tuli	fire	**tule/n**	**tul/ta**	
tuuli	wind	**tuule/n**	**tuul/ta**	
ääni	sound	**ääne/n**	**ään/tä**	
lumi	snow	**lume/n**	**lun/ta**	(*Note*: m → n)
pieni	small	**piene/n**	**pien/tä**	

The **-e** of the inflectional stem is dropped before the partitive singular ending only when it is preceded by certain consonants. The following rule holds:

> In the partitive singular **-e-** is dropped if the preceding consonant is **l**, **r**, or **n**; or **t** occurring after these or after a vowel.

§18.4　VESI NOMINALS

The rule given above also covers **vesi** nominals. These are a group of words with a basic form in **-si** and an inflectional stem in **-te-**.

> In **vesi** nominals **-si** alternates with **-te-**; before the plural **-i-**, **-te-** changes to **-s-**; **-te-** is subject to consonant gradation (§15).

To illustrate the inflectional stem not subject to consonant gradation let us take the illative singular, e.g. **vete/en** 'into the water'.

		Inflectional stem followed by:			
Basic form		*Case (except partitive)*	*Partitive*	*Plural*	*Possessive suffix*
vesi	water	**vete/en**	**vet/tä**	**ves/i/ssä**	**vete/ni**
käsi	hand	**käte/en**	**kät/tä**	**käsi/ssä**	**käte/ni**
uusi	new	**uute/en**	**uut/ta**	**uus/i/ssa**	–
viisi	five	**viite/en**	**viit/tä**	**viis/i/ssä**	–
tosi	true	**tote/en**	**tot/ta**	**tos/i/ssa**	–
kansi	cover	**kante/en**	**kant/ta**	**kans/i/ssa**	**kante/ni**
varsi	handle	**varte/en**	**vart/ta**	**vars/i/ssa**	**varte/ni**

No alternation			*Alternation*	
vete/nä	as water		+ **vede/n**	of the water
vete/en	into the water		+ **vede/t**	waters
vete/mme	our water		+ **vede/ssä**	in the water
vete/nne	your water		+ **vede/stä**	out of the water
vete/ni	my water		+ **vede/llä**	with water

§19   NOMINALS WITH A BASIC FORM IN **-e**

The second group of nominals with a special inflectional stem is (almost entirely) made up of nominals with a basic form ending in **-e**. The other inflected forms are made from a stem ending in a long **-ee**. The following points should also be noted.

The partitive singular is formed by adding the ending **-tta ~ -ttä** directly to the basic form.

The rules of consonant gradation apply to the basic form and to the partitive singular, not to the inflectional stem, which has a long vowel (§15.3).

The **-ee-** of the inflectional stem shortens before the plural **-i-** (§16.2).

			Inflectional stem followed by:		
Basic		*Partitive*	*Case*	*Plural*	*Possessive*
form		*singular*	*(except*		*suffix*
			part. sing.)		
perhe	family	**perhe/ttä**	**perhee/n**	**perhe/i/ssä**	**perhee/ni**
vene	boat	**vene/ttä**	**venee/n**	**vene/i/ssä**	**venee/ni**
joukkue	team	**joukkue/tta**	**joukkuee/n**	**joukkue/i/ssa**	**joukkuee/ni**
+ **liike**	shop	+ **liike/ttä**	**liikkee/n**	**liikke/i/ssä**	**liikkee/ni**
+ **suhde**	relation	+ **suhde/tta**	**suhtee/n**	**suhte/i/ssa**	**suhtee/ni**
kone	machine	**kone/tta**	**konee/n**	**kone/i/ssa**	**konee/ni**
+ **tarve**	need	+ **tarve/tta**	**tarpee/n**	**tarpe/i/ssa**	**tarpee/ni**
+ **sade**	rain	+ **sade/tta**	**satee/n**	**sate/i/ssa**	**satee/ni**
+ **ote**	grasp	+ **ote/tta**	**ottee/n**	**otte/i/ssa**	**ottee/ni**
+ **liikenne**	traffic	+ **liikenne/ttä**	**liikentee/n**	**liikente/i/ssä**	**liikentee/ni**

Strong grade		*Weak grade*	
liikkee/n	of the movement	+ **liike**	movement
liikkee/t	movements		(*nom. sing.*)
liikkee/ssä	in the movement	+ **liike/ttä**	movement
liikke/i/ssä	in the movements		(*part. sing.*)

Strong grade		*Weak grade*
lii<u>kk</u>ee/stä	out of the movement	
lii<u>kk</u>e/i/stä	out of the movements	
lii<u>kk</u>ee/mme	our movement	
lii<u>kk</u>ee/nne	your movement	

Almost all nominals with a basic form in **-e** are declined in this way. For exceptions, see the end of §18.2.

§20 NOMINALS WITH A BASIC FORM ENDING IN A CONSONANT

The third nominal stem type consists of nominals with a basic form ending in a consonant. Several sub-groups need to be distinguished (§20.1–8), but they all have the following features in common.

> The inflectional stem often ends in the vowel **-e**, and the final consonant of the basic form alternates with other sounds.
>
> The partitive singular is generally formed with the ending **-ta ~ -tä**, which is attached directly to the basic form (cf. §19).
>
> Consonant gradation affects the basic form and the partitive singular.
>
> The final vowel of the inflectional stem (usually **-e**) changes before the plural **-i-**.

§20.1 IHMINEN NOMINALS

The most important sub-group of these nominals is made up of those ending in **-nen**, the type **ihminen** 'person'.

> In **ihminen** nominals **-nen** changes to **-se-** in the inflectional stem; the partitive singular is formed from the inflectional stem with the final **-e** dropped.

Basic form		Inflectional stem followed by:			
		Case (except part. sing.)	Partitive	Plural	Possessive suffix
ihminen	person	ihmise/n	ihmis/tä	ihmis/i/ssä	ihmise/ni
nainen	woman	naise/n	nais/ta	nais/i/ssa	naise/ni
yleinen	general	yleise/n	yleis/tä	yleis/i/ssä	–
hevonen	horse	hevose/n	hevos/ta	hevos/i/ssa	hevose/ni
punainen	red	punaise/n	punais/ta	punais/i/ssa	–
toinen	another	toise/n	tois/ta	tois/i/ssa	–
jokainen	every	jokaise/n	jokais/ta	–	–

§20.2 AJATUS NOMINALS

There are two groups of nominals with a basic form ending in a short vowel + s. The most common of these is the type **ajatus** 'thought' (cf. §20.3).

> In **ajatus** nominals -s changes to -kse- in the inflectional stem; the partitive singular is formed directly from the basic form.

Basic form		Partitive singular	Inflectional stem followed by:		Possessive suffix
			Case (except part. sing.)	Plural	
ajatus	thought	ajatus/ta	ajatukse/n	ajatuks/i/ssa	ajatukse/ni
kysymys	question	kysymys/tä	kysymykse/n	kysymyks/i/ssä	kysymykse/ni
vastaus	answer	vastaus/ta	vastaukse/n	vastauks/i/ssa	vastaukse/ni
teos	work	teos/ta	teokse/n	teoks/i/ssa	teokse/ni
rakennus	building	rakennus/ta	rakennukse/n	rakennuks/i/ssa	rakennukse/ni
hallitus	government	hallitus/ta	hallitukse/n	hallituks/i/ssa	hallitukse/ni
päätös	decision	päätös/tä	päätökse/n	päätöks/i/ssä	päätökse/ni

§20.3 TAIVAS NOMINALS

In nominals like **taivas** 'heaven' the -s of the basic form alternates with a vowel identical with the preceding vowel.

> In **taivas** nominals -s changes in the inflectional stem to a vowel identical with the preceding vowel; the partitive singular is formed directly from the basic form.

Basic form		Partitive singular	*Inflectional stem followed by:*		
			Case (except part. sing.)	Plural	Possessive suffix
taivas	heaven	taivas/ta	taivaa/n	taiva/i/ssa	taivaa/ni
valmis	ready	valmis/ta	valmii/n	valmi/i/ssa	–
+ rikas	rich	+ rikas/ta	rikkaa/n	rikka/i/ssa	–
oppilas	pupil	oppilas/ta	oppilaa/n	oppila/i/ssa	oppilaa/ni
+ tehdas	factory	+ tehdas/ta	tehtaa/n	tehta/i/ssa	tehtaa/ni
+ porras	step	+ porras/ta	portaa/n	porta/i/ssa	portaa/ni
+ kirkas	bright	+ kirkas/ta	kirkkaa/n	kirkka/i/ssa	–

Strong grade		*Weak grade*	
tehtaa/n	of the factory	+ tehdas	factory
tehtaa/t	factories		(*nom. sing.*)
tehtaa/ssa	in the factory	+ tehdas/ta	factory
tehta/i/ssa	in the factories		(*part. sing.*)
tehtaa/sta	out of the factory		
tehta/i/sta	out of the factories		
tehtaa/mme	our factory		
tehtaa/nne	your factory		

§20.4   HYVYYS NOMINALS

The third group of nominals with a basic form ending in **-s** is the type **hyvyys** 'goodness'. This includes all nouns with a final **-s** preceded by a long vowel, and many nouns with two different vowels preceding the final **-s**. All the words in this group are derived forms, cf. **hyvä** 'good' – **hyv/yys** 'goodness', **kaunis** 'beautiful' – **kaune/us** 'beauty', **osa** 'part' – **os/uus** 'share'. They have several special sound alternations.

In **hyvyys** nominals **-s** changes to **-te-** in the inflectional stem of the singular; before the plural **-i**, **-s** changes to **-ks-**; the partitive singular is formed from the inflectional stem and **-e-** is dropped.

Basic form		Partitive singular	*Inflectional stem followed by:*		
			Case (except part. sing.)	Plural	Possessive suffix
hyvyys	goodness	hyvyyt/tä	+ hyvyyde/n	hyvyyks/i/ä	hyvyyte/ni
korkeus	height	korkeut/ta	+ korkeude/n	korkeuks/i/a	korkeute/ni
rakkaus	love	rakkaut/ta	+ rakkaude/n	rakkauks/i/ssa	rakkaute/ni
totuus	truth	totuut/ta	+ totuude/n	totuuks/i/ssa	totuute/ni

Strong grade		*Weak grade*	
totuutee/n	into truth	+ **totuude/n**	of truth
totuute/na	as truth	+ **totuude/ssa**	in truth
totuute/mme	our truth	+ **totuude/sta**	out of truth
		+ **totuude/lla**	with truth

§20.5 AVAIN NOMINALS

Most of the words inflected like **avain** 'key' are derived with the ending **-in** (cf. §93.1). The stem alternates between **-in-** and **-ime-**, and the partitive singular is made from the basic form.

				Inflectional stem followed by:		
Basic		*Partitive*	*Case*	*Plural*		*Possessive*
form		*singular*	*(except part. sing.)*			*suffix*
avain	key	**avain/ta**	**avaime/n**	**avaim/i/ssa**		**avaime/ni**
puhelin	telephone	**puhelin/ta**	**puhelime/n**	**puhelim/i/ssa**		**puhelime/ni**
kirjain	letter	**kirjain/ta**	**kirjaime/n**	**kirjaim/i/ssa**		**kirjaime/ni**

§20.6 TYÖTÖN NOMINALS

Derived nominals of the type **työ/tön** 'unemployed' are very common. The partitive singular is made from the basic form. The other inflected forms are based on a stem where **-ton ~ -tön** alternates with **-ttoma- ~ -ttömä-**. In the plural **-a-/-ä-** is dropped (§16.7–8).

			Inflectional stem followed by:	
Basic		*Partitive*	*Case*	*Plural*
form		*singular*	*(except part. sing.)*	
työ/tön	unemployed	**työ/tön/tä**	**työ/ttömä/n**	**työ/ttöm/i/ssä**
onne/ton	unhappy	**onne/ton/ta**	**onne/ttoma/n**	**onne/ttom/i/ssa**
tie/tön	without roads	**tie/tön/tä**	**tie/ttömä/n**	**tie/ttöm/i/ssä**

§20.7 ASKEL NOMINALS

There are a few dozen nominals ending in a consonant which form another small sub-group. The two final sounds of the basic form are generally **-el** or **-en**. The partitive singular is made from the basic form. The inflectional stem adds an **-e-** (which is dropped before the plural **-i-**).

Basic form		Partitive singular	*Inflectional stem followed by:* Case (except part. sing.)	Plural	Possessive suffix
askel	step	**askel/ta**	**askele/n**	**askel/i/ssa**	**askele/ni**
sävel	tune	**sävel/tä**	**sävele/n**	**sävel/i/ssä**	**sävele/ni**
jäsen	member	**jäsen/tä**	**jäsene/n**	**jäsen/i/ssä**	**jäsene/ni**

§20.8   LYHYT NOMINALS

There are a few nominals ending in **-ut** or **-yt**, where in the inflectional stem the **-t** changes to **-e-**, which is then dropped before the plural **-i-**. The group includes **kevyt** 'light', **lyhyt** 'short', **ohut** 'thin', **olut** 'beer'. The nouns **mies** 'man' and **kevät** 'spring' also have unusual declensions.

Basic form		Partitive singular	*Inflectional stem followed by:* Case (except part. sing.)	Plural	Possessive suffix
lyhyt	short	**lyhyt/tä**	**lyhye/n**	**lyhy/i/ssä**	–
olut	beer	**olut/ta**	**olue/n**	**olu(e)/i/ssa**	**olue/ni**
mies	man	**mies/tä**	**miehe/n**	**mieh/i/ssä**	**miehe/ni**
kevät	spring	**kevät/tä**	**kevää/n**	**kevä/i/ssä**	**kevää/ni**

New loan words ending in a final consonant form their inflectional stem by adding the vowel **i**, which changes to **e** before the plural **-i-** (§16.6). Cf. **stadion** 'stadium': **stadioni/n**, **stadioni/a**, **stadione/i/ta**. Loan words with a final **-s**, however, generally decline like **ajatus** nominals (§20.2), e.g. **anis** 'aniseed': **anikse/n**, **anikse/ssa**, **anis/ta** (part. sing.).

6 THE CONJUGATION OF VERBS

- *General*
- *Infinitive endings*
- *Inflectional stems*

§21 GENERAL

Verb forms are built up like nominals by adding endings to stems. Verbs differ from nominals in that they do not have an independent basic form as such to which inflectional endings could be attached, as is the case with nominals: cf. the basic form **auto** 'car' and the inflected forms **auto/n**, **auto/ssa, auto/i/hin**.

The dictionary form of Finnish verbs, i.e. the shorter form of the first infinitive, already has an ending, e.g. **osta/a** '(to) buy', **vastat/a** '(to) answer', **juo/da** '(to) drink'. Before other verb forms can be made one must first take off the infinitive ending from the stem, to which other endings are then added, cf. **osta/a** '(to) buy' : **osta/isi/n** 'I would buy', **osta/nut** 'bought'.

Some verbs have more than one stem, in which case one is formed from the other, e.g. **vastat/a** '(to) answer' : **vastaa/n** 'I answer' and **tul/la** '(to) come' : **tule/n** 'I come'. Consonant gradation (§15) and vowel changes before **-i-** (§16) affect verbs in much the same way as nominals, e.g. **anta/a** '(to) give' : **anna/n** 'I give' (consonant gradation) : **anno/i/n** 'I gave' (vowel change, and also consonant gradation).

The stems needed for the conjugation of verbs are the infinitive stem, which is arrived at after the infinitive endings are detached according to the rules given in §22, and the inflectional stem, which can be formed from the infinitive stem and to which e.g. the personal endings are added (§23). The rules for the formation of the inflectional stem are given in §23.

The following examples illustrate the use of the first infinitive (cf. also §74).

Haluan *juo/da* olutta.	I want to *drink* some beer.
Tahtoisitko *syö/dä*?	Would you like to *eat*?
Yritän *sano/a* asiat selvästi.	I try to *say* the things clearly.
Minun täytyy *lähte/ä*.	I must *leave*.
Saako täällä *laula/a*?	Can one *sing* here?

Nyt sinun pitää *lopetta/a*.	Now you must *stop*.
Tässä on mukava *istu/a*.	It is nice to *sit* here.
Olisi kiva *men/nä* ulos.	It would be nice to *go* out.

§22 INFINITIVE ENDINGS

The first infinitive has four endings, (1) **-a** ~ **-ä**, (2) **-da** ~ **-dä**, (3) **-ta** ~ **-tä**, and (4) **-la** ~ **-lä**, **-ra** ~ **-rä**, **-na** ~ **-nä**. The most common one is **-a** ~ **-ä**. All the infinitive endings are preceded by the infinitive stem.

> The ending **-a** ~ **-ä** occurs when the infinitive stem ends in a short vowel.

anta/a	give	**kysy/ä**	ask
alka/a	begin	**lähte/ä**	leave
katso/a	look	**pitä/ä**	hold
puhu/a	talk	**tietä/ä**	know

> The ending **-a** ~ **-ä** also occurs when the infinitive stem ends in a short vowel followed by **t** (usually **-at/a**, **-ät/ä**).

huomat/a	notice	**herät/ä**	awake
halut/a	want	**hypät/ä**	jump
korjat/a	repair	**määrät/ä**	order
vastat/a	answer	**kerät/ä**	collect

> The ending **-da** ~ **-dä** occurs when the infinitive stem ends in a long vowel or a diphthong.

saa/da	get	**jää/dä**	remain
tuo/da	bring	**vie/dä**	take
voi/da	be able	**syö/dä**	eat
luennoi/da	lecture	**pysäköi/dä**	park

> The ending **-ta** ~ **-tä** occurs when the infinitive stem ends in **-s**.

nou<u>s</u>/<u>ta</u>	rise	**pää<u>s</u>/<u>tä</u>**	be allowed
juo<u>s</u>/<u>ta</u>	run	**tönäi<u>s</u>/<u>tä</u>**	shove
mumi<u>s</u>/<u>ta</u>	mumble	**pe<u>s</u>/<u>tä</u>**	wash
valai<u>s</u>/<u>ta</u>	light	**vili<u>s</u>/<u>tä</u>**	swarm

---

The endings **-la ~ -lä, -na ~ -nä, -ra ~ -rä** occur when the infinitive stem ends in an identical consonant (**-l, -n, -r**).

---

tu<u>l</u>/<u>la</u>	come	**viete<u>l</u>/<u>lä</u>**	entice
o<u>l</u>/<u>la</u>	be	**nie<u>l</u>/<u>lä</u>**	swallow
ajate<u>l</u>/<u>la</u>	think	**hymyi<u>l</u>/<u>lä</u>**	smile
pa<u>n</u>/<u>na</u>	put	**me<u>n</u>/<u>nä</u>**	go
pu<u>r</u>/<u>ra</u>	bite		

The most important types are those exemplified by **anta/a** and **huomat/a**. **Saa/da** verbs are also important. There are not many verbs with infinitives ending in **-na ~ -nä** and **-ra ~ -rä**.

In **anta/a** and **saa/da** verbs all inflected forms are based on the infinitive stem. But also in the other verb groups at least some forms are based on this stem. The following rule states which inflected forms of all verbs are made from the infinitive stem.

With all verbs the infinitive stem is used to form:

1 the past participle (§61)
2 most imperative forms (§66)
3 potential forms (§67)
4 passive forms (§69–72)
5 the second infinitive (§76)

---

§23 INFLECTIONAL STEMS

This section shows how the five groups of verbs introduced above form their inflectional stems (§23.1–4); it concludes with a few special cases (§23.5–6). All forms except those mentioned in the above rule are made from the inflectional stem. For each verb, two examples of the inflectional stem are given in order to illustrate the effect of consonant gradation (e.g. **a<u>nt</u>a/a** '(to) give' : **a<u>nn</u>a/n** 'I give').

§23.1   ANTA/A VERBS

Anta/a verbs, where the infinitive ending occurs after a short vowel, do not have a separate inflectional stem; other endings are added directly to the infinitive stem. The + symbol indicates consonant gradation.

> **Anta/a** verbs have only an infinitive stem.

Infinitive		*First person sing.*		*Third person sing.*	
osta/a	buy	osta/n	I buy	osta/a	he buys
alka/a	begin	+ ala/n		alka/a	
ymmärtä/ä	understand	+ ymmärrä/n		ymmärtä/ä	
etsi/ä	look for	etsi/n		etsi/i	
luke/a	read	+ lue/n		luke/e	
neuvo/a	advise	neuvo/n		neuvo/o	
unohta/a	forget	+ unohda/n		unohta/a	
herättä/ä	wake up	+ herätä/n		herättä/ä	
kysy/ä	ask	kysy/n		kysy/y	

§23.2   HUOMAT/A VERBS

Huomat/a verbs, which generally end in **-at/a**, **-ät/ä**, are a very important group ('contracted verbs'). The relation here between the infinitive stem and the inflectional stem is a complex one. The **-t-** of the infinitive alternates with **-a-/-ä-** and consonant gradation applies to the infinitive, whereas there is no alternation in the inflectional stem (§15.4).

> In **huomat/a** verbs the **-t-** of the infinitive stem changes to **-a-** or **-ä-** according to vowel harmony; consonant gradation affects the infinitive stem.

Infinitive		*First person sing.*		*Third person sing.*	
huomat/a	notice	huomaa/n	I notice	huomaa	he notices
osat/a	know how	osaa/n		osaa	
+ hypät/ä	jump	hyppää/n		hyppää	
seurat/a	follow	seuraa/n		seuraa	
tarjot/a	offer	tarjoa/n		tarjoa/a	
halut/a	want	halua/n		halua/a	
+ pelät/ä	fear	pelkää/n		pelkää	
määrät/ä	order	määrää/n		määrää	
+ veikat/a	bet	veikkaa/n		veikkaa	

Infinitive		First person sing.	Third person sing.
+ **haka<u>t</u>/a**	hew	**hakka<u>a</u>/n**	**hakka<u>a</u>**
+ **maa<u>t</u>/a**	lie	**maka<u>a</u>/n**	**maka<u>a</u>**
+ **tava<u>t</u>/a**	meet	**tapa<u>a</u>/n**	**tapa<u>a</u>**
+ **kado<u>t</u>/a**	disappear	**kato<u>a</u>/n**	**kato<u>a</u>/a**
vara<u>t</u>/a	reserve	**vara<u>a</u>/n**	**vara<u>a</u>**

§23.3 SAA/DA VERBS

The third group, **saa/da** verbs, where the infinitive ending occurs after a long vowel or a diphthong, is similar to the **anta/a** group in that these verbs too have only an infinitive stem.

Saa/da verbs have only an infinitive stem.

Infinitive		First person sing.		Third person sing.	
saa/da	get	**saa/n**	I get	**saa**	he gets
myy/dä	sell	**myy/n**		**myy**	
juo/da	drink	**juo/n**		**juo**	
voi/da	be able	**voi/n**		**voi**	
luennoi/da	lecture	**luennoi/n**		**luennoi**	
kanavoi/da	direct	**kanavoi/n**		**kanavoi**	
pysäköi/dä	park	**pysäköi/n**		**pysäköi**	
<u>teh</u>/<u>dä</u>	do	+ **tee/n**		**teke/e**	
<u>näh</u>/<u>dä</u>	see	+ **näe/n**		**näke/e**	

The common verbs **teh/dä** 'do' and **näh/dä** 'see' are exceptional, since they have an inflectional stem ending in **-ke-**, with **-k** alternating with the **-h-** of the infinitive stem.

§23.4 NOUS/TA AND TUL/LA VERBS

These two groups form their inflectional stem by adding **-e-** to the infinitive.

The inflectional stem of **nous/ta** and **tul/la** verbs is formed by adding **-e-** to the infinitive stem.

Infinitive		First person sing.		Third person sing.	
nou<u>s</u>/ta	rise	**nou<u>se</u>/n**	I rise	**nou<u>se</u>/e**	he rises
pe<u>s</u>/tä	wash	**pe<u>se</u>/n**		**pe<u>se</u>/e**	

Infinitive		*First person sing.*	*Third person sing.*
tul/la	come	tul**e**/n	tul**e**/e
men/nä	go	men**e**/n	men**e**/e
hymyil/lä	smile	hymyil**e**/n	hymyil**e**/e
+ ajatel/la	think	ajattel**e**/n	ajattel**e**/e
kiistel/lä	dispute	kiistel**e**/n	kiistel**e**/e
+ työskennel/lä	work	työskentel**e**/n	työskentel**e**/e
julkais/ta	publish	julkais**e**/n	julkais**e**/e

In these verbs too, consonant gradation occurs in the infinitive stem (§15.4), e.g. **ajatel/la** '(to) think' : **ajattele/n** 'I think'.

§23.5 TARVIT/A VERBS

Infinitives ending in **-it/a**, **-it/ä**, e.g. **tarvit/a** 'need', are similar to **huomat/a** verbs (§23.2), but their inflectional stem is formed differently:

> The inflectional stem of **tarvit/a** verbs is formed by adding **-se-** to the infinitive stem.

Infinitive		*First person sing.*		*Third person sing.*	
tarvit/a	need	**tarvitse/n**	I need	**tarvitse/e**	he needs
ansait/a	earn	**ansaitse/n**		**ansaitse/e**	
hallit/a	rule	**hallitse/n**		**hallitse/e**	
harkit/a	consider	**harkitse/n**		**harkitse/e**	
häirit/ä	disturb	**häiritse/n**		**häiritse/e**	

§23.6 LÄMMET/Ä VERBS

Infinitives ending in **-et/a**, **-et/ä** like **lämmet/ä** 'get warm' also form their inflectional stem in a different way (cf. §23.2).

> In **lämmet/ä** verbs the **-t-** of the infinitive stem changes to **-ne-** in the inflectional stem.

Infinitive		*First person sing.*		*Third person sing.*	
+ **lämmet/ä**	get warm	**lämpene/n**	I get warm	**lämpene/e**	he gets warm
vanhet/a	grow old	**vanhene/n**		**vanhene/e**	
+ **paet/a**	flee	**pakene/n**		**pakene/e**	
+ **kalvet/a**	turn pale	**kalpene/n**		**kalpene/e**	
laajet/a	grow wider	**laajene/n**		**laajene/e**	

7 BASIC SENTENCE STRUCTURE

- *Present tense personal endings*
- *The nominative (basic form of nominals)*
- *Singular and plural*
- *The verb **olla** '(to) be'*
- *'To have' in Finnish*
- *Negative sentences*
- *Questions and answers*
- *Concord of attributes*

§24 PRESENT TENSE PERSONAL ENDINGS

Finnish has three grammatical persons, each occurring in the singular and the plural. They correspond to the following pronouns.

minä	I	**me**	we
sinä	you (sing.)	**te**	you (pl.)
hän; se	he, she; it	**he, ne**	they

The third person singular covers all singular nominals except the pronouns **minä** and **sinä**, and the third person plural covers all plural nominals except the pronouns **me** and **te**. Finite verb forms (§13) show concord of person with the grammatical subject. The persons have their own endings, which are added to the verb stem (the third person singular often has no ending).

	Singular	*Plural*
First person	**-n**	**-mme**
Second person	**-t**	**-tte**
Third person	(cf. below)	**-vat ~ -vät**

These endings are attached to the inflectional stem (§23) after any tense and mood endings (§13). In the third person singular of the present indicative the final vowel of the stem is lengthened.

In the third person singular of the present indicative the short vowel following the final consonant or syllable boundary of the inflectional stem is lengthened.

	Singular		*Plural*	
First person	(**minä**) **osta/n**	I buy	(**me**) **osta/mme**	we buy
	(**minä**) **sano/n**	I say	(**me**) **sano/mme**	we say
	(**minä**) **saa/n**	I get	(**me**) **saa/mme**	we get
	(**minä**) **syö/n**	I eat	(**me**) **syö/mme**	we eat
	(**minä**) **tule/n**	I come	(**me**) **tule/mme**	we come
Second person	(**sinä**) **osta/t**	you buy	(**te**) **osta/tte**	you buy
	(**sinä**) **sano/t**	you say	(**te**) **sano/tte**	you say
	(**sinä**) **saa/t**	you get	(**te**) **saa/tte**	you get
	(**sinä**) **syö/t**	you eat	(**te**) **syö/tte**	you eat
	(**sinä**) **tule/t**	you come	(**te**) **tule/tte**	you come
Third person	**hän osta/a**	he/she buys	**he osta/vat**	they buy
	Pekka sano/o	Pekka says	**he sano/vat**	they say
	tyttö saa	the girl gets	**tytöt saa/vat**	the girls get
	mies syö	the man eats	**miehet syö/vät**	the men eat
	auto tule/e	the car comes	**autot tule/vat**	the cars come

A long vowel, and the second vowel of a diphthong, are not lengthened in the third person singular, cf. **Kalle saa** 'Kalle gets'; **Kalle syö** 'Kalle eats'. Note words such as **halua/a** 'wants', **kohoa/a** 'rises', where vowel lengthening occurs after a syllable boundary (cf. §9). The independent subject words of the third person cannot usually be omitted, but subject pronouns in the first and second persons often are, in which case the personal ending of the verb is all that indicates the person (shown in brackets above).

First and second person subject pronouns (**minä**, **sinä**, **me**, **te**) are often omitted.

The second person plural ending **-tte** is also used as a polite form addressed to a single person. The form **osta/tte** can thus mean 'you (pl.) buy' or 'you (sing., polite) buy'.

Consonant gradation applies in the first and second persons of many verbs on condition that the ending is not preceded by a long vowel (§15.2, §15.4). Examples follow of **anta/a** 'give', **otta/a** 'take' and **vetä/ä** 'pull'.

	Singular	*Plural*
First person	**anna/n**	**anna/mme**
	ota/n	**ota/mme**
	vedä/n	**vedä/mme**
Second person	**anna/t**	**anna/tte**

	ota/t	**ota/tte**
	vedä/t	**vedä/tte**
Third person	**anta/a**	**anta/vat**
	otta/a	**otta/vat**
	vetä/ä	**vetä/vät**

In these forms there is no consonant gradation in **huomat/a** verbs on account of the long vowel, cf. **hyppää/n** 'I jump', **hyppää/t** 'you jump', **hän hyppää** 'he/she jumps'. The following examples illustrate the personal endings of the most important verb types (cf. §23).

etsi/ä	*look for*	**luke/a**	*read*	**lentä/ä**	*fly*
etsi/n	etsi/mme	lue/n	lue/mme	lennä/n	lennä/mme
etsi/t	etsi/tte	lue/t	lue/tte	lennä/t	lennä/tte
etsi/i	etsi/vät	luke/e	luke/vat	lentä/ä	lentä/vät

osat/a	*know how*	**maat/a**	*lie*	**halut/a**	*want*
osaa/n	osaa/mme	makaa/n	makaa/mme	halua/n	halua/mme
osaa/t	osaa/tte	makaa/t	makaa/tte	halua/t	halua/tte
osaa	osaa/vat	makaa	makaa/vat	halua/a	halua/vat

saa/da	*get*	**juo/da**	*drink*	**myy/dä**	*sell*
saa/n	saa/mme	juo/n	juo/mme	myy/n	myy/mme
saa/t	saa/tte	juo/t	juo/tte	myy/t	myy/tte
saa	saa/vat	juo	juo/vat	myy	myy/vät

nous/ta	*rise*	**tul/la**	*come*	**men/nä**	*go*
nouse/n	nouse/mme	tule/n	tule/mme	mene/n	mene/mme
nouse/t	nouse/tte	tule/t	tule/tte	mene/t	mene/tte
nouse/e	nouse/vat	tule/e	tule/vat	mene/e	mene/vät

tarvit/a	*need*	**ansait/a**	*earn*	**häirit/ä**	*disturb*
tarvitse/n	tarvitse/mme	ansaitse/n	ansaitse/mme	häiritse/n	häiritse/mme
tarvitse/t	tarvitse/tte	ansaitse/t	ansaitse/tte	häiritse/t	häiritse/tte
tarvitse/e	tarvitse/vat	ansaitse/e	ansaitse/vat	häiritse/e	häiritse/vät

§25 THE NOMINATIVE (BASIC FORM OF NOMINALS)

The nominative is the basis upon which the Finnish case system is built. The nominative is the primary form of nominals in dictionaries, and it is also the most common case of most nominal words. The functions of the nominative are seen most clearly when it is compared with the partitive, the second basic case in the system. The partitive often expresses an indefinite, non-limited quantity of something, allowing the possibility that there may exist more of it. The nominative, on the other hand, expresses either a concrete or abstract whole or a definite, limited, total quantity.

§25.1   NOMINATIVE ENDINGS

The nominative has

1   no ending in the singular
2   the ending **-t** in the plural

Nominative singular		Nominative plural	
auto	car	**auto/t**	the cars
maa	country	**maa/t**	the countries
talo	house	**talo/t**	the houses
hylly	shelf	**hylly/t**	the shelves
nainen	woman	**naise/t**	the women (cf. §20.1)
kivi	stone	**kive/t**	the stones (cf. §18.2)
käsi	hand	**käde/t**	the hands (cf. §18.4)

There are no articles in Finnish corresponding to the way the difference between definite and indefinite meaning is expressed e.g. in English (the car, a car). Whether the Finnish expression **auto** is to be interpreted as definite or indefinite is often indicated by the word order of the sentence in question (§25.3). The nominative plural, e.g. **auto/t**, almost always has the meaning 'definite'.

§25.2   NON-DIVISIBLE AND DIVISIBLE NOUNS

In order to explain the use of the nominative we also need to make a distinction with respect to the partitive. A noun is *non-divisible* (countable) if it refers to a more or less concrete entity that cannot be divided into smaller parts in such a way that the parts share the quality of the whole. Non-divisible nouns can be counted (one *x*, two *x*'s, etc.). Examples: **auto** 'car', **talo** 'house', **hylly** 'shelf', **nainen** 'woman', **käsi** 'hand', **sielu** 'soul'. (In English these nouns would be classified as singular count nouns.)

A noun is *divisible* (non-countable) if it refers to a concrete mass or an abstract entity that can be divided into parts in such a way that the parts share the quality of the whole. Examples: **kahvi** 'coffee', **maito** 'milk', **rauta** 'iron', **kulta** 'gold', **olut** 'beer', **vesi** 'water', **vahvuus** 'strength', **rakkaus** 'love'. Divisible nouns cannot normally be counted.

§25.3   USE OF THE NOMINATIVE

The use of the nominative depends on three factors: whether the noun is divisible or non-divisible, whether a divisible word is definite or indefinite, and sometimes whether the noun is singular or plural. Four rules follow below.

> (1) Singular, non-divisible subject nouns appear in the nominative and express
>   (a) definite meaning at the beginning of the sentence
>   (b) indefinite meaning at the end of the sentence.

Auto on kadulla.	*The car* is in the street.
Kadulla on *auto*.	There is *a car* in the street.
Nainen on talossa.	*The woman* is in the house.
Talossa on *nainen*.	There is *a woman* in the house.
Kirja ilmestyi.	*The book* was published.
Ilmestyi *kirja*.	*A book* was published.
Pullo on kaapissa.	*The bottle* is in the cupboard.
Kaapissa on *pullo*.	There is *a bottle* in the cupboard.

Nouns at the beginning of a sentence are generally interpreted as definite, i.e. to be known in the sense that the hearer (reader) knows what they refer to.

Sentences where both subject and object are non-divisible are often ambiguous as regards definiteness:

Mies osti *kirjan*.	*A/the man* bought *a/the book*.
Nainen hankki *auton*.	*A/the woman* got *a/the car*.

If the word order is inverted, with the object at the beginning and the subject at the end, the object is interpreted as definite (known) and the subject as indefinite (new):

Kirjan osti mies.	*A* man bought *the book./*
	The book was bought by *a man*.

Singular non-divisible predicate nouns (complements) are always in the nominative.

Pekka on *mies*.	Pekka is *a man*.
Tuula on *nainen*.	Tuula is *a woman*.
Tämä on *pöytä*.	This is *a table*.
Tuo on *auto*.	That is *a car*.
Auto tuo on!	That's *a car*! (with emphasis)
Paavo on *opettaja*.	Paavo is *a teacher*.

Singular predicative adjectives are also in the nominative if the subject is a non-divisible word.

Auto on *sininen*.	The car is *blue*.

Tuo vene on *kallis.*	That boat is *expensive.*
Kalle on *pitkä.*	Kalle is *tall.*
Ajatuksesi oli *hyvä.*	Your idea was *good.*
Kone on *likainen.*	The machine is *dirty.*

---

(2) Non-divisible plural nouns with definite meaning take the ending **-t**.

Auto/t **ovat kadulla.**	*The cars* are in the street.
Kadulla ovat *auto/t.*	In the street are *the cars!*
Miehe/t **tulivat kotiin.**	*The men* came home.
Kirja/t **maksavat 10 mk.**	*The books* cost 10 marks.
Ministeri/t **lähtivät lomalle.**	*The ministers* went on holiday.
Pekka osti *kirja/t.*	Pekka bought *the books.*
Leena näki *laiva/t.*	Leena saw *the ships.*
Syön nämä *omena/t.*	I'll eat these *apples.*

---

(3) Divisible nouns with definite (total, limited) meaning are in the nominative singular.

Ruoka **maistuu hyvältä.**	*(The) food* tastes good.
Kahvi **on kupissa.**	The *coffee* is in the cup.
Liha **maksaa paljon.**	*(The) meat* is expensive.
Aika **loppuu.**	*(The) time* is up.
Osta *olut!* (cf. §37, §38)	Buy *the beer!*
Kahvi **juotiin.** (cf. §37, §38)	The *coffee* was drunk.
Tämä on Pekan *maito.*	This is Pekka's *milk.*
Maito **on valkoista.**	*(The) milk* is white.
Ilma **on kirkas.**	The *air* is clear.

---

(4) The subject is always in the nominative if
    (a) the verb has an object
    (b) the verb is **olla** '(to) be' and a complement follows.

Poika **potkii palloa.**	*A/the boy* kicks a/the ball.	(4a)
Pojat **potkivat palloa.**	*(The) boys* kick a/the ball.	(4a)
Kahvi **on hyvää.**	*(The) coffee* is good.	(4b)
Mikään **ei ole mahdotonta.**	*Nothing* is impossible.	(4b)

§26 SINGULAR AND PLURAL

Nominals inflect for singular and plural. The singular always has no ending. The plural has two endings, **-t** and **-i-**. The ending **-t** occurs only in the nominative and accusative (§37, §38), and **-i-** in all other cases.

	Singular		*Plural*	
Nominative	**talo**	house	**talo/t**	the houses
Genitive	**talo/n**	of the house	**talo/j/en**	of the houses
Partitive	**talo/a**	house	**talo/j/a**	houses
Inessive	**talo/ssa**	in the house	**talo/i/ssa**	in the houses
Elative	**talo/sta**	out of the house	**talo/i/sta**	out of the houses
Illative	**talo/on**	into the house	**talo/i/hin**	into the houses
Adessive	**talo/lla**	on the house	**talo/i/lla**	on the houses
Ablative	**talo/lta**	off the house	**talo/i/lta**	off the houses
Allative	**talo/lle**	onto the house	**talo/i/lle**	onto the houses
Essive	**talo/na**	as a house	**talo/i/na**	as houses
Translative	**talo/ksi**	to a house	**talo/i/ksi**	to (become) houses

> The plural **-i-** changes to **-j-** between two vowels.

This rule concerns the genitive plural and the partitive plural: **hylly/j/en** 'of the shelves', **hylly/j/ä** 'shelves', **pullo/j/en** 'of the bottles', **pullo/j/a** 'bottles', **tyttö/j/en** 'of the girls', **tyttö/j/ä** 'girls'.

All plural forms are made from the inflectional stem (§18–20), and before the plural **-i-** the vowel changes apply (§16). The table below illustrates the formation of the plural.

Nominative singular		*Inflectional stem*	(cf. §)	*Nominative plural*	*Inessive plural*	*Vowel change (cf. §)*
pullo	bottle	pullo/n	–	pullo/t	pullo/i/ssa	–
katu	street	kadu/n	–	kadu/t	kadu/i/ssa	–
maa	country	maa/n	–	maa/t	ma/i/ssa	16.2
risti	cross	risti/n	18.1	risti/t	riste/i/ssä	16.6
kivi	stone	kive/n	18.2	kive/t	kiv/i/ssä	16.5
lehti	newspaper	lehde/n	18.2	lehde/t	lehd/i/ssä	16.5
meri	sea	mere/n	18.3	mere/t	mer/i/ssä	16.5
vesi	water	vede/n	18.4	vede/t	ves/i/ssä	16.5; 18.4
kone	machine	konee/n	19	konee/t	kone/i/ssa	16.2
liike	movement	liikkee/n	19	liikkee/t	liikke/i/ssä	16.2
työ	work	työ/n	–	työ/t	tö/i/ssä	16.3
hai	shark	hai/n	–	hai/t	ha/i/ssa	16.4

Nominative singular		Inflectional stem	(cf. §)	Nominative plural	Inessive plural	Vowel change (cf. §)
seinä	wall	seinä/n	–	seinä/**t**	sein/**i**/ssä	16.7
vanha	old	vanha/n	–	vanha/**t**	vanh**o**/**i**/ssa	16.8
tavara	thing	tavara/n	–	tavara/**t**	tavar**o**/**i**/ssa	16.8
koira	dog	koira/n	–	koira/**t**	koir/**i**/ssa	16.8
ihminen	person	ihmi**se**/n	20.1	ihmise/**t**	ihmis/**i**/ssä	16.5
vanhus	old person	vanhu**kse**/n	20.2	vanhukse/**t**	vanhu**ks**/**i**/ssa	16.5
taivas	heaven	taiv**aa**/n	20.3	taivaa/**t**	taiva/**i**/ssa	16.2
rikas	rich	rikk**aa**/n	20.3	rikkaa/**t**	rikka/**i**/ssa	16.2
totuus	truth	totuu**de**/n	20.4	totuude/**t**	totuu**ks**/**i**/ssa	16.5; ks: 20.4
avain	key	avai**me**/n	20.5	avaime/**t**	avaim/**i**/ssa	16.5
työtön	unemployed	työttö**mä**/n	20.6	työttömä/**t**	työttöm/**i**/ssä	16.7
jäsen	member	jäse**ne**/n	20.7	jäsene/**t**	jäsen/**i**/ssä	16.5
mies	man	mie**he**/n	20.8	miehe/**t**	mieh/**i**/ssä	16.5

There are many nouns which appear only in the plural even though they refer to a singular concept. Plural words of this kind include:

Nominative plural		Inessive plural
kasvot	face	**kasvoissa**
housut	trousers	**housuissa**
sakset	scissors	**saksissa**
kärryt	cart	**kärryissä**
häät	wedding	**häissä**
tanssit	dance	**tansseissa**
arpajaiset	lottery	**arpajaisissa**

§27   THE VERB **OLLA** '(TO) BE'

The conjugation of the verb **olla** is exceptional in the third person. The inflectional stem is formed by adding **-e-** (§23.4).

(minä) ole/n	I am	(me) ole/mme	we are
(sinä) ole/t	you are	(te) ole/tte	you are
hän on	he/she is	he o/vat	they are

The ending **-e-** is dropped before the past tense ending **-i-** and also before the conditional **-isi-** (§16.5).

(minä) ol/i/n	I was	(me) ol/i/mme	we were
(sinä) ol/i/t	you were	(te) ol/i/tte	you were
hän ol/i	he/she was	he ol/i/vat	they were
(minä) ol/isi/n	I would be	(me) ol/isi/mme	we would be
(sinä) ol/isi/t	you would be	(te) ol/isi/tte	you would be
hän ol/isi	he/she would be	he ol/isi/vat	they would be

§28 'TO HAVE' IN FINNISH

In the Finnish possessive structure the possessor appears in the adessive case **-lla ~ -llä**; the form **on** of the verb **olla** follows, and then the person or thing possessed.

> Possessor + **-lla ~ -llä** + **on** + person or thing possessed.

Paavo/lla on uusi pyörä.	Paavo has a new bicycle ('at' Paavo is . . .).
Isä/llä on kaksi autoa.	Father has two cars.
Suome/lla on hyvät mahdollisuudet.	Finland has good chances.
Äidi/llä on silmälasit.	Mother has glasses.

The adessive forms of the personal pronouns are very common.

minu/lla on	I have	**mei/llä on**	we have
sinu/lla on	you have	**tei/llä on**	you have
häne/llä on	he/she has	**hei/llä on**	they have

For inalienable possession or 'intimate connection' the inessive case **-ssa ~ -ssä** is used instead of the adessive.

Maa/ssa on uusi hallitus.	The country has a new government.
Venee/ssä on pitkä masto.	The boat has a tall mast.
Puu/ssa on vihreät lehdet.	The tree has green leaves.
Auto/ssa on neljä pyörää.	The car has four wheels.

§29 NEGATIVE SENTENCES

There is no invariable negation word in Finnish negative sentences. Negation is expressed by an inflected verb, which shows concord of grammatical person with the subject of the sentence like any other finite verb.

	Singular	*Plural*
First person	**en**	**emme**
Second person	**et**	**ette**
Third person	**ei**	**eivät**

The negative forms of the present indicative are based on this negation verb, which is followed by the inflectional stem (§23) of the main verb, without any personal ending and in the weak grade (§15) except before a long vowel.

Negation verb   +   Inflectional stem of main verb
+ personal ending   in weak grade (unless before long vowel)

The changes caused by consonant gradation are important: cf. **anta/a** '(to) give' : **hän anta/a** 'he/she gives', **anna/n** 'I give', **anna/tte** 'you (pl.) give'. Further examples follow of the present indicative negative. The form of the main verb can always be derived by detaching the first or second person ending from the present affirmative.

Affirmative		*Negative*	
tulet	you come	**et tule**	you do not come
luemme	we read	**emme lue**	we do not read
he lukevat	they read	**he eivät lue**	they do not read
hän lukee	he/she reads	**hän ei lue**	he/she does not read
hyppään	I jump	**en hyppää**	I do not jump
hyppäätte	you (pl.) jump	**ette hyppää**	you (pl.) do not jump
se vetää	it pulls	**se ei vedä**	it does not pull
vedän	I pull	**en vedä**	I do not pull
he vetävät	they pull	**he eivät vedä**	they do not pull
vedämme	we pull	**emme vedä**	we do not pull
hän tarvitsee	he/she needs	**hän ei tarvitse**	he/she does not need

The negative forms of **olla** all contain the stem **ole-**.

en ole	I am not	**emme ole**	we are not
et ole	you are not	**ette ole**	you are not
ei ole	(he/she) is not	**eivät ole**	(they) are not

The negative forms of other tenses will be presented later together with the tenses themselves (§63). The following rule concerning negative sentences is an important one.

In negative sentences the following constituents are in the partitive:

(1) the object
(2) that which is possessed
(3) that which does not exist

(1) **Emme juo** *olut/ta.* We do not drink *beer*.
 Ettekö näe *auto/a?* Don't you see *the car?*
 En tunne *hän/tä.* I don't know *him/her.*
 He eivät omista *vene/ttä.* They do not own *a boat*.

(2) **Minulla ei ole** *auto/a.* I don't have *a car*.
 Meillä ei ole *punaviini/ä.* We don't have any *red wine*.
 Eikö teillä ole *lämmin/tä ruoka/a?* Don't you have any *warm food?*
 Maassa ei ole *hallitus/ta.* The country has no *government*.

(3) **Kadulla ei ole** *auto/a.* There is no *car* in the street.
 Kotona ei ole *isä/ä.* There is no *father* at home.
 Jääkaapissa ei ole *maito/a.* There is no *milk* in the fridge.
 Komerossa ei ole *vaatte/i/ta.* There are no *clothes* in the
         cupboard.

§30 QUESTIONS AND ANSWERS

§30.1 QUESTIONS WITH **-KO** ~ **-KÖ** ('YES/NO' QUESTIONS)

Direct questions that can be answered by 'yes' or 'no' are formed by moving the word being questioned to the beginning of the sentence and adding to it the enclitic particle **-ko** ~ **-kö**, which is almost always the last ending of the word. The word questioned is most commonly the verb. If we take the sentence **Pekka saapui Turkuun aamulla** 'Pekka arrived at Turku in the morning', we can form the following questions:

Saapu/i/ko Pekka Turkuun aamulla?
Did Pekka arrive at Turku in the morning?

Pekka/ko saapui Turkuun aamulla?
Was it Pekka who arrived at Turku in the morning?

Turku/un/ko Pekka saapui aamulla?
Was it at Turku that Pekka arrived in the morning?

Aamu/lla/ko Pekka saapui Turkuun?
Was it in the morning that Pekka arrived at Turku?

Here are some more examples of the formation of these direct questions.

Mene/t/kö ulos? Are you going out?
Ole/t/ko sairas? Are you ill?
Sa/isi/n/ko oluen? Could I have a beer?
Pitä/ä/kö Jussi Marjasta? Does Jussi like Marja?
Tietä/vät/kö he, että tulen? Do they know that I am coming?
Puu/ko tämä on? Is this a TREE? (capital letters
       indicating emphasis)

Ruotsi/ssa/ko Kalle on?   Is Kalle in SWEDEN?
Häne/t/kö sinä tapasit?   Was it him/her that you met?
Presidenti/ksi/kö Koivisto valittiin? Was Koivisto elected PRESIDENT?

There are many ways of answering such questions in the affirmative. The word being questioned is often repeated (in the right person, if it is a verb, and without the ending **-ko ~ -kö**). If the word questioned is a verb one can also answer **kyllä** 'yes', and if it is some other word one can answer **niin** (literally: 'so'). Both **kyllä** and **niin** can be used with a repetition of the word questioned. The word **joo** 'yes, yeah' is used mostly in the spoken language.

Question	*Various affirmative answers*
Tul/i/ko Pekka Turkuun?	**– Tuli.**
Did Pekka come to Turku?	**– Kyllä tuli.**
	– Kyllä.
Ole/t/ko sairas?	**– Olen.**
Are you ill?	**– Kyllä olen.**
	– Kyllä.
Mene/tte/kö tanssimaan?	**– Menemme.**
Are you going dancing?	**– Kyllä menemme.**
	– Kyllä.
O/vat/ko lapset ulkona?	**– Ovat.**
Are the children outside?	**– Kyllä ovat.**
	– Kyllä.
Auto/n/ko ostitte?	**– Niin.**
Was it a car that you bought?	**– Niin, auton.**
	– Auton.
Mäntynieme/ssä/kö presidentti	**– Niin.**
asuu?	**– Niin, Mäntyniemessä.**
Is it at Mäntyniemi that the	**– Mäntyniemessä.**
president lives?	

Negative answers to direct questions are formed from the negation verb (§28), which must be in the right person and may be followed by the inflectional stem of the main verb with no personal ending.

Question	*Negative answer*
Mene/e/kö Tauno Kotkaan?	**– Ei (mene).**
Is Tauno going to Kotka?	
Ole/t/ko kovin sairas?	**– En (ole).**
Are you very ill?	

Syö/tte/kö hernekeittoa?	**– Emme (syö).**
Do you eat pea-soup?	**– En (syö).**
O/vat/ko kirjat laukussa?	**– Eivät (ole).**
Are the books in the bag?	
Viljo/ko siellä on?	**– Ei (vaan Auli).**
Is that Viljo there?	No (it's Auli).
Juna/lla/ko tulitte?	**– Emme (vaan linja-autolla).**
Did you come by train?	No (by bus).

A question can be made especially polite by using the conditional ending **-isi-** and/or the particle **-han ~ -hän**.

Sa/isi/n/ko pullon punaviiniä?	Could I have a bottle of red wine?
Sa/isi/n/ko/han kylmän oluen?	Might I have a cold beer?
On/ko/han Viljo Kohonen tavattavissa?	I wonder if Viljo Kohonen is in?
Ol/isi/ko/han teillä nailonsukkia?	I wonder if you might have any nylon stockings?

The ending **-ko ~ -kö** is also used in indirect questions.

En tiedä, men/i/kö Auli kotiin.	I don't know if Auli went home.
Kysy, on/ko heillä lämmintä ruokaa.	Ask if they have warm food.
Ole/t/ko varma, saa/ko sinne mennä?	Are you sure that (*lit.* whether) one can go there?
Kerro, maistu/i/ko ruoka hyvältä.	Say whether the food tasted good.

§30.2   QUESTION-WORD QUESTIONS ('WH'-QUESTIONS)

The second main class of questions is question-word questions, which are answered more precisely (not just 'yes' or 'no'). The most important question words in Finnish are the following (cf. §56):

mikä	what, which (more concrete, definite meaning)
mitä	what, which (more abstract, indefinite meaning; partitive of **mikä**)
millainen	what kind of
missä	where
mistä	from where, whence
mihin	where to, whither (more precise)
minne	where to, whither (less precise)
miten	how, in what way
koska	when
milloin	when
kuka	who
kuinka	how
kumpi	which of two

Mikä, **kuka** and **millainen** decline in different cases like ordinary nominals. In fact, **mitä**, **missä**, **mistä** and **mihin** are inflected forms of the pronoun **mikä**. **Kenen** 'whose' is the genitive of the pronoun **kuka**.

Question	*Answer*
Mikä **tämä on?**	**(Se on) kynä.**
What is this?	(It is) a pen.
Mitä **tämä on?**	**(Se on) olutta.**
What is this?	(It is) beer.
Missä **Auli on?**	**(Auli on) luennolla.**
Where is Auli?	(Auli is) at the lecture.
Mistä **tulet?**	**(Tulen) Oslosta.**
Where do you come *from*?	(I come) from Oslo.
Mihin **panen vaatteeni?**	**(Pane ne) sohvalle.**
Where shall I put my clothes?	(Put them) on the sofa.
Millainen **mies hän on?**	**(Hän on) mukava (mies).**
What kind of a man is he?	(He is a) nice (man).
Koska **John tuli Suomeen?**	**(Hän tuli Suomeen) viime vuonna.**
When did John come to Finland?	(He came to Finland) last year.
Kuka **tuo pitkä nainen on?**	**(Hän on) Tyyne Nyrkiö.**
Who is that tall woman?	(She is) Tyyne Nyrkiö.
Kuinka **paljon pullo olutta maksaa?**	**(Se maksaa) kolme markkaa.**
How much does a bottle of beer cost?	(It costs) three marks.
Kenen **lasi tämä on?**	**(Se on) Jorman.**
Whose glass is this?	(It is) Jorma's.
Kenellä **pallo on?**	**(Pallo on) minulla.**
Who has got the ball? (lit. *'At'* whom is . . .)	I have. (lit. [The ball is] 'at' me.)

§31 CONCORD OF ATTRIBUTES

Attributes are modifiers of nouns. There are two kinds of attributes occurring before the noun: pronoun attributes (**tämä auto** '*this* car') and adjective attributes (**sininen auto** 'a *blue* car'). Both agree with the headword in case and number.

Attributes agree with the headword in case and number.

---

iso auto	a big car
iso/t auto/t	the big cars
iso/ssa auto/ssa	in the big car
iso/i/ssa auto/i/ssa	in the big cars
sininen kukka	a blue flower
sinise/t kuka/t	the blue flowers
sinise/ssä kuka/ssa	in the blue flower
sinis/i/ssä kuk/i/ssa	in the blue flowers
tuo punainen kukka	that red flower
tuo/n punaise/n kuka/n	of that red flower
tuo/ssa punaise/ssa kuka/ssa	in that red flower
nuo punaise/t kuka/t	those red flowers
no/i/lla punais/i/lla kuk/i/lla	with those red flowers
tämä vanha kahvi	this old coffee
tä/tä vanha/a kahvi/a	this old coffee (part.)
tä/stä vanha/sta kahvi/sta	out of this old coffee
tä/llä vanha/lla kahvi/lla	with this old coffee

Attributes occurring before plural headwords (§26) are always in the plural, but such expressions may refer to either singular or plural concepts.

kaunii/t kasvo/t	a beautiful face/the beautiful faces
nämä kasvo/t	this face/these faces
terävä/t sakse/t	sharp scissors (one pair or several)
harma/i/ssa housu/i/ssa	in grey trousers
yhde/t sakse/t	one pair of scissors
kahde/t kasvo/t	two faces

There are a few adjectives or adjective-like words which are exceptions to the concord rule and do not agree with the headword. The most common ones are: **ensi** 'first', **eri** 'different', **joka** 'every', **koko** 'whole', **pikku** 'little', **viime** 'last', cf. **ensi kerra/lla** 'next time'; **viime talve/na** 'last winter'; **koko kaupungi/ssa** 'in the whole town'; **joka ihmise/lle** 'to every person'; **eri sängy/ssä** 'in a different bed'.

There are several idiomatic two-word expressions where the words are inflected in different cases:

mi/llä tavo/i/n	in which way (adessive sg. and instructive pl.)
si/llä tapa/a	in this way (adessive sg. and partitive sg.)

8 THE PARTITIVE

- *Formation of the partitive*
- *Use of the partitive*

After the nominative, the most important case in Finnish is the partitive. In many instances the nominative and the partitive are in opposition to each other. Both may appear as the case of the subject, object and complement (for the object, see also §37).

The nominative expresses a concrete or abstract whole or a definite quantity (§25). The partitive often expresses an indefinite, non-limited quantity of something, allowing the possibility that more of it may exist.

§32 FORMATION OF THE PARTITIVE

§32.1 PARTITIVE SINGULAR

In the singular the partitive has three endings: **-a ~ -ä**, **-ta ~ -tä**, **-tta ~ -ttä**. The first two also appear in the plural.

> The ending **-a ~ -ä** occurs when the inflectional stem ends in a consonant followed by a short vowel (which is not an **-e-** that may be dropped).

Basic form		Inflectional stem (gen. sing.)	Cf. §	Partitive singular
oma	own	oma/n	–	oma/**a**
päivä	day	päivä/n	–	päivä/**ä**
vanha	old	vanha/n	–	vanha/**a**
elämä	life	elämä/n	–	elämä/**ä**
talo	house	talo/n	–	talo/**a**
tuoli	chair	tuoli/n	–	tuoli/**a**
hetki	moment	hetke/n	18.2	hetke/**ä**
katu	street	kadu/n	–	katu/**a**
käsky	order	käsky/n	–	käsky/**ä**
Suomi	Finland	Suome/n	18.2	Suome/**a**
koti	home	kodi/n	–	koti/**a**

Basic form		Inflectional stem (gen. sing.)	Cf. §	Partitive singular
kaupunki	town	kaupungi/n	–	kaupunki/**a**
kivi	stone	kive/n	18.2	kive/**ä**
presidentti	president	presidenti/n	–	presidentti/**ä**
Helsinki	Helsinki	Helsingi/n	–	Helsinki/**ä**
kaikki	all	kaike/n	18.2	kaikke/**a**
onni	luck	onne/n	18.2	onne/**a**
asia	matter	asia/n	–	asia/**a**
ainoa	only	ainoa/n	–	ainoa/**a**
tärkeä	important	tärkeä/n	–	tarkeä/**ä**
vaikea	difficult	vaikea/n	–	vaikea/**a**

Words ending in **-ea**, **-eä** in particular may also take the longer ending **-ta** ~ **-tä**, e.g. **korkea/a** ~ **korkea/ta** 'high', **pehmeä/ä** ~ **pehmeä/tä** 'soft'.

The ending **-ta** ~ **-tä** occurs after

(a) a basic form ending in a long vowel or a diphthong
(b) an inflectional stem ending in a consonant + **-e-** which has then been dropped
(c) a basic form ending in a consonant
(d) a monosyllabic pronoun stem

	Basic form		Inflectional stem (gen. sing.)	Cf. §	Partitive singular
(a)	**maa**	country	maa/n	–	maa/**ta**
	syy	reason	syy/n	–	syy/**tä**
	tie	road	tie/n	–	tie/**tä**
	Porvoo	(place name)	Porvoo/n	–	Porvoo/**ta**
	työ	work	työ/n	–	työ/**tä**
	pää	head	pää/n	–	pää/**tä**
	yö	night	yö/n	–	yö/**tä**
	kuu	moon	kuu/n	–	kuu/**ta**
(b)	**kieli**	language	kiele/n	18.3	kiel/**tä**
	pieni	small	piene/n	18.3	pien/**tä**
	lumi	snow	lume/n	18.3	lun/**ta** (NB: **n**)
	ääni	sound	ääne/n	18.3	ään/**tä**
	meri	sea	mere/n	18.3	mer/**ta** (-**ta**!)
	veri	blood	vere/n	18.3	ver/**ta** (-**ta**!)
	vesi	water	vede/n	18.4	vet/**tä**
	uusi	new	uude/n	18.4	uut/**ta**

Basic form		*Inflectional stem (gen. sing.)*	*Cf. §*	*Partitive singular*
kansi	cover	kann**e**/n	18.4	kant/**ta**
ihminen	person	ihmis**e**/n	20.1	ihmis/**tä**
Virtanen	(surname)	Virtas**e**/n	20.1	Virtas/**ta**
tavallinen	ordinary	tavallis**e**/n	20.1	tavallis/**ta**
hyvyys	goodness	hyvyyd**e**/n	20.4	hyvyyt/**tä**
likaisuus	dirtiness	likaisuud**e**/n	20.4	likaisuut/**ta**
(c) **ajatus**	thought	ajatukse/n	20.2	ajatus/**ta**
kysymys	question	kysymykse/n	20.2	kysymys/**tä**
kiitos	thanks	kiitokse/n	20.2	kiitos/**ta**
taivas	heaven	taivaa/n	20.3	taivas/**ta**
kirves	axe	kirvee/n	20.3	kirves/**tä**
puhelin	telephone	puhelime/n	20.6	puhelin/**ta**
arvoton	valueless	arvottoma/n	20.6	arvoton/**ta**
askel	pace	askele/n	20.7	askel/**ta**
mies	man	miehe/n	20.8	mies/**tä**
olut	beer	olue/n	20.8	olut/**ta**
(d) **tuo**	that	tuo/n	–	tuo/**ta**
tämä	this	tämä/n	–	tä/**tä**
se	it	se/n	–	si/**tä**
joka	which (relative)	jonka	–	jo/**ta**
mikä	which	minkä	–	mi/**tä**
kuka	who	kene/n	–	ke/**tä**

The partitive ending for words ending in **-io, -iö** is **-ta ~ -tä**, e.g. **valtio/ta** 'state', **radio/ta** 'radio', **keittiö/tä** 'kitchen', **yhtiö/tä** 'company'.

The ending **-tta ~ -ttä** is attached to basic forms ending in **-e-** (§19).

Basic form		*Inflectional stem (gen. sing.)*	*Partitive singular*
perhe	family	perhee/n	perhe/**ttä**
suhde	relation	suhtee/n	suhde/**tta**
liikenne	traffic	liikentee/n	liikenne/**ttä**
kone	machine	konee/n	kone/**tta**
tunne	feeling	tuntee/n	tunne/**tta**
kirje	letter	kirjee/n	kirje/**ttä**
virhe	mistake	virhee/n	virhe/**ttä**

However, the words **itse** 'self', **kolme** 'three' and **nukke** 'doll', and proper names like **Kalle**, **Raahe**, **Ville**, take the ending **-a ~ -ä**.

§32.2   PARTITIVE PLURAL

In the plural the partitive has two endings, **-a** ~ **-ä** and **-ta** ~ **-tä**, which are added to the inflectional stem after the plural **-i-** (§26). The plural **-i-** causes vowel changes in the stem (§16), and between vowels **-i-** changes to **-j-** (§26). Consonant gradation is rare in the partitive plural, since the endings do not fulfil the basic conditions for alternation (§15.2).

> The ending **-a** ~ **-ä** is always used when the inflectional stem of the singular ends in a short vowel.

Basic form		Inflectional stem	Cf. §	Partitive singular	Partitive plural
talo	house	talo/n	–	talo/a	talo/j/**a**
katu	street	kadu/n	–	katu/a	katu/j/**a**
tunti	hour	tunni/n	–	tunti/a	tunte/j/**a**
lasi	glass	lasi/n	–	lasi/a	lase/j/**a**
kivi	stone	kive/n	18.2	kive/ä	kiv/i/**ä**
lehti	newspaper	lehde/n	18.2	lehte/ä	leht/i/**ä**
tuuli	wind	tuule/n	18.3	tuul/ta	tuul/i/**a**
pieni	small	piene/n	18.3	pien/tä	pien/i/**ä**
käsi	hand	käde/n	18.4	kät/tä	käs/i/**ä**
kansi	cover	kanne/n	18.4	kant/ta	kans/i/**a**
päivä	day	päivä/n	–	päivä/ä	päiv/i/**ä**
sama	same	sama/n	–	sama/a	samo/j/**a**
poika	boy	poja/n	–	poika/a	poik/i/**a**
kirja	book	kirja/n	–	kirja/a	kirjo/j/**a**
nainen	woman	naise/n	20.1	nais/ta	nais/i/**a**
yleinen	general	yleise/n	20.1	yleis/tä	yleis/i/**ä**
sormus	ring	sormukse/n	20.2	sormus/ta	sormuks/i/**a**
nuoruus	youth	nuoruude/n	20.4	nuoruut/ta	nuoruuks/i/**a**
avain	key	avaime/n	20.5	avain/ta	avaim/i/**a**
koditon	homeless	kodittoma/n	20.6	koditon/ta	kodittom/i/**a**
jäsen	member	jäsene/n	20.7	jäsen/tä	jäsen/i/**ä**
mies	man	miehe/n	20.8	mies/tä	mieh/i/**ä**

In words of three or more syllables such as **kanava** 'canal', **aurinko** 'sun', **ammatti** 'profession', the ending **-a** ~ **-ä** occurs when the last vowel of the stem is dropped, and otherwise when the penultimate syllable of the word ends in a consonant (**pääl.lik.kö** 'chief', **au.rin.ko** 'sun') or in two vowels (**rat.kai.su** 'decision').

Basic form		Inflectional stem	Partitive singular	Partitive plural
aurinko	sun	auringo/n	aurinko/a	aurinko/j/**a**
ammatti	profession	ammati/n	ammatti/a	ammatte/j/**a**
hedelmä	fruit	hedelmä/n	hedelmä/ä	hedelm/i/**ä**
ystävä	friend	ystävä/n	ystävä/ä	ystäv/i/**ä**
metalli	metal	metalli/n	metalli/a	metalle/j/**a**
kysely	inquiry	kysely/n	kysely/ä	kysely/j/**ä**
päällikkö	chief	päällikö/n	päällikkö/ä	päällikkö/j/**ä**
ratkaisu	decision	ratkaisu/n	ratkaisu/a	ratkaisu/j/**a**
omena	apple	omena/n	omena/a	omen/i/**a**

The ending **-ta ~ -tä** is used when the inflectional stem of the singular ends in two vowels.

Basic form		Inflectional stem	Cf. §	Partitive singular	Partitive plural
maa	country	maa/n	–	maa/ta	ma/i/**ta**
kuu	moon	kuu/n	–	kuu/ta	ku/i/**ta**
syy	reason	syy/n	–	syy/tä	sy/i/**tä**
vapaa	free	vapaa/n	–	vapaa/ta	vapa/i/**ta**
perhe	family	perhee/n	19	perhe/ttä	perhe/i/**tä**
lääke	medicine	lääkkee/n	19	lääke/ttä	lääkke/i/**tä**
aine	substance	ainee/n	19	aine/tta	aine/i/**tä**
tie	road	tie/n	–	tie/tä	te/i/**tä**
tuo	that	tuo/n	–	tuo/ta	no/i/**ta**
työ	work	työ/n	–	työ/tä	tö/i/**tä**
rikas	rich	rikkaa/n	20.3	rikas/ta	rikka/i/**ta**
hammas	tooth	hampaa/n	20.3	hammas/ta	hampa/i/**ta**
kallis	expensive	kallii/n	20.3	kallis/ta	kalli/i/**ta**
ohut	thin	ohue/n	20.8	ohut/ta	ohu/i/**ta**
lyhyt	short	lyhye/n	20.8	lyhyt/tä	lyhy/i/**tä**
asia	matter	asia/n	–	asia/a	asio/i/**ta**
tärkeä	important	tärkeä/n	–	tärkeä/ä	tärke/i/**tä**
ainoa	only	ainoa/n	–	ainoa/a	aino/i/**ta**
komea	fine	komea/n	–	komea/a	kome/i/**ta**

Many nouns of three or more syllables, with a penultimate syllable ending in short vowel, take the partitive plural ending **-ta ~ -tä**. This also applies to nouns ending in **-kka ~ -kkä** and **-la ~ -lä**.

Basic form		Partitive singular	Partitive plural
lukija	reader	lukija/a	lukijo/i/**ta**
kulkija	wanderer	kulkija/a	kulkijo/i/**ta**
lusikka	spoon	lusikka/a	lusiko/i/**ta**
kahvila	café	kahvila/a	kahvilo/i/**ta**
käymälä	toilet	käymälä/ä	käymälö/i/**tä**
omena	apple	omena/a	omeno/i/**ta**
päärynä	pear	päärynä/ä	päärynö/i/**tä**
peruna	potato	peruna/a	peruno/i/**ta**
tavara	thing	tavara/a	tavaro/i/**ta**
ankkuri	anchor	ankkuri/a	ankkure/i/**ta**
arvelu	supposition	arvelu/a	arvelu/i/**ta**

In many words of this type both **-ta** ~ **-tä** and **-a** ~ **-ä** are possible, but consonant gradation then affects the stem differently depending on the form chosen; for example **päällikkö/j/ä** : **päällikö/i/tä** 'chiefs', **lusiko/i/ta** : **lusikko/j/a** 'spoons', **sairaalo/i/ta** : **sairaalo/j/a** 'hospitals', **omen/i/a** : **omeno/i/ta** 'apples'.

Adjectives of three or more syllables form their partitive plural in the normal way by adding the ending **-a** ~ **-ä** (cf. §16).

Basic form		Partitive singular	Partitive plural
ahkera	hard-working	ahkera/a	ahker/i/**a**
ankara	severe	ankara/a	ankar/i/**a**
hämärä	dim	hämärä/ä	hämär/i/**ä**
vikkelä	quick	vikkelä/ä	vikkel/i/**ä**

The following pronoun forms are important:

Basic form		Partitive singular	Partitive plural
minä	I	minu/**a**	
sinä	you (sing.)	sinu/**a**	
hän	he/she	hän/**tä**	
me	we		me/i/**tä**
te	you (pl.)		te/i/**tä**
he	they		he/i/**tä**
se	it	si/**tä**	ni/i/**tä**
tämä	this	tä/**tä**	nä/i/**tä**
tuo	that	tuo/**ta**	no/i/**ta**

§33   USE OF THE PARTITIVE

§33.1   PARTITIVE SUBJECT

It is helpful to compare the use of the partitive with that of the nominative (§25.3): these two cases are semantically complementary to each other. The following rule concerns the use of the partitive as a subject and object case.

> With divisible words the partitive expresses an indefinite, non-limited quantity.

Typical uses of the partitive are thus **vet/tä** 'water', **valo/a** 'light', **rakkaut/ta** 'love', **tuole/j/a** 'chairs', **auto/j/a** 'cars'. The following rule concerns the partitive subject.

> In sentences with a partitive subject
>
> 1   the subject is generally at the end of the sentence
> 2   the finite verb is always in the third person singular

The examples below are divided into two groups: divisible indefinite singular words (indefinite mass nouns), and divisible indefinite plural forms of words that are non-divisible in the singular (i.e. indefinite plural count forms).

> (1) Divisible subjects expressing an indefinite quantity are in the partitive singular (mass, abstract and collective words).

Purkissa on _leipä/ä_.	There is (*some*) *bread* in the tin.
Pullossa on _maito/a_.	There is (*some*) *milk* in the bottle.
Torille tuli _kansa/a_.	*People* came to the market place.
Huoneessa on _valo/a_.	There is (*some*) *light* in the room.
Kellariinkin valui _vet/tä_.	(*Some*) *water* leaked into the cellar, too.
Suomessa on vielä _puhdas/ta ilma/a_.	Finland still has *clean air*.
Täällä tapahtuu _kaikenlais/ta_.	'Here there happens *everything possible.*'
	(i.e. 'All kinds of things happen here.')
Kaikenlais/ta täällä tapahtuu.	'*Everything possible* happens here.'
	('All kinds of things happen here.')

| **Jääkaapissa on** *olut/ta.* | In the fridge there is *(some)* *beer.* |
| *Olut/ta* **jääkaapissa on!** | There is *(some)* BEER in the fridge! |

The sentences above should be compared with the following ones, where the subject expresses a definite (total) amount. These subjects are normally at the beginning of the sentence.

Leipä **on purkissa.**	*The bread* is in the tin.
Maito **on pullossa.**	*The milk* is in the bottle.
Kansa **tuli torille.**	*The people* came to the market place.
Vesi **valui kellariin.**	*The water* leaked into the cellar.
Kulta **löytyi Outokummusta.**	*The gold* was found at Outokumpu.

---

(2) Plural subject nouns (non-divisible in the singular expressing an indefinite quantity) appear in the partitive plural.

Kadulla on *auto/j/a.*	There are *cars* in the street.
Liikkui *huhu/j/a.*	There were *(lit.* 'moved') *rumours* around.
Täällä on *pien/i/ä laps/i/a.*	There are *small children* here.
Ihmis/i/ä **kuolee joka päivä.**	*(Some) people* die every day.
Syntyi *vaikeuks/i/a.*	*Difficulties* arose.
Minulla on *mon/i/a ystäv/i/ä.*	I have *many friends.*
Onko Kallella *laps/i/a?*	Does Kalle have *any children?*
Sellais/i/a virhe/i/tä **esiintyy usein.**	*Such mistakes* occur often.

The corresponding 'total' subjects (usually, but not always, definite in English) are in the nominative plural, and the finite verb then shows concord of person with the subject.

Auto/t **ovat kadulla.**	*The cars* are in the street.
Lapse/t **ovat täällä.**	*The children* are here.
Ihmise/t **kuolevat.**	*People* die (i.e. *all* people).
Laiva/t **tulevat satamaan.**	*The ships* come to the harbour.
Vaikeude/t **eivät tule yksin.**	*Difficulties* do not come singly (*all,* not just some).

---

(3) The partitive is used if the existence of the entity referred to by the subject word is completely denied (i.e. in most negative sentences).

| **Kadulla ei ole** *auto/a.* | There is no *car* in the street. |
| **Maassa ei ole** *hallitus/ta.* | The country has no *government.* |

Minulla ei ole *tieto/a* **siitä.**	I have no *knowledge* of it.
Koti/a **ei enää ollut.**	*Home* was no longer.
Täällä ei ole *yhtään tuttu/a.*	There is not *a single person* I know here.
Juna/a **ei vielä näy.**	The train is not yet in sight (*lit.* 'is not seen').

However, if for example the actual existence of something is not completely denied but only its being in a particular place, the nominative is used.

Auto **ei ole kadulla.**	The car is not in the street.
Hallitus **ei ole Turussa.**	The government is not in Turku.
Juna **ei ole asemalla.**	The train is not in the station.

The partitive can sometimes also be the subject case of non-divisible words, in interrogative sentences expecting a negative answer.

Onko teillä *tä/tä kirja/a?*	Do you have *this book*?
Tuleeko hänestä *lääkäri/ä?*	Will he really become *a doctor*? (*lit.* 'Will out of him come a doctor?')

§33.2 PARTITIVE OBJECT

The cases of the object are partitive and accusative, as the cases of the subject are nominative and partitive. The accusative object in some ways corresponds to the nominative subject (for the different accusative endings see §38: the most common is **-n**).

Accusative object

Minä ostan *auto/n.*	I('ll) buy *a/the car.*
Silja joi *maido/n.*	Silja drank (up) *the milk.*
Osta *auto.*	Buy *a/the car.*
Auto/t **hankittiin halvalla.**	The cars were obtained cheaply (*lit.* 'One obtained . . .').
Ostamme *auto/t.*	We('ll) buy *the cars.*

Like the nominative subject, the accusative object expresses a whole or a definite quantity. The partitive usually expresses an indefinite quantity (Rule (3) below), but as one of the object cases it also has other functions (Rules (1) and (2)).

---

(1) The object of a negative sentence is almost always in the partitive.

En osta *auto/a.*	I don't/won't buy *a/the car.*
Pekka ei nähnyt *Leena/a.*	Pekka did not see *Leena.*
Silja ei juo *maito/a.*	Silja does not drink (*the*) *milk.*
En tunne *Kekkos/ta.*	I do not know *Kekkonen.*

Paavo ei syö *puuro/a.*	Paavo does not eat (*the*) *porridge.*
Etkö opiskele *suome/a?*	Don't you study *Finnish?*
He eivät ymmärrä *tä/tä.*	They don't understand *this.*
En ole koskaan tavannut *hän/tä.*	I have never met *him/her.*
Si/tä **emme vielä tiedä.**	*That* we don't know yet.
Janne ei lue *sanomaleht/i/ä.*	Janne does not read (*the*) *newspapers.*
En tunne *no/i/ta mieh/i/ä.*	I don't know *those men.*
Ettekö ole lukeneet *nä/i/tä kirjo/j/a?*	Haven't you read *these books?*

This rule always applies. It makes no difference whether the meaning of the object is definite or indefinite. The same negative sentence thus corresponds to two different affirmative sentences.

Affirmative   *Negative*

Silja joi *maido/n.*
Silja drank *the milk.*

Silja ei juonut *maito/a.*
Silja didn't drink *the/any milk.*

Silja joi *maito/a.*
Silja drank (*some*) *milk.*

---

(2)(a) The object is in the partitive if the action expressed by the verb does not lead to any 'important' final result (i.e. the action is irresultative).

In English this use of the partitive often corresponds to the progressive form of the verb ('be + -ing'); see the translation of the examples below. The accusative, on the other hand, indicates that the action expressed by the verb *has* led to an important result (is resultative).

Irresultative *(partitive object)*	*Resultative* *(accusative object)*
Tyttö luki *läksy/ä.*	**Tyttö luki** *läksy/n.*
The girl *was doing* her homework (i.e. had not yet finished).	The girl *did* (i.e. finished) her homework.
Väinö rakensi *talo/a.*	**Väinö rakensi** *talo/n.*
Väinö *was building* a/the house.	Väinö *built* a/the house.
Väinö rakentaa *talo/a.*	**Väinö rakentaa** *talo/n.*
Väinö *is building* a/the house.	Väinö *will build* a/the house.

Hän ajaa *auto/a*.
He/she *is driving* a/the car.

Hän ajaa *auto/n* **talliin.**
He/she *drives* the car into the garage.

Presidentti ampui *lintu/a*.
The president *shot at* (or: *shot and wounded)* a/the bird.

Presidentti ampui *linnu/n*.
The president *shot (and probably killed)* a/the bird.

Kalle lämmittää *sauna/a*.
Kalle *is warming up* the sauna.

Kalle lämmittää *sauna/n*.
Kalle *will warm up* the sauna.

Many verbs are intrinsically irresultative, and their objects are thus generally in the partitive. One important group of such verbs is those expressing an emotion or state of mind.

rakasta/a	love	**vihat/a**	hate
pelät/ä	fear	**kaivat/a**	miss, long for
kunnioitta/a	honour	**sur/ra**	grieve
arvosta/a	value	**valitta/a**	complain
katu/a	regret	**sääli/ä**	pity
kiittä/ä	thank	**harrasta/a**	be interested in
kiinnosta/a	interest	**huvitta/a**	amuse
miellyttä/ä	please	**moitti/a**	blame
arvostel/la	criticize	**haukku/a**	scold
loukat/a	insult	**syyttä/ä**	accuse
uhat/a	threaten	**kiusat/a**	annoy

---

(2)(b) The object of verbs of emotion is in the partitive.

Minä rakastan *sinu/a*!   I love *you*!
Rakastan *tuo/ta nais/ta*.   I love *that woman*.
Suomi kiinnostaa *minu/a*.   Finland interests *me*.
Pelkäätkö *koir/i/a*?   Are you afraid of *dogs*?
Ahtisaari kiitti *hallitus/ta*.   Ahtisaari thanked *the government*.
Säälin *hän/tä*.   I pity *him/her*.
Tauno kaipaa *jo/ta/kin uut/ta*.   Tauno longs for *something new*.

There are also other verbs which have an irresultative meaning and therefore very often take the partitive object.

jatka/a	continue	**puolusta/a**	defend
verrat/a	compare	**seurat/a**	follow
ehdotta/a	suggest	**tarkoitta/a**	mean
vastusta/a	oppose	**vaikeutta/a**	make difficult
edusta/a	represent	**korosta/a**	emphasize
ajatel/la	think	**heikentä/ä**	weaken

Ajattelen *sinu/a.*	I think of *you.*
Keihänen jatkoi *tominta/a.*	Keihänen continued *his business.*
Joku seuraa *minu/a.*	Someone is following *me.*
Voiko *suome/a* **verrata ruotsiin?**	Can one compare *Finnish* to Swedish?
***Mi/tä* sinä tarkoitat?**	*What* do you mean?
Lipponen edustaa	Lipponen represents *the Social*
sosialidemokraatte/j/a.	*Democrats.*

---

(3) The object is in the partitive when it expresses an indefinite, non-limited quantity (divisible words and plural words).

Partitive object
(indefinite quantity)

Accusative object
(definite quantity)

Ostan *jäätelö/ä.*
I('ll) buy *some ice-cream.*

Ostan *jäätelö/n.*
I('ll) buy *an/the ice-cream.*

Pekka juo *olut/ta.*
Pekka drinks *beer/*is drinking
(*some*) *beer.*

Pekka juo *olue/n.*
Pekka (will) drink *a/the beer.*

Opitko *suome/a?*
Are you learning (*some*) *Finnish?*
(Also: Did you learn ...)

Opin *suomen kiele/n.*
I learned *the Finnish language.*

Näen *ihmis/i/ä.*
I see (*some*) *people.*

Näen *ihmise/t.*
I see *the people.*

Tuula tapaa *viera/i/ta.*
Tuula meets/is meeting *some guests.*

Tuula tapaa *vieraa/t.*
Tuula meets *the guests.*

Nieminen myy *metsä/ä.*
Nieminen sells/is selling *some forest.*

Nieminen myy *metsä/n.*
Nieminen sells/will sell *the forest.*

§33.3   PARTITIVE COMPLEMENT

A complement is a constituent occurring after the verb **olla**, expressing some characteristic of the subject, e.g. **nainen** and **mukava** in the sentences **Marketta on nainen** 'Marketta is a woman' and **Marketta on mukava** 'Marketta is nice'. The cases of the complement are nominative and partitive, and occasionally also genitive (e.g. **Auto on minu/n** 'The car is mine'). When the complement is an adjective the following rules hold.

A singular adjective complement (i.e. a predicative adjective) is in the partitive when the subject is divisible.

Maito on *valkois/ta.*	(The) milk is *white.*
Rauta on *kova/a.*	(The) iron is *hard.*
Kahvi on *kuuma/a.*	(The) coffee is *hot.*

Tämä on *merkillis/tä*.	This is *peculiar*.
Musiikki on *kaunis/ta*.	(The) music is *beautiful*.
Rehellisyys on *harvinais/ta*.	Honesty is *rare*.
Uiminen on *hauska/a*.	Swimming is *nice*.

When the subject is non-divisible, the adjective complement is normally in the nominative.

Heidän koiransa on *valkoinen*.	Their dog is *white*.
Tämä pala on *kova*.	This bit is *hard*.
Kuppi on *kuuma*.	The cup is *hot*.
Hän on *merkillinen*.	He/she is *funny*.
Autoni ei ole *kaunis*.	My car is not *beautiful*.

An adjective complement is also in the partitive when the subject is an infinitive or a subordinate clause, or when there is no subject.

On *ilmeis/tä*, **että ...**	It is *clear* that ...
On *paras/ta* **lähteä.**	It is *best* to leave.
Luennolla oli *hauska/a*.	It was *nice* at the lecture.
	(*lit.* 'At the lecture was nice.')

With some adjectives both nominative and partitive are equally possible as complement cases; often the nominative is better.

Minun on *vaikea*(*a*) **tulla.**	It is *difficult* for me to come.
Oli *hauska*(*a*) **tutustua.**	It was *nice* to meet (you).
Ei ole *helppo*(*a*) **päättää.**	It is not *easy* to decide.

If the subject is plural, the adjective complement must also be in the plural (concord), and is usually in the partitive plural. But the nominative plural is often equally possible; this form is obligatory if the subject is a plural invariable word (§26) or if the concept referred to by the subject is clearly of limited scope.

A plural adjective complement (predicative adjective) is generally in the partitive, but it takes the nominative if the subject is an invariable plural or refers to a clearly limited concept.

Oletteko *ilois/i/a*?	Are you (pl.) *glad*?
Omenat ovat *tanskalais/i/a*.	The apples are *Danish*.
Nämä kirjat ovat *kalli/i/ta*.	These books are *expensive*.
Tulppaanit ovat *punais/i/a*.	The tulips are *red*.
He ovat *miellyttäv/i/ä*.	They are *pleasant*.
Voileivät ovat *hyv/i/ä*.	The sandwiches are *good*.

In sentences like the above the nominative is also possible: **Nämä kirjat ovat kallii/t**; **Tulppaanit ovat punaise/t**; **Voileivät ovat hyvä/t**. In the following examples, however, the nominative is obligatory; the subject is either an invariable plural or a word referring to a part of the body.

Jalat ovat *likaise/t*.	The feet are *dirty*.
Saappaat ovat *pitkä/t*.	The boots are *tall*.
Kasvot olivat *valkoise/t*.	The face was *white*.
Sakset ovat *terävä/t*.	The scissors are *sharp*.
Housut ovat *harmaa/t*.	The trousers are *grey*.

Noun complements can also be either nominative or partitive.

A noun complement is in the partitive when it expresses an indefinite quantity of a substance, group or species.

Oletteko *ruotsalais/i/a?*	Are you (pl.) *Swedish?*
Olemme *suomalais/i/a*.	We are *Finnish*.
He ovat *nais/i/a*.	They are *women*.
Tuoli on *puu/ta*.	The chair is (made) *of wood*.
Paitani on *villa/a*.	My shirt is (made) *of wool*.
Aika on *raha/a*.	Time is *money*.
Tämä on *punaviini/ä*.	This is *red wine*.

The noun complement is otherwise in the nominative when it is a non-divisible word and refers to a definite quantity.

Keijo on *mies*.	Keijo is *a man*.
Tämä on *auto*.	This is *a car*.
Olavi Järvinen on *lääkäri*.	Olavi Järvinen is *a doctor*.
Tässä on *viini!*	This (*lit.* 'here') is (*the*) *wine!*

§33.4   THE PARTITIVE IN EXPRESSIONS OF QUANTITY

The partitive is used in expressions of quantity, i.e. after numerals and words like **monta** 'many', **paljon** 'much', **vähän** '(a) little, few' (except when the numeral is inflected, see §52.2).

The partitive singular is used after numerals (except **yksi** 'one').

yksi tyttö	one girl
kaksi tyttö/ä	two girls
viisi tyttö/ä	five girls
neljä maa/ta	four countries
yhdeksän vene/ttä	nine boats
kaksikymmentä kirja/a	twenty books
sata mies/tä	a hundred men
monta nais/ta	many women

After other expressions of quantity the partitive singular is used for divisible words and the partitive plural for non-divisible words.

vähän maito/a	(a) little milk
vähän auto/j/a	few cars
paljon olut/ta	much beer

puoli tunti/a	half an hour
kuppi kuuma/a kahvi/a	a cup of hot coffee
kaksi kuppi/a kylmä/ä tee/tä	two cups of cold tea
lasi punaviini/ä	a glass of red wine
kilo omeno/i/ta	a kilo of apples
kaksi kilo/a appelsiine/j/a	two kilos of oranges
joukko ihmis/i/ä	a crowd of people
pari kenk/i/ä	a pair of shoes
pala leipä/ä	a bit of bread
pussi sokeri/a	a bag of sugar

If the numeral expression is the subject of the sentence, the finite verb is then in the third person singular.

Kaksi miestä *kulke/e* **kadulla.**   Two men *walk/are walking* in the street.
(Compare: **Miehet** *kulke/vat* **kadulla.**   The men *walk/are walking* in the street.

Neljä pääministeriä   Four prime ministers *meet/are*
   kokoontu/u **Helsinkiin.**   *meeting* in Helsinki.
(Compare: **Pääministerit**   The prime ministers *meet/are*
   kokoontu/vat **Helsinkiin.**   *meeting* in Helsinki.)

If the numeral is in a case other than the nominative, the whole phrase of which the numeral is a part must be in the same case (concord, §52.2).

Ajamme Helsinkiin *kahde/lla auto/lla.*
We drive/are driving to Helsinki *in two cars.*

Minulla ei ole *kolme/a velje/ä.*
I don't have *three brothers.*

Kirjoitin kirjan *kuude/ssa viiko/ssa.*
I wrote a/the book *in six weeks.*

§33.5   THE PARTITIVE WITH PRE- AND POSTPOSITIONS

There are several prepositions and a few postpositions which require the partitive for the word they modify, e.g. the prepositions **lähellä** 'near', **ilman** 'without', **ennen** 'before', **pitkin** 'along', **kohti** 'towards', **vasten** 'against', and the postpositions **kohtaan** 'towards', **varten** 'for'.

Tuletko kotiin *ennen* **joulu/a?**   Are you coming home *before* Christmas?
Pertti selviää *ilman* **auto/a.**   Pertti manages *without* a car.
He kävelivät *pitkin* **silta/a.**   They walked *along* the bridge.
Tunnen sääliä sinu/a *kohtaan.*   I feel pity *for* (lit. 'towards') you.
Tä/tä *varten* **olemme tulleet.**   This is what we have come *for.* (*lit.* 'For this we have come.')

9 THE GENITIVE, POSSESSIVE SUFFIXES AND THE ACCUSATIVE

- *Formation of the genitive*
- *Use of the genitive*
- *Possessive suffixes*
- *What is the accusative?*
- *The accusative endings*
- *Quantity adverbs taking an object case*

This chapter deals with two cases, the genitive and the accusative, and also the possessive suffixes, which are a class of endings distinct from case forms. The accusative is not really a case form proper but a collective name for certain cases used for the object (nominative, genitive and **-t** accusative) which are in opposition to the partitive. The genitive and the possessive suffixes are related since they both often express possession.

§34 FORMATION OF THE GENITIVE

§34.1 GENITIVE SINGULAR

The genitive singular ending is always **-n**, which is added to the inflectional stem. As the genitive ending consists of only one consonant, it usually causes consonant gradation (weak grade) in the inflectional stem (§15). This does not apply to nominals ending in **-e** (§19), nor to some ending in a consonant (§20), where the basic form and the partitive singular take the weak grade and other cases the strong grade.

> The genitive singular ending is **-n**, which is added to the inflectional stem.

Basic form		Genitive	Cf. §
Rauno	(masculine name)	Rauno/**n**	–
puu	tree, wood	puu/**n**	–
Suvikki	(feminine name)	Suviki/**n**	–
Kaisu	(feminine name)	Kaisu/**n**	–

Basic form		Genitive	Cf. §
teltta	tent	telta/**n**	–
tunti	hour	tunni/**n**	–
onni	luck	onne/**n**	18.2
Suomi	Finland	Suome/**n**	18.2
saari	island	saare/**n**	18.3
tuli	fire	tule/**n**	18.3
käsi	hand	käde/**n**	18.4
varsi	handle	varre/**n**	18.4
laite	appliance	laittee/**n**	19
kone	machine	konee/**n**	19
Järvinen	(surname)	Järvise/**n**	20.1
toinen	other	toise/**n**	20.1
teos	work	teokse/**n**	20.2
tehdas	factory	tehtaa/**n**	20.3
taivas	heaven, sky	taivaa/**n**	20.3
rakkaus	love	rakkaude/**n**	20.4
puhelin	telephone	puhelime/**n**	20.5
isätön	fatherless	isättömä/**n**	20.6
sävel	tune	sävele/**n**	20.7
mies	man	miehe/**n**	20.8
kevät	spring	kevää/**n**	20.8

If the genitive singular of nominals is known, the inflectional stem can always be found by removing the **-n** ending. Most other case forms are formed by adding the necessary number and case endings to this stem.

§34.2   GENITIVE PLURAL

The genitive plural is the most complex of the Finnish case forms. The most common endings are **-den** (which can always be changed to **-tten**) and **-en**, which are normally added after the ending **-i-** of the plural stem (§16, §26). In some declension types the ending **-ten** is also used, added to the consonant stem of the singular (especially in **ihminen** words, §20.1). It is usually worth comparing the formation of the genitive plural with that of the partitive plural.

> The genitive plural ending is **-den** if the partitive plural ending is **-ta ~ -tä** (i.e. if the inflectional stem ends in two vowels, and also in some monosyllabic words, §32.2).

Basic form		Inflectional stem (gen. sing.)	Cf. §	Partitive plural	Genitive plural
maa	country	maa/n	–	ma/i/ta	ma/i/**den**
puu	tree, wood	puu/n	–	pu/i/ta	pu/i/**den**
vapaa	free	vapaa/n	–	vapa/i/ta	vapa/i/**den**
este	obstacle	estee/n	19	este/i/tä	este/i/**den**
peite	cover	peittee/n	19	peitte/i/tä	peitte/i/**den**
hammas	tooth	hampaa/n	20.3	hampa/i/ta	hampa/i/**den**
hidas	slow	hitaa/n	20.3	hita/i/ta	hita/i/**den**
korkea	high	korkea/n	–	korke/i/ta	korke/i/**den**
tärkeä	important	tärkeä/n	–	tärke/i/tä	tärke/i/**den**
asia	matter	asia/n	–	asio/i/ta	asio/i/**den**
lukija	reader	lukija/n	–	lukijo/i/ta	lukijo/i/**den**
tavara	thing	tavara/n	–	tavaro/i/ta	tavaro/i/**den**
peruna	potato	peruna/n	–	peruno/i/ta	peruno/i/**den**
ankkuri	anchor	ankkuri/n	–	ankkure/i/ta	ankkure/i/**den** (~ankkuri/**en**)
kukkula	hill	kukkula/n	–	kukkulo/i/ta	kukkulo/i/**den**

> The ending **-den** can always be replaced by the ending **-tten**.

Compare **ma/i/den** ~ **ma/i/tten**, **este/i/den** ~ **este/i/tten**, **korke/i/den** ~ **korke/i/tten**, etc.

> The genitive plural ending is **-en** if the partitive plural ending is **-a** ~ **-ä** (i.e. if the inflectional stem ends in a consonant followed by a short vowel, and also in some polysyllabic words, §32.2).

Basic form		Inflectional stem (gen. sing.)	Cf. §	Partitive plural	Genitive plural
katto	roof	kato/n	–	katto/j/a	katto/j/**en**
karhu	bear	karhu/n	–	karhu/j/a	karhu/j/**en**
kala	fish	kala/n	–	kalo/j/a	kalo/j/**en**
muna	egg	muna/n	–	mun/i/a	mun/i/**en**
isä	father	isä/n	–	is/i/ä	is/i/**en**
tunti	hour	tunni/n	–	tunte/j/a	tunti/**en**
lasi	glass	lasi/n	–	lase/j/a	lasi/**en**
ovi	door	ove/n	18.2	ov/i/a	ov/i/**en**

Basic form		Inflectional stem (gen. sing.)	Cf. §	Partitive plural	Genitive plural
kaikki	all	kaike/n	18.2	kaikk/i/a	kaikk/i/**en**
kieli	language	kiele/n	18.3	kiel/i/ä	kiel/i/**en**
sieni	mushroom	siene/n	18.3	sien/i/ä	sien/i/**en**
käsi	hand	käde/n	18.4	käs/i/ä	käs/i/**en**
viisi	five	viide/n	18.4	viis/i/ä	viis/i/**en**
hevonen	horse	hevose/n	20.1	hevos/i/a	hevos/i/**en**
nainen	woman	naise/n	20.1	nais/i/a	nais/i/**en**
kokous	meeting	kokoukse/n	20.2	kokouks/i/a	kokouks/i/**en**
sormus	ring	sormukse/n	20.2	sormuks/i/a	sormuks/i/**en**
totuus	truth	totuude/n	20.4	totuuks/i/a	totuuks/i/**en**
vaikeus	difficulty	vaikeude/n	20.4	vaikeuks/i/a	vaikeuks/i/**en**
avain	key	avaime/n	20.5	avaim/i/a	avaim/i/**en**
työtön	unemployed	työttömä/n	20.6	työttöm/i/ä	työttöm/i/**en**
askel	pace	askele/n	20.7	askel/i/a	askel/i/**en**
mies	man	miehe/n	20.8	mieh/i/ä	mieh/i/**en**
hedelmä	fruit	hedelmä/n	–	hedelm/i/ä	hedelm/i/**en**
sopiva	suitable	sopiva/n	–	sopiv/i/a	sopiv/i/**en**
hämärä	dim	hämärä/n	–	hämär/i/ä	hämär/i/**en**
asema	station	asema/n	–	asem/i/a	asem/i/**en**
opettaja	teacher	opettaja/n	–	opettaj/i/a	opettaj/i/**en**
aurinko	sun	auringo/n	–	aurinko/j/a	aurinko/j/**en**
ammatti	profession	ammati/n	–	ammatte/j/a	ammatti/**en**
päällikkö	chief	päällikö/n	–	päällikkö/j/ä	päällikkö/j/**en**

In many words of three or more syllables both **-den** and **-en** are possible, but in some words the effect of consonant gradation must then be noted: **päällikö/i/den ~ päällikkö/j/en**, **ammate/i/den ~ ammatti/en**, **ankkure/i/den ~ ankkuri/en**.

Sometimes the genitive plural can also be formed using the ending **-ten**, which is added to a basic form ending in a consonant (§32.1, group (c)), or to a consonant stem formed after the final vowel has been dropped (§32.1, group (b)). These words always have a partitive sg. form in **–ta~–tä**. This ending is particularly common with **ihminen** words (§20.1).

> If the partitive singular is **–ta~–tä** the genitive plural ending is **-ten**, which is added to the same consonant stem.

Basic form		Inflectional stem (gen. sing.)	Cf. §	Genitive plural	Or (for most types seldom)
kieli	language	kiele/n	18.3	kiel/**ten**	~ kiel/i/**en**
pieni	small	piene/n	18.3	pien/**ten**	~ pien/i/**en**
nuori	young	nuore/n	18.3	nuor/**ten**	~ nuor/i/**en**
nainen	woman	naise/n	20.1	nais/**ten**	~ (nais/i/**en**)
ruotsalainen	Swedish	ruotsalaise/n	20.1	ruotsalais/**ten**	~ (ruotsalais/i/**en**)
ostos	purchase	ostokse/n	20.2	ostos/**ten**	~ ostoks/i/**en**
hammas	tooth	hampaa/n	20.3	hammas/**ten**	~ hampa/i/**den**
kallis	expensive	kallii/n	20.3	kallis/**ten**	~ kalli/i/**den**
puhelin	telephone	puhelime/n	20.5	puhelin/**ten**	~ puhelim/i/**en**
askel	pace	askele/n	20.7	askel/**ten**	~ askel/i/**en**
mies	man	miehe/n	20.8	mies/**ten**	~ mieh/i/**en**

§35   USE OF THE GENITIVE

The genitive often marks the possessor, belonging to someone or something, or origin.

Presidenti/n nimi on Ahtisaaari.
The President's name is Ahtisaari.

Auli/n auto on keltainen.
Auli's car is yellow.

Ihmise/n elämä on lyhyt.
Man's life is short.

Kaarle Kustaa on *ruotsalais/ten* kuningas.
Carl Gustaf is the King *of the Swedes.*

Oletko juonut *Aura/n* olutta?
Have you drunk *Aura* beer?

Mies/ten vaatteet ovat pohjakerroksessa.
Men's clothes are on the ground floor.

Öljyma/i/den politiikka kovenee.
The policies *of the oil countries* are getting tougher.

Kirjo/j/en sisältö on muuttunut.
The content *of (the) books* has changed.

Genitive expressions like the following are typical to Finnish; in many European languages the corresponding forms are preposition or adjective structures or compound nouns.

Turu/n kaupunki	the city *of Turku*
Helsingi/n yliopisto	*Helsinki* University
englanni/n kieli	the *English* language
Venäjä/n ulkoministeri	the Foreign Minister *of Russia*
Summa/n taistelut	the battles *of Summa*
Niemise/n perhe	the *Nieminen* family
Virtase/n Reino	Reino *Virtanen* (colloquial)
Lapi/n mies	a man *from Lapland*
maido/n hinta	the price *of milk*
Suome/n kansa	the *Finnish* people
Pohjoisma/i/den neuvosto	the Council *of the Nordic Countries*
Ranska/n vallankumous	the *French* Revolution
kadu/n mies	the man *in the street*
ruotsi/n kiele/n opettaja	*a Swedish language* teacher
Espanja/n matka	a trip *to Spain*

The genitive is the case of the subject with some verbs of necessity or obligation (**täytyy** 'must', **on pakko** 'have to', etc.), and some verbs with a modal meaning (e.g. **kannattaa** 'be worth (doing sth.)', **sopii** 'may', **onnistuu** 'succeed').

Minu/n **täytyy lähteä**.	*I* must leave.
He/i/dän **täytyy lähteä**.	*They* must leave.
Saksalais/ten **täytyy lähteä**.	*The Germans* must leave.
Suome/n **kannattaa yrittää**.	It is worth *Finland* trying.
Vireni/n **onnistui voittaa**.	*Viren* succeeded in winning.
Mies/ten **on pakko poistua**.	*The men* have to go away.
Sinu/n **ei pidä uskoa kaikkea**.	*You* must not believe everything.

(In traditional Finnish grammar these genitives are not always analysed as subjects, but are called dative adverbials. The two basic subject cases are nominative and partitive (§25.3, §33.1).)

The genitive is also the case of the subject (traditionally: the dative adverbial) in expressions like **on hyvä** 'be good', **on paha** 'be bad' and **on hauska** 'be nice'.

Minu/n **on hyvä olla**.	*I* feel good.
Mauno/n **oli hauska päästä kotiin**.	It was nice *for Mauno* to get home.
Suomalais/ten **oli paha palata**.	*The Finns* felt bad about returning.
Mikä *Tuula/n* **on?**	What's up *with Tuula*?

The subjects of many participle and infinitive constructions also appear in the genitive.

Talve/n **tullessa ...**	When *winter* comes ... (*lit.* 'Winter coming ...')
Kesä/n **tultua ...**	*Spring* having come ...

kaikk/i/en tuntema kirjailija   a writer known *by everyone*
Näin *Ulla/n* tulevan.   I saw *Ulla* coming.
Huomasin *Kalle/n* tulleen.   I noticed *Kalle* had come.

And finally, many postpositions require the genitive for the headwords they modify.

pöydä/n *alla*	*under* the table
kesä/n *aikana*	*during* the summer
auto/n *jäljessä*	*after* the car
huonee/n *keskellä*	*in the middle of* the room
äidi/n *luo*	*to* mother
Virolaise/n *mielestä*	*in* Virolainen's opinion
talo/n *sisällä*	*inside* the house
raha/n *tähden*	*for the sake of* money
isä/n *vieressä*	*next to* father
tämä/n *yhteydessä*	*in connection with* this
tori/n *ympärillä*	*around* the market place

§36   POSSESSIVE SUFFIXES

Finnish does not have independent possessive pronouns as such, marking possession for the different grammatical persons; this function is fulfilled by the genitive forms of the personal pronouns.

minä	I	**minu/n**	my
sinä	you (sing.)	**sinu/n**	your (sing.)
hän	he, she	**häne/n**	his, her
me	we	**mei/dän**	our
te	you (pl.)	**tei/dän**	your (pl.)
he	they	**hei/dän**	their

The word signifying what is possessed also takes an ending, a possessive suffix, which varies with the person (concord; third person singular and plural have the same ending).

	Singular	*Plural*
First person	**-ni**	**-mme**
Second person	**-si**	**-nne**
Third person	**-nsa ~ -nsä**	**-nsa ~ -nsä**

Genitive personal pronouns in the first and second persons can be omitted when they occur together with a possessive suffix.

(minun) velje/**ni**	my brother
(minun) äiti/**ni**	my mother
(sinun) sisare/**si**	your sister
hänen poika/**nsa**	his/her son
hänen isä/**nsä**	his/her father
(meidän) talo/**mme**	our house
(meidän) perhee/**mme**	our family
(teidän) paikka/**nne**	your place
(teidän) kirja/**nne**	your book
heidän talo/**nsa**	their house
heidän ystävä/**nsä**	their friend

The omission of the first and second person pronouns is particularly common when the person is identical with that of the subject of the sentence and the possessive expression has another function (e.g. object).

Otan *kirja/ni*.	I('ll) take *my book*.
Myyttekö *auto/nne*?	Are you selling *your car*?
Löydätkö *avaime/si*?	Can you find *your key*?
Teemme *parhaa/mme*.	We are doing *our best*.
Emme muuta *asunno/sta/mme*.	We are not moving *out of our flat*.

Third person pronouns can normally only be omitted when they have the same reference as the subject of the sentence; they then correspond to possessive pronouns in many other languages.

Hän ajaa *auto/nsa* **kotiin**.	He drives *his car* home.
Kalle ajaa *auto/nsa* **kotiin**.	Kalle drives *his car* home.
He juovat *olue/nsa*.	They drink *their beer*.
Miehet juovat *olue/nsa*.	The men drink *their beer*.
Presidentti lähtee *linna/a/nsa*.	The President goes to *his palace*.

Compare the following sentences where the third person pronoun does not refer back to the subject.

Kalle ajaa *hänen auto/nsa* **kotiin**.
Kalle drives *his/her car* home (i.e. *someone else's car*).

Amerikkalaiset tapaavat *heidän edustaja/nsa*.
The Americans meet *their representatives* (not their own but e.g. the other side's).

Within the word, possessive suffixes always occur after case endings but before enclitic particles.

auto/lla/<u>ni</u>	with *my* car
auto/sta/<u>si</u>	out of *your* car
maa/ta/<u>mme</u>	*our* country (part.)
poika/<u>nne</u>/kin	*your* son too
äidi/ltä/<u>ni</u>/hän	from *my* mother + emphasis
isä/lle/<u>si</u>/kö	to *your* father?

When a possessive suffix occurs after a case form ending in a consonant the following alternation takes place:

> The final consonant of a case ending is dropped when followed by a possessive suffix.

This deletion particularly applies to the genitive singular ending **-n**, the genitive plural endings **-iden** ~ **-itten** ~ **-en** ~ **-ten**, the nominative plural ending **-t** and the illative endings **-Vn** ~ **-hVn** ~ **-seen** ~ **-siin**.

Root + case		*Root + case + possessive suffix*	
laiva/<u>n</u>	of the ship	**laiva/ /ni**	my ship's
tytö/<u>n</u>	of the girl	**tyttö/ /mme**	our girl's
talo/<u>t</u>	the houses	**talo/ /nne**	your houses
lauku/<u>t</u>	the bags	**laukku/ /si**	your bags
auto/<u>on</u>	into the car	**auto/<u>o</u>/ni**	into my car
maa/<u>han</u>	into the country	**maa/<u>ha</u>/nsa**	into his country

Note especially that on account of this dropping of the final consonant several case forms look the same when followed by a possessive suffix: nominative singular and plural, and genitive singular.

Veneeni **on uusi.**	*My boat* is new.
Veneeni **ovat uudet.**	*My boats* are new.
Veneeni **nimi on Tarantella.**	*My boat's* name is Tarantella.
Oletko nähnyt *veneeni?*	Have you seen *my boat(s)*?

Notice that it is the concord in the verb that differentiates the first two sentences above (**on** 'is' and **ovat** 'are').

It is apparent from what has been said so far that consonant gradation does not occur directly before a possessive suffix; cf. the inflection of the noun **laukku** 'bag'.

(minun) lau<u>kk</u>u/ni	**(meidän) lau<u>kk</u>u/mme**
(sinun) lau<u>kk</u>u/si	**(teidän) lau<u>kk</u>u/nne**
hänen lau<u>kk</u>u/nsa	**heidän lau<u>kk</u>u/nsa**

Because of the deletion of the final consonant, (**minun**) **laukku/ni** for instance may mean 'my bag', 'my bags', or 'of my bag'.

In the nominative singular the possessive suffix is always added to the inflectional stem.

Basic form	Inflectional stem + possessive suffix		Cf. §
ovi	ove/mme	our door	18.2
ääni	ääne/si	your voice	18.3
käsi	käte/ni	my hand	18.4
kone	konee/nne	your machine	19
hevonen	hevose/nsa	his/her/their horse	20.1
kysymys	kysymykse/si	your question	20.2
kirves	kirvee/nsä	his/her/their axe	20.3

If the third person possessive suffix occurs after a case ending in a short vowel, its form is usually **-Vn** (vowel + **-n**), where the vowel is identical with the immediately preceding vowel. The ending **-nsa ~ -nsä** is occasionally also possible with such forms, and it is always the ending used after cases other than those ending in a short vowel.

heidän talo/ssa/an	in their house
hänen auto/lla/an	with his/her car
heidän isä/lle/en	to their father
hänen äidi/ltä/än	from his/her mother
äiti/ä/än	his/her mother (part.)
pää/tä/än	his/her head (part.)
maa/ta/an	his/her country (part.)

Compare the following forms where the third person possessive suffix is not preceded by a case ending of the type defined above.

heidän talo/o/nsa	into their house (illat.)
hänen auto/nsa	his/her car (nom. or gen.)
heidän isä/ä/nsä	their father (part. or illat.)
hänen äiti/nsä	his/her mother (nom. or gen.)

§37   WHAT IS THE ACCUSATIVE?

The accusative is not a uniform morphological case form as such, but a collective name given to a certain set of cases when they mark the object of the sentence. These cases are: nominative singular, which of course has no ending (Ø); genitive singular, with the ending **-n**; the **-t** accusative ending peculiar to personal pronouns; and the nominative plural in **-t**. The accusative, i.e. this set of case forms, appears as the case of the object in opposition to the partitive.

When determining the particular case of the object one must first check whether any of the conditions for the partitive hold (§33.2); if so, the object must be in the partitive. The partitive is thus a 'stronger' object case than the accusative. Only after this, if none of the partitive object conditions are fulfilled, can one proceed to determine which of the accusative endings is the correct one.

> The object is in the partitive if any of the partitive conditions (§33.2) hold; if not, the object takes one of the accusative endings (Ø, **-n**, **-t**).

The partitive object occurs in three instances: (a) in negative sentences, (b) when the action expressed by the verb is irresultative, and (c) when the object expresses an indefinite quantity.

(a) **En tunne** *tuo/ta mies/tä*.   I don't know *that man*.
   Risto ei lue *sanomalehte/ä*.   Risto does not read *the newspaper*.

(b) **Reino lukee** *hyvä/ä kirja/a*.   Reino is reading *a good book*.
   He katsovat *ottelu/a*.   They are watching *the match*.

(c) **Opiskelemme suomen** *kiel/tä*.   We study/are studying the Finnish
                                          language.
   Ostatteko *olut/ta?*   Will you buy (*some*) *beer*?

The case of the object is therefore accusative only if (a) the sentence is affirmative, and also (b) the action of the verb is resultative, or (c) the object is a whole or a definite quantity. With respect to (c), the accusative may be compared to the nominative when the nominative marks the subject (§25.3).

> The accusative expresses
>
> (a) resultative action
> (b) a whole or a definite quantity in affirmative sentences.

Accusative object   *Partitive object*

(a) **Tuula kirjoittaa** *kirjee/n*.   **Tuula kirjoittaa** *kirje/ttä*.
   Tuula writes *a/the letter*.   Tuula is writing *a/the letter*.

   Hän kantoi *kassi/n* **kotiin**. **Hän kantoi** *kassi/a*.
   He carried *the bag* home.   He was carrying *a/the bag*.

Suurensin *valokuva/n*.
I enlarged *the photo* (e.g. to a given size).

Suurensin *valokuva/a*.
I was enlarging *a/the photo*.
Or: I enlarged *a/the photo* (a bit, but I could have made it bigger still).

(b) Ostin *leivä/n*.
I bought *the bread/a loaf of bread*.

Ostin *leipä/ä*.
I bought *some bread*.

Syötkö *kala/n*?
Will you eat *a/the fish*?[1]

Syötkö *kala/a*?
Do you eat *fish*?

Tunnen *ruotsalaise/t*.
I know *the Swedes*.

Tunnen *ruotsalais/i/a*.
I know *some Swedes*.

All the accusative endings Ø, **-n** and **-t** share these basic meanings. The following section deals with the factors determining when each of these endings should be used.

§38   THE ACCUSATIVE ENDINGS

When is each accusative ending used? We can formulate three rules:

---

(1) The **-t** accusative always marks the object
  (a) in the plural
  (b) in personal pronouns.

---

(1)(a) **Luen *kirja/t*.**   I'll read *the books*.
Kansa valitsee   The people elect *the Members of*
**   *kansanedustaja/t*.**   *Parliament.*
Vien *kirjee/t* postiin.   I will take *the letters* to the post.
Isä vie *lapse/t* kouluun.   Father takes *the children* to school.
Vie *lapse/t* kouluun.   Take *the children* to school.
***Lapse/t* vietiin kouluun.**   *The children* were taken to school.
Tunnetko *nämä maa/t*?   Do you know *these countries*?
Sylvi avasi *ikkuna/t*.   Sylvi opened *the windows*.
Hallitus korvaa *vahingo/t*.   The government will repay *the damage.*
Huomenna ostan *uude/t*   Tomorrow I will buy a pair of *new*
**   *kengä/t*.**   *shoes.*
Minun täytyy ostaa *kirja/t*.   I must buy *the books*.

---

1 *Translator's note*: structures like this, with a present tense resultative verb + an accusative object, often correspond to the English future form with 'will' rather than the simple present, otherwise the resultative sense is lost.

The use of the plural **-t** here follows exactly the same rules as the plural **-t** for the subject (§25.3).

When they function as the object, personal pronouns take the ending **-t**: **minu/t, sinu/t, häne/t; meidä/t, teidä/t, heidä/t.**

(1)(b) **Risto vei *minu/t* elokuviin.**   Risto took *me* to the cinema.
 Vie *minu/t* elokuviin!   Take *me* to the cinema!
 Oletko nähnyt *häne/t*?   Have you seen *him/her*?
 **Neiti Mäkinen saattaa *teidä/t*   Miss Mäkinen will escort *you* to
 ovelle.**   the door.
 Saatanko *sinu/t* kotiin?   Shall I take *you* home?
 Kyllä Tuula tuntee *heidä/t*.   Tuula knows *them* all right.
 Tuo *häne/t* tänne!   Bring *him/her* here!
 ***Minu/t* vietiin elokuviin.**   *I* was taken to the cinema.

If the object is *singular* (and is not one of the personal pronouns **minä** : **minu/t, sinä** : **sinu/t, hän** : **häne/t**) there are two possibilities. Sometimes the ending is **-n**, and sometimes there is no ending (Ø). A singular object takes no ending if the predicate verb is first or second person imperative, passive, or a verb expressing obligation with a subject in the genitive (§35). Otherwise a singular object takes the ending **-n**.

---

(2) A singular accusative object
 (a) usually takes **-n**
 (b) takes no ending with verbs in first and second person imperative, passive verbs, and some verbs of obligation

---

(Minä) ostan *kirja/n*.   I will buy *a/the book*.
Tunsitko *Olli Nuutise/n*?   Did you know *Olli Nuutinen*?
Isä vie *lapse/n* kouluun.   Father takes *the child* to school.
Irma avaa *ikkuna/n*.   Irma opens *the window*.
**Join *kupi/n* kahvia ja söin   I drank *a cup* of coffee and ate *a
 leivokse/n*.**   tart*.
**Hallitukse/n* muodostaa Paavo   *The government* is/will be formed
 Lipponen.**   by Paavo Lipponen.
**Ilkka ostaa *sormukse/n*   Ilkka will buy *a ring* for his wife.
 vaimolleen.**

Pekka Pekkanen saa *paika/n*.   Pekka Pekkanen gets/will get *the job*.
Poliisit pysäyttävät *liikentee/n*.   The police stop *the traffic*.
**Kommunistit esittävät *uude/n*   The communists put forward *a new
 ehdotukse/n*.**   proposal*.
**Rakennamme *tehtaa/n*   We (will) build *a/the factory* at
 Tampereelle.**   Tampere.

Osta *kirja*!	Buy (sing.) *a book*!
Ostakaa *kirja*!	Buy (pl.) *a book*!
Ostakaamme *kirja*!	Let us buy *a book*!
Kirjoita *kirje* **loppuun!**	Finish writing *the letter*! (*lit.* 'Write the letter to the end!')
Viekää *koira* **pois!**	Take (pl.) *the dog* away!
Ostettiin *kirja.*	*A book* was bought. ('One bought a book.')
Ostetaan *kirja.*	Let's buy *a book*. ('One buys a book.')
Koira **vietiin pois.**	*The dog* was taken away.
Onko *kirje* **kirjoitettu loppuun?**	Is *the letter* finished?
Kalle Nieminen **nähtiin viimeksi Kuopiossa.**	*Kalle Nieminen* was last seen in Kuopio.
Minun täytyy ostaa *kirja.*	I must buy *a/the book.*
Sinun on pakko viedä *kirje* **postiin.**	You have to take *the letter* to the post.
Nyt *koira* **on vietävä ulos.**	Now *the dog* must be taken out.
Teidän pitäisi tavata *Raija.*	You should meet *Raija*.
Meidän täytyy hyväksyä *tämä.*	We must accept *this*.

The third important accusative rule concerns numerals:

---

(3) Numerals (except **yksi** 'one') have no accusative ending.

Kadulla näin *kolme* **ihmistä.**	I saw *three* people in the street.
Saanko *kaksi* **tuoppia olutta?**	Can I have *two* tankards of beer?
Väinö söi *kuusi* **appelsiinia.**	Väinö ate *six* oranges.
Kansa valitsee *kaksisataa* **kansanedustajaa.**	The people elect *two hundred* Members of Parliament.

But:

Saanko *yhde/n kupi/n* **kahvia?**	Can I have *one cup* of coffee?
Reijo lainaa *yhde/n kirja/n.*	Reijo borrows *one book*.

Note once again the point made above (§36) concerning possessive suffixes: because of the omission of the final consonant some forms coincide.

Without possessive suffix	*With possessive suffix*
Ostin *auto/n.*	**Ostin** *auto/ni.*
I bought *a/the car.*	I bought *my car.*
Ostin *auto/t.*	**Ostin** *auto/ni.*
I bought *the cars.*	I bought *my cars.*
Ostin *auto/n* **moottorin.**	**Ostin** *auto/ni* **moottorin.**
I bought the engine *of the car.*	I bought the engine *of my car.*

In conclusion it should be stressed that the partitive rules always take precedence over the accusative rules. For example, in negative sentences the object is always in the partitive regardless of what the accusative ending would be in the corresponding affirmative sentences.

Affirmative (accusative)	*Negative (partitive)*
Luen *kirja/t*.	**En lue *kirjo/j/a*.**
I read *the books*.	I don't read *books*.
Tunnen *nämä maa/t*.	**En tunne *nä/i/tä ma/i/ta*.**
I know *these countries*.	I don't know *these countries*.
Risto vie *minu/t* elokuviin.	**Risto ei vie *minu/a* elokuviin.**
Risto will take *me* to the cinema.	Risto will not take *me* to the cinema.
Näen *häne/t*.	**En näe *hän/tä*.**
I see *him/her*.	I don't see *him/her*.
Ostan *kirja/n*.	**En osta *kirja/a*.**
I (will) buy *a/the book*.	I will not buy *a/the book*.
Pekka Virtanen saa *paika/n*.	**Pekka Virtanen ei saa *paikka/a*.**
Pekka Virtanen will get *the job*.	Pekka Virtanen will not get *the job*.
Sinun on pakko viedä *kirje* postiin.	**Sinun ei ole pakko viedä *kirje/ttä* postiin**.
You have to take *the letter* to the post.	You do not have to take *the letter* to the post.
Pertti ostaa *neljä* vihkoa.	**Pertti ei osta *neljä/ä* vihkoa.**
Pertti buys/will buy *four* notebooks.	Pertti does/will not buy *four* notebooks.
Juotko *kaksi* kuppia kahvia?	**Etkö juo *kah/ta* kuppia kahvia?**
Will you drink *two* cups of coffee?	Won't you drink *two* cups of coffee?

§39   QUANTITY ADVERBS TAKING AN OBJECT CASE

There are some expressions of quantity which are similar to objects in that they take partitive or accusative endings in accordance with the normal rules for objects. These expressions include those answering the questions 'how long?', 'how far?', 'how many times?', and 'which time (in order)?'.

Olen ollut Suomessa *viiko/n*.	I have been *a week* in Finland.
En ole ollut Suomessa *viikko/a*.	I have not been *a week* in Finland.
Ole Suomessa *viikko*!	Stay *a week* in Finland!
Suomessa ollaan *viikko*.	We (*lit.* 'one') will stay *a week* in Finland.

Viren juoksee *kilometri/n.*	Viren will run *a kilometre.*
Viren ei juokse *kilometri/ä.*	Viren will not run *a kilometre.*
Juokse *kilometri!*	Run *a kilometre!*
Olen nähnyt hänet *kaksi kertaa.*	I have seen him/her *twice* ('two times').
En ole nähnyt häntä *kah/ta kertaa.*	I have not seen him/her *twice.*

10 THE SIX LOCAL CASES

- *General*
- *Inessive*
- *Elative*
- *Illative*
- *Adessive*
- *Ablative*
- *Allative*
- *Directional verbs*
- *Place names*

§40 GENERAL

Six of the 15 Finnish cases form a sub-system of their own since their basic function is the expression of *place* and *direction*. This important set of local cases consists of the inessive **-ssa ~ -ssä**, the elative **-sta ~ -stä**, the illative **-Vn ~ -hVn ~ -seen ~ -siin** (where **V** stands for any vowel), the adessive **-lla ~ -llä**, the ablative **-lta ~ -ltä** and the allative **-lle**.

The system of local cases is structured according to two dimensions. One is location: 'inside' (or in immediate contact with) vs. 'outside'. And the other is direction: 'static', 'movement towards' and 'movement away from'. The six cases can be set out as follows; the table includes only one variant for each case ending.

		Location	
		Inside	*Outside*
	Static	**-ssa**	**-lla**
Direction	*Away from*	**-sta**	**-lta**
	Towards	**-Vn**	**-lle**

The use of the local cases is illustrated in the house diagram below; *x* indicates 'static' location.

It must be remembered that the local cases also have many other meanings apart from place and direction. Some may express for example time, reason, instrument or manner.

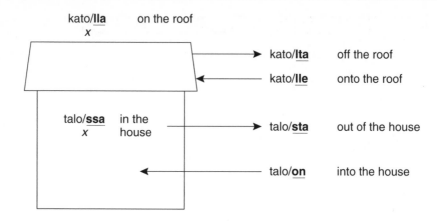

kato/**lla**   on the roof
   x

kato/**lta**   off the roof

kato/**lle**   onto the roof

talo/**ssa**   in the
   x   house

talo/**sta**   out of the house

talo/**on**   into the house

§41   INESSIVE

The inessive ending is **-ssa** ~ **-ssä**; in the singular this is added directly to the inflectional stem (§18–20), and in the plural it is added after the plural **-i-** following the inflectional stem (§26). Because the inessive ending begins with two consonants the rules of consonant gradation apply in the normal way (§15). In **vene** words (§19) and words with a basic form ending in a consonant (§20), the inflectional stem appears in the strong grade.

> The basic meaning of the inessive is 'location inside something', sometimes 'direct contact'.

Basic form	Inessive singular		Inessive plural	
talo	**talo/ssa**	in the house	**talo/i/ssa**	in the houses
puu	**puu/ssa**	in the tree	**pu/i/ssa**	in the trees
maa	**maa/ssa**	in the country	**ma/i/ssa**	in the countries
tunti	**tunni/ssa**	in the hour	**tunne/i/ssa**	in the hours
kivi	**kive/ssä**	in the stone	**kiv/i/ssä**	in the stones
käsi	**käde/ssä**	in the hand	**käs/i/ssä**	in the hands
liike	**liikkee/ssä**	in the shop	**liikke/i/ssä**	in the shops
nainen	**naise/ssa**	in the woman	**nais/i/ssa**	in the women
ajatus	**ajatukse/ssa**	in the thought	**ajatuks/i/ssa**	in the thoughts
syvyys	**syvyyde/ssä**	in the depth	**syvyyks/i/ssä**	in the depths
avain	**avaime/ssa**	in the key	**avaim/i/ssa**	in the keys

It is fairly rare for the inessive to mean 'direct contact', but there are a few common expressions of this kind.

Minulla on sukat *jala/ssa.*
I have socks on my feet (*lit. 'in the foot'*).

Pekalla on hansikkaat *käde/ssä.*
Pekka has gloves on his hands (*'in the hand'*).

Venee/ssä **on kaksi mastoa.**
The boat (*'in the boat'*) has two masts.

Tuopi/ssa **on korvat.**
The tankard (*'in the tankard'*) has handles.

Onko sinulla hattu *pää/ssä?*
Do you have a hat on your head (*'in the head'*)?

Laiva on *laituri/ssa.*
The ship is at (*'in'*) *the quay.*

The inessive is common in expressions of time, when it indicates the period of time during which an action takes place.

Luin kirjan *tunni/ssa.*
I read the book *in an hour.*

Pimenee *kymmene/ssä minuuti/ssa.*
It gets dark *in ten minutes.*

Hän luki lääkäriksi *viide/ssä vuode/ssa.*
He qualified as a doctor *in five years.*

Päivä/ssä **pääsee Helsingistä Kuopioon.**
One can get from Helsinki to Kuopio *in a day.*

Tulen Norjaan *ensi kuu/ssa.*
I'm coming to Norway *next month.*

Sometimes the inessive is used to mark a substance covering something.

Talo on *tule/ssa.*	The house is on (*'in'*) *fire.*
Nenä oli *vere/ssä.*	The nose was bloody (*'in blood'*).
Aurajoki on *jää/ssä.*	The river Aura is frozen (*'in ice'*).
Lasi on *huurtee/ssa.*	The glass is covered with frost (*'is in frost'*).

Concord rules apply in the normal way: pronouns and adjectival modifiers inflect in the same case and number as the headword (§31).

iso/ssa talo/ssa	in the big house
tä/ssä talo/ssa	in this house
piene/ssä auto/ssa	in the small car
iso/i/ssa talo/i/ssa	in the big houses
tavallise/ssa liikkee/ssä	in an ordinary shop

tavallis/i/ssa liikke/i/ssä	in ordinary shops
toise/ssa maa/ssa	in another country
tois/i/ssa ma/i/ssa	in other countries

§42   ELATIVE

The elative ending is **-sta ~ -stä**, which is added to the inflectional stem and causes consonant gradation in the same way as the inessive. The basic meaning of the elative is 'out from inside'.

> The basic meaning of the elative is 'out from inside', sometimes 'origin' or 'direction away from surface contact'.

Basic form	Elative singular		Elative plural
talo	talo/sta	out of the house	talo/i/sta
maa	maa/sta	out of the country	ma/i/sta
kivi	kive/stä	out of the stone	kiv/i/stä
vesi	vede/stä	out of the water	ves/i/stä
ihminen	ihmise/stä	out of the person	ihmis/i/stä
tiede	tietee/stä	out of science	tiete/i/stä

The sentences below illustrate this basic meaning.

Sylvi nousee *sängy/stä* kello kahdeksan.
Sylvi gets *out of bed* at eight o'clock.

Noudan paketin *posti/sta*.
I'll fetch the parcel *from the post office*.

***Mi/stä* Teuvo tulee?**
Where does Teuvo come *from*?

Hän tulee *Kemi/stä*.
He comes *from Kemi*.

Nousemme *juna/sta* satamassa.
We get *out of the train* at the harbour.

Älä juo olutta *pullo/sta*!
Don't drink beer *from the bottle*!

Pekka tulee *koulu/sta*.
Pekka comes *from school*.

Merimiehet karkasivat *laiva/sta*.
The sailors deserted (*'from'*) *the ship*.

Vesi loppuu *kaivo/sta.*
The well runs out of water ('the water finishes *from the well*').

Tulen *hammaslääkäri/stä.*
I am coming *from the dentist.*

Mi/stä **löysit kynäsi?**
('*From*') *where* did you find your pen?

Otan hatun *pää/stä/ni.*
I take my hat *off my head.*

Jyväskylä/stä **Helsinkiin**
from Jyväskylä to Helsinki

Johtaja on palannut *Brasilia/sta.*
The director has returned *from Brazil.*

The elative is also often used for adverbials occurring after certain verbs. These verbs include those of speaking, writing, thinking, understanding, liking and knowing.

Pentti kertoo *matka/sta/an.*	Pentti tells *about his trip.*
Hän puhuu *kokemuks/i/sta/an.*	He speaks *of his experiences.*
Mitä ajattelet *Vennamo/sta?*	What do you think *of Vennamo?*
Mitä luulet *tä/stä?*	What do you think *of this?*
En pidä *musta/sta kahvi/sta.*	I don't like *black coffee.*
Minä pidän *Liisa/sta.*	I like *Liisa.*
Mi/stä **sen tiedät?**	How ('*from what*') do you know?

The elative can also indicate the substance something is made of, origin, and cause.

Pöytä on tehty *puu/sta.*	The table is made *of wood.*
Teen puvun *villa/sta.*	I will make the dress *out of wool.*
Häne/stä **tulee lääkäri.**	He will be ('*out of him* will come') a doctor.
isä/stä **poikaan**	*from father* to son
kolme/sta **neljään kilometriä**	*from three* to four kilometres
Witold on *Puola/sta.*	Witold is *from Poland.*
Lapsi itkee *pelo/sta.*	The child is crying with ('*from*') *fear.*
Hän hymyili *onne/sta.*	He smiled *with happiness.*
Mi/stä **syy/stä Ahti lähti?**	For ('*from*') *what reason* did Ahti leave?

Note also the following additional functions of the elative:

kaksi *te/i/stä*	two *of you*
viisi *nais/i/sta*	five *of the women*

Kiitos *ruua/sta.*	Thank you *for the food.*
Maksan 100 mk *taki/sta.*	I will pay 100 marks *for the coat.*
Minu/sta **hän on sairas.**	In my opinion (*'of me'*) he is ill.
aamu/sta **iltaan**	*from morning* to evening
Hän on ollut täällä *viime*	He has been here *since last year.*
vuode/sta.	

Concord rules operate in the usual way (§31):

piene/stä talo/sta	out of the small house
varhaise/sta aamu/sta	from early morning
tä/stä auto/sta	out of this car
mu/i/sta ma/i/sta	from other countries

§43   ILLATIVE

The illative has three different endings: **-Vn** and **-hVn** (where **V** is always a vowel identical with the immediately preceding vowel), and **-seen**. The illative plural ending is also occasionally **-siin**. Consonant gradation does not occur before the illative ending (§15). The basic meaning is 'into'.

> The basic meaning of the illative is '(direction) into', sometimes 'end point of a change or movement'.

The ending **-Vn** occurs after inflectional stems ending in a short vowel (also in the plural; if the plural stem ends in two vowels the illative ending is **-hVn**).

Basic form	Illative singular		Illative plural
talo	**talo/on**	into the house	**talo/i/hin**
koulu	**koulu/un**	to school	**koulu/i/hin**
kaupunki	**kaupunki/in**	to the town	**kaupunke/i/hin**
lehti	**lehte/en**	into the newspaper	**leht/i/in**
kivi	**kive/en**	into the stone	**kiv/i/in**
käsi	**käte/en**	into the hand	**käs/i/in**
meri	**mere/en**	into the sea	**mer/i/in**
kunta	**kunta/an**	into the commune	**kunt/i/in**
ihminen	**ihmise/en**	into the person	**ihmis/i/in**
ajatus	**ajatukse/en**	into the thought	**ajatuks/i/in**
avain	**avaime/en**	into the key	**avaim/i/in**
korkea	**korkea/an**	into the high	**korke/i/hin** (**-siin**)
sairaala	**sairaala/an**	into (the) hospital	**sairaalo/i/hin**

The ending **-hVn** occurs after monosyllabic inflectional stems (both singular and plural) and also after plural stems ending in two vowels.

Basic form	Illative singular		Illative plural
maa	maa/**han**	into the country	ma/i/**hin**
tie	tie/**hen**	to the road	te/i/**hin**
työ	työ/**hön**	to work	tö/i/**hin**
suu	suu/**hun**	into the mouth	su/i/**hin**
tämä	tä/**hän**	into this	nä/i/**hin**
tuo	tuo/**hon**	into that	no/i/**hin**
joka	jo/**hon**	into which	jo/i/**hin**
mikä	mi/**hin**	into which	mi/**hin**
pullo	pullo/**on**	into the bottle	pullo/i/**hin**
kala	kala/**an**	into the fish	kalo/i/**hin**
vaikea	vaikea/**an**	into the difficult	vaike/i/**siin** (-**hin**)
purkki	purkki/**in**	into the tin	purkke/i/**hin**

The ending **-seen** occurs after polysyllabic inflectional stems ending in a long vowel; the illative plural is then either **-siin** or **-hin**.

Basic form	Illative singular		Illative plural
vapaa	vapaa/**seen**	into the free	vapa/i/**siin** (-**hin**)
harmaa	harmaa/**seen**	into the grey	harma/i/**siin** (-**hin**)
perhe	perhee/**seen**	into the family	perhe/i/**siin** (-**hin**)
tiede	tietee/**seen**	into science	tiete/i/**siin** (-**hin**)
rikas	rikkaa/**seen**	into the rich	rikka/i/**siin** (-**hin**)
taivas	taivaa/**seen**	to heaven/ into the sky	taiva/i/**siin** (-**hin**)

The examples below illustrate the use of the illative in its basic meaning.

Isä ajaa auton *autotalli/in.*
Father drives the car *into the garage.*

Panetko sokeria *kahvi/in?*
Do you put sugar *into (your) coffee?*

Hän pani avaimen *lukko/on.*
He put the key *into the lock.*

Kyllä minä vastaan *puhelime/en.*
Yes, I (will) answer *the phone.*

Lähetän kirjeen *Tukholma/an.*
I (will) send a letter *to Stockholm.*

Seija laski paketin *maa/han*.
Seija put the parcel *on the ground*.

Kesällä aion matkustaa *Tanska/an*.
In the summer I intend to travel *to Denmark*.

Kuningatar lähtee *Lontoo/seen*.
The queen is going *to London*.

Lintu rakensi pesänsä *puu/hun*.
The bird built its nest *in the tree*.

Mi/hin ma/i/hin **Koivisto lähtee tänä vuonna?**
Which countries is Koivisto going *to* this year?

Aurinko laskee *länte/en*.
The sun sets *in the west*.

Aamulla kaikki menevät *työ/hön*.
In the morning everyone goes *to work*.

Pekka menee *koulu/un*.
Pekka goes *to school*.

Aion mennä *sänky/yn*.
I intend to go/am going *to bed*.

Muutamme *uute/en paikka/an*.
We are moving *to a new place*.

Nixon ei joutunut *vankila/an*.
Nixon did not have to go *to prison*.

The illative is also used for the end point of a movement or change, or the surface which a movement is directed towards and comes into direct contact with.

Käte/en **tuli haava**.
The hand was wounded ('*into the hand* came a wound').

Lamppu ripustetaan *katto/on*.
The light is hung from ('*into*') *the ceiling*.

Emäntä panee ruuan *pöytä/än*.
The hostess puts the food *onto the table*.

Lapsi panee lakin *pää/hän*.
The child puts the cap *on* (*his*) *head*.

Pane kengät *jalka/an*!
Put shoes on your feet ('*into the foot*')!

Opettaja löi nyrkin *pöytä/än.*
The teacher banged his fist *on the table.*

The illative also occurs in time expressions, indicating the later of two time limits or the time by which an action has not taken place.

viikosta *viikko/on*	from week *to week*
aamusta *ilta/an*	from morning *to evening*
tammikuusta *maaliskuu/hun*	from January *to March*

En ole käynyt Ruotsissa *vuote/en.*
I haven't been to Sweden *for a year.*

Pekka ei ole ollut kotona *kolme/en viikko/on.*
Pekka has not been home *for three weeks.*

En ole nähnyt häntä *pari/in tunti/in.*
I haven't seen him *for a couple of hours.*

Concord rules operate in the normal way.

piene/en kaupunki/in	into a small town
pien/i/in kaupunke/i/hin	into small towns
korkea/an puu/hun	into a high tree
kaikk/i/in kone/i/siin	into all the machines

The final consonant of the illative ending is dropped before possessive suffixes.

talo/on	into the house
talo/o/ni	into my house
talo/o/mme	into our house
talo/i/hin	into the houses
talo/i/hi/nne	into your houses

§44   ADESSIVE

The three cases presented above, the inessive, elative and illative, are the internal local cases: **talo/ssa** 'in the house', **talo/sta** 'out of the house', **talo/on** 'into the house'. The corresponding external local cases are the adessive, ablative and allative, cf. **kadu/lla** 'in the street', **kadu/lta** 'from the street', **kadu/lle** 'to the street', and **Peka/lla** ' "at" Pekka', **Peka/lta** 'from Pekka', **Peka/lle** 'to Pekka'.

The adessive often means location 'on top of' or 'near', 'owner', or 'instrument' by means of which an action is performed.

Basic form	Adessive singular		Adessive plural
pöytä	pöydä/**llä**	on the table	pöyd/i/**llä**
katu	kadu/**lla**	in the street	kadu/i/**lla**
auto	auto/**lla**	by car	auto/i/**lla**
ihminen	ihmise/**llä**	'at' the person	ihmis/i/**llä**
kone	konee/**lla**	with a machine	kone/i/**lla**
vastaus	vastaukse/**lla**	with the answer	vastauks/i/**lla**

The basic meanings of the adessive are illustrated in the sentences below.

Matto on *lattia/lla.*	The mat is *on the floor.*
Kupit ovat *pöydä/llä.*	The cups are *on the table.*
Onko juna jo *asema/lla?*	Is the train already *at the station?*
Vaatteeni ovat *tuoli/lla.*	My clothes are *on the chair.*
Auto on jo *lauta/lla.*	The car is already *on the ferry.*
Kokous on *Ylioppilastalo/lla.*	The meeting is *at the Student House.*
Vainikkala on *Venäjän raja/lla.*	Vainikkala is *at the Russian border.*
Penkki on *peräseinä/llä.*	The bench is *on the back wall.*
Puukko on *vyö/llä.*	The knife is *in the belt.*
Poja/lla/ni **on kolme lasta.**	*My son* has three children.
Minu/lla **ei ole rahaa.**	*I* have no money.
Perti/llä **on uusi vene.**	*Pertti* has a new boat.
Isä/llä **on harmaat hiukset.**	(My) *father* has grey hair.
Matkustamme Kuopioon *juna/lla.*	We travel to Kuopio *by train.*
Hän kirjoittaa *kynä/llä.*	He writes *with a pen.*
Syön keittoa *lusika/lla.*	I eat soup *with a spoon.*

The adessive is also used in time expressions, especially those where the headword is not preceded by attributes (time expressions containing attributes are frequently in the essive **-na** ~ **-nä**, §49). If the headword is **hetki** 'moment', **tunti** 'hour', **viikko** 'week', **kausi** 'period', or **vuosisata** 'century', however, the case is invariably the adessive.

Talve/lla **voi hiihtää.**	*In winter* one can ski.
Päivä/llä **teen työtä.**	*In the day* I work.
Yö/llä **pitäisi nukkua.**	*At night* one should sleep.
Tä/llä hetke/llä **en voi tulla.**	*At the moment* I can't come.

Viime tunni/lla **puhuimme objektista.**
In the last lesson we spoke about the object.

Ensi viiko/lla **lähden Lappiin.**
Next week I am going to Lapland.

The adessive can also express manner.

Tä/llä tava/lla **ei voi tehdä.**   One can't do (it) *this way.*
Puhukaa *kova/lla ääne/llä.*   Speak *in a loud voice.*
Tulen *miele/llä/ni.*   I'll come *with pleasure.*

Attributes agree in the normal way.

kolme/lla auto/lla   in ('*with*') three cars
pitkä/llä kadu/lla   *in* the long street
tä/llä pöydä/llä   *on* this table
vanha/lla miehe/llä   '*at*' the old man

§45   ABLATIVE

The ablative ending is **-lta ~ -ltä**, which is added to the inflectional stem in both singular and plural and causes consonant gradation.

> The ablative expresses movement 'off or from a surface' or 'from near' or 'from someone'.

Basic form	*Ablative singular*		*Ablative plural*
maa	**maa/lta**	from the country	**ma/i/lta**
pöytä	**pöydä/ltä**	off the table	**pöyd/i/ltä**
meri	**mere/ltä**	from the sea	**mer/i/ltä**
ihminen	**ihmise/ltä**	from the person	**ihmis/i/ltä**
mies	**miehe/ltä**	from the man	**mieh/i/ltä**

There follow a few examples of the use of the ablative.

Juna lähtee *asema/lta.*   The train leaves *from the station.*
Otatko maton *lattia/lta?*   Will you take the mat (up) *off the floor?*
Reino nousi *penki/ltä.*   Reino got up *from the bench.*
Linja-auto ajoi *tie/ltä.*   The bus drove *off the road.*
Tuula tulee *kaupungi/lta.*   Tuula comes *from the town.*

Huomenna johtaja palaa *kesäloma/lta/an.*
Tomorrow the director is returning *from his summer holiday.*

Raitiovaunu kääntyy *Aurakadu/lta* **Eerikinkadulle.**
The tram turns *from Aura Street* into Eric's Street.

Tänään tuli kirje *poja/lta/ni.*
Today there came a letter *from my son.*

Lainaan rahaa *äidi/ltä.*
I'll borrow money *from mother.*

Kysy *häne/ltä,* **missä posti on.**
Ask (*'from'*) *him* where the post office is.

Ostan auton *Niemise/ltä.*
I will buy the car *from Nieminen.*

Pyydän *sinu/lta* **anteeksi.**
I beg your pardon ('pardon *from you').*

Anoin *rehtori/lta* **lupaa.**
I applied for permission *from the headmaster.*

Laulaja/lta **meni ääni.**
The singer lost (*'from the singer* went') his voice.

Poja/lta **katkesi jalka.**
The boy broke his leg (*'from the boy* broke the leg').

Kaikki jää *minu/lta* **kesken.**
I never finish anything ('everything remains unfinished *from me').*

The ablative also expresses *time, measure,* and sometimes a *property* of something.

Viini on *vuode/lta* **1879.**
The wine is *from the year* 1879.

Lopetamme *tä/ltä päivä/ltä.*
We will finish *for today.*

Opetus alkaa *kello yhdeksä/ltä.*
Teaching begins *at nine o'clock.*

Lounas on *kello kahde/lta/toista.*
Lunch is *at twelve o'clock.*

Perunat maksavat markan *kilo/lta.*
The potatoes cost a mark *a kilo.*

Maito maksaa kaksi markkaa *litra/lta.*
Milk costs two marks *a litre.*

Kankaan hinta on 25 mk *metri/ltä.*
The price of the material is 25 marks *a metre.*

Hän on *luontee/lta/an* **vilkas.**
He is lively *by nature.*

Olen *paino/lta/ni* **normaali.**
I am of normal weight ('normal *of my weight').*

Particular attention should be paid to the sense-perception verbs **näyttää** 'seem, look', **tuntua** 'seem, feel', **maistua** 'taste' and **kuulostaa** 'sound', which take an ablative adverbial (complement).

Tämä näyttää *kumma/lta.*	This looks *odd.*
Puku näyttää *hyvä/ltä.*	The dress looks *good.*
Ehdotus tuntuu *huono/lta.*	The suggestion seems *bad.*
Laulu tuntui *mukava/lta.*	The song seemed *nice.*
Ruoka maistuu *huono/lta.*	The food tastes *bad.*
Kuulostaa *mainio/lta.*	(That) sounds *excellent.*

Concord rules operate as usual.

mi/ltä laituri/lta?	from what platform?
likaise/lta lattia/lta	from the dirty floor
tuo/lta vanha/lta naise/lta	from that old lady

§46   ALLATIVE

The allative ending is **-lle**, which is added to the inflectional stem in the singular and plural and causes consonant gradation.

> The allative expresses movement 'towards a surface' or 'to someone'.

Basic form	Allative singular		Allative plural
katto	**kato/lle**	onto the roof	**kato/i/lle**
tuoli	**tuoli/lle**	onto the chair	**tuole/i/lle**
nainen	**naise/lle**	to the woman	**nais/i/lle**
tyttö	**tytö/lle**	to the girl	**tytö/i/lle**

The use of the allative is illustrated in the following sentences.

Kirja putosi *lattia/lle.*	The book fell *onto the floor.*
Pane tyynyt *sohva/lle!*	Put the cushions *on the sofa!*
Istuudun *tuoli/lle.*	I sit down *on the chair.*
Lähdemmekö *ostoks/i/lle?*	Shall we go shopping (*'to the purchases'*)?
Kuka vie koiran *kävely/lle?*	Who will take the dog *for a walk?*
Menen *parvekkee/lle.*	I am going *onto the balcony.*
Älä sylje *lattia/lle!*	Don't spit *on the floor!*
Tapio lähtee *matka/lle* **huomenna.**	Tapio is going away (*'to a trip'*) tomorrow.
Illalla menemme *Ylioppilastalo/lle.*	In the evening we are going *to the Student House.*

Lähdemmekö *asema/lle?*
Shall we go *to the station?*

Hän on muuttanut *Kauppiaankadu/lle.*
He has moved *to Merchant's Street.*

Oikea/lle **vai** *vasemma/lle?*
To the right or *to the left?*

Puhun *sinu/lle.*
I talk *to you.*

Kerro asia *minu/lle.*
Tell me about it ('tell the matter *to me').*

Annan lahjan *vaimo/lle/ni.*
I give a present *to my wife.*

Näytän *te/i/lle* **tien.**
I'll show *you* the way.

Tarjoamme *viera/i/lle* **illallisen.**
We offer *the guests* a dinner.

Opetan suomea *skandinaave/i/lle.*
I teach Finnish *to Scandinavians.*

The perception verbs taking a structure with the ablative (§45) can also take the allative, but in the standard language the ablative is more common.

Tämä näyttää kumma/lle ~ **kumma/lta.**   This looks odd.
Ruoka maistui huono/lle ~ **huono/lta.**   The food tasted bad.

Finally, a few examples of concord.

tä/lle miehe/lle	to this man
pitkä/lle kävely/lle	for a long walk
likaise/lle lattia/lle	onto the dirty floor
kaik/i/lle nä/i/lle laps/i/lle	to all these children

§47   DIRECTIONAL VERBS

The set of local cases has a natural threefold division (§40): both internal and external local cases can express static location, movement towards or movement away from. In Finnish, adverbials associated with some verbs expressing change or direction appear in one of the directional cases (elative, illative, ablative, allative), whereas in many Indo-European languages the equivalent expression would contain a 'static' preposition. These verbs include **etsiä** 'look for', **jättää** 'leave', **jäädä** 'stay', **löytää** 'find', **ostaa** 'buy', **pysähtyä** 'stop (intrans.)', **pysäyttää** 'stop (trans.)', **rakentaa** 'build' and **unohtaa** 'forget'.

Hän etsii avainta *tasku/sta.*	He looks *in his pocket* for the key.
Hän löytää kolikon *kadu/lta.*	He finds the coin *in the street.*
Hän löytää avaimen *tasku/sta.*	He finds the key *in his pocket.*
Elanno/sta **löysin uudet kengät.**	I found new shoes *at Elanto.*
Aion jäädä *Ruotsi/in.*	I intend to stay *in Sweden.*

Paavo jäi *luoka/lle.*
Paavo failed to pass into the next form ('stayed *in the class*').

Jätän auton *autotalli/in.*
I will leave the car *in the garage.*

Onko hän unohtanut avaimen *lukko/on?*
Has he left ('forgotten') the key *in the lock?*

Unohdin kirjat *huonee/see/ni.*
I left ('forgot') the books *in my room.*

Ostan olutta *Alko/sta.*
I'll buy some beer *in Alko.*

Ostammeko kartan *kirjakaupa/sta?*
Shall we buy a map *at the bookshop?*

Rakennamme uuden hotellin *Turku/un.*
We shall build a new hotel *in Turku.*

Juna pysähtyi *asema/lle.*
The train stopped *at the station.*

Poliisi pysäytti auton *kadunkulma/an.*
The policeman stopped the car *at the corner of the street.*

§48   PLACE NAMES

Place names decline either in the internal local cases (inessive, elative, illative) or in the external ones (adessive, ablative, allative). The internal cases are more common. The names of countries almost always decline in the internal local cases.

Suome/ssa	in Finland
Suome/sta	from Finland
Suome/en	to Finland
Tanska/ssa	in Denmark
Unkari/in	to Hungary
Sveitsi/stä	from Switzerland

Englanti/**in**	to England
Neuvostoliito/**ssa**	in the Soviet Union
Neuvostoliitto/**on**	to the Soviet Union
Yhdysvallo/i/**sta**	from the United States
Yhdysvalto/i/**hin**	to the United States
NB: **Venäjä/llä**	in Russia

The names of most towns and other municipalities also decline in the
internal local cases, but there are some exceptions.

Helsingi/**ssä**	in Helsinki
Turu/**ssa**	in Turku
Oulu/**sta**	from Oulu
Pori/**in**	to Pori
Jyväskylä/**ssä**	in Jyväskylä
Kuopio/**sta**	from Kuopio
Tukholma/**an**	to Stockholm
Moskova/**ssa**	in Moscow
Lontoo/**seen**	to London
Pariisi/**ssa**	in Paris
Tamperee/**lla**	in Tampere
Tamperee/**lta**	from Tampere
Tamperee/**lle**	to Tampere
Rauma/**lla**	in Rauma
Riihimäe/**ltä**	from Riihimäki
Rovanieme/**llä**	in Rovaniemi
Seinäjoe/**lla**	in Seinäjoki

11 OTHER CASES

- *Essive*
- *Translative*
- *Abessive, comitative and instructive*

§49 ESSIVE

The essive ending is **-na ~ -nä**, which is added to the inflectional stem in the singular and plural. The structure of the essive ending is such that it does not cause consonant gradation (§15.2). The essive usually expresses a (temporary) state or function, sometimes circumstances, conditions or causes. The essive is also used in time expressions.

Basic form	Essive singular		Essive plural
auto	**auto/na**	as a car	**auto/i/na**
ihminen	**ihmise/nä**	as a person	**ihmis/i/nä**
nuori	**nuore/na**	(as a) young (person)	**nuor/i/na**
vanha	**vanha/na**	(as an) old (person)	**vanho/i/na**

Heikki on Jämsässä *lääkäri/nä*.
Heikki is (working *as*) a *doctor* in Jämsä.

Olemme siellä *vuokralais/i/na*.
We are *lodgers* there.

Lähetän ilmoituksen *pikakirjee/nä*.
I will send the notice *as an express letter.*

Kuka siellä on *apu/na*?
Who is helping ('*as a help*') there?

Pidämme ehdotusta *järkevä/nä*.
We regard the proposal *as sensible.*

Olen Suomessa *turisti/na*.
I am *a tourist* in Finland.

Pentti oli kolme viikkoa *sairaa/na*.
Pentti was *ill* for three weeks.

Viini kelpaa *kylmä/nä/kin*.
Wine is good even *when cold.*

Minulla on *tapa/na* polttaa vain illalla.
I have *a habit* of smoking only in the evening.

Pekka lähti *iloise/na* luennolle.
Pekka went cheerfully ('*as cheerful*') to the lecture.

Syön puuron *kuuma/na*.
I will eat the porridge *hot*.

Pysyykö ilma *kirkkaa/na*?
Will the air stay *clear*?

Arto tuli *väsynee/nä* kotiin.
Arto came home *tired*.

The essive is used in time expressions when the reference is to festivals and days of the week, and usually when the headword denoting time is preceded by an attribute (cf. §44).

***Joulu/na* olin kotona.**
At Christmas I was at home.

***Itsenäisyyspäivä/nä* presidentillä on vastaanotto.**
On Independence Day the president has a reception.

***Juhannukse/na* aion purjehtia.**
At midsummer I'm going sailing.

Tuletko meille *lauantai/na*?
Will you come round ('to us') *on Saturday*?

***Perjantai/na* kaikki menevät saunaan.**
On Friday everyone goes to sauna.

Minulla on luento *maanantai/na*. I have a lecture *on Monday*.
***Sunnuntai/na* täytyy levätä.** *On Sunday* one must rest.
***Viime talve/na* olin sairaana.** *Last winter* I was ill.
***Ensi kesä/nä* lähden Italia/an.** *Next summer* I'm going to Italy.
***Erää/nä päivä/nä* tapasin hänet.** *One day* I met him/her.
***Kahte/na yö/nä* on ollut hallaa.** *On two nights* there has been frost.
***Mi/nä päivä/nä* hän tulee?** *What day* is he coming?

***Kuum/i/na kes/i/nä* on paljon kärpäsiä.**
In hot summers there are lots of flies.

***Tä/nä vuon/na* inflaatio on taas noussut.**
This year inflation has risen again.

Tammikuun *seitsemänte/nä päivä/nä*.
On the seventh (day) of January.

Note that the words **ensi** 'next' and **viime** 'last' do not obey the concord rules for attributes, cf. **ensi talve/na** 'next winter', **viime talve/na** 'last winter'.

§50 TRANSLATIVE

The translative ending is **-ksi**, which is added to the inflectional stem in the singular and plural and causes consonant gradation (the ending begins with two consonants). The translative generally expresses a state, property, function or position into which something or someone enters, or the end point of a movement or change.

Basic form	Translative singular		Translative plural
auto	**auto/ksi**	to (become) a car	**auto/i/ksi**
pieni	**piene/ksi**	to (become) little	**pien/i/ksi**
lahja	**lahja/ksi**	to (become) a present, as a present	**lahjo/i/ksi**
rengas	**renkaa/ksi**	to (become) a ring	**renka/i/ksi**

Lauri tuli *iloise/ksi.*	Lauri became *pleased.*
Isä on tullut *vanha/ksi.*	Father has become *old.*
Tuletko *kipeä/ksi?*	Are you becoming *ill?*
Tyttö aikoo *insinööri/ksi.*	The girl intends to become *an engineer.*
Pekka antoi kirjan *lahja/ksi.*	Pekka gave the book *as a present.*

Juotko lasin *tyhjä/ksi?*
Will you empty your glass ('drink your glass *empty*')?

Poikasi on kasvanut *pitkä/ksi.*
Your son has grown *tall.*

Jalat käyvät *kanke/i/ksi.*
(One's) legs go *stiff.*

Kirjoitan kirjan *valmii/ksi.*
I shall finish writing the book ('write the book *finished*').

Olot muuttuivat *normaale/i/ksi.*
The conditions became *normal.*

Pääsetkö *opettaja/ksi* **Helsinkiin?**
Will you be able *to become a teacher* in Helsinki?

Tämä riittää *perustelu/ksi.*
This suffices *as an explanation.*

Auli luuli minua *norjalaise/ksi.*
Auli thought me *a Norwegian.*

Turkua sanotaan *vanha/ksi kaupungi/ksi*.
Turku is said to be *an old city*.

Vennamoa ei saa kutsua *idiooti/ksi*.
Vennamo must not be called *an idiot*.

Opettaja puhuu *suome/ksi*.	The teacher speaks *in Finnish*.
Kaikki esitelmät ovat *ruotsi/ksi*.	All the lectures are *in Swedish*.
Mitä 'auto' on *englanni/ksi*?	What is 'auto' *in English*?
Tule vähän *lähemmä/ksi*!	Come a bit *closer*!
Siirtykää hiukan *kauemma/ksi*!	Move a little *further away*!
Nouse *ylemmä/ksi*!	Get up *higher*!

The translative also expresses time, in particular time by which something happens or during which something happens, or the point of time until which something is postponed.

Tulen kotiin *joulu/ksi*.
I'll come home *for Christmas*.

Onko meillä ohjelmaa *iltapäivä/ksi*?
Do we have a programme *for the afternoon*?

Minun täytyy ehtiä kotiin kello *kolme/ksi*.
I must get home *by three*.

Pekka lähtee Espanjaan *viiko/ksi*.
Pekka is going to Spain *for a week*.

Poistun *kahde/ksi tunni/ksi*.
I shall be away for *two hours*.

Ostatko ruokaa *sunnuntai/ksi*?
Will you buy some food *for Sunday*?

Lykkäämme kokouksen *huomise/ksi*.
We shall postpone the meeting *until tomorrow*.

Maksu siirtyy *myöhemmä/ksi*.
The payment is transferred to a later date ('*to later*').

Note the contrast between the essive and the translative in pairs such as the following.

Tulen kotiin *joulu/ksi*.	I'll come home *for Christmas*.
***Joulu/na* olen kotona.**	*At Christmas* I am/shall be at home.
Ostatko ruokaa *sunnuntai/ksi*?	Will you buy some food *for Sunday*?
***Sunnuntai/na* emme mene kirkkoon.**	*On Sunday* we do not go to church.

Kesä/ksi **lähden Suomeen.**   I am going to Finland *for the summer.*
Kesä/llä **olen Suomessa.**   *In the summer* I shall be in Finland.

When the translative ending is followed by a possessive suffix the final
-i changes to **-e-**.

Tuletko *vaimo/kse/ni?*   Will you become *my wife?*
Laulan *oma/ksi ilo/kse/ni.*   I sing *for my own pleasure.*

Juomme maljan *sinun kunnia/kse/si.*
We drink a toast in ('*to*') *your honour.*

He ottavat lapsen *oma/kse/en.*
They adopt ('take') the child *as their own.*

§51   ABESSIVE, COMITATIVE AND INSTRUCTIVE

These three cases are all rare; the instructive and the comitative appear
mainly in fixed expressions like idioms.

The abessive ending is **-tta ~ -ttä**, which is added to the inflectional
stem in the singular and plural and causes consonant gradation. Its
meaning is 'without'.

Hän lähti ulkomaille *raha/tta* **ja** *passi/tta.*
He went abroad *without money* and *without a passport.*

Hänet tuomittiin *syy/ttä.*
He was condemned *without cause.*

Joka *kuri/tta* **kasvaa, se** *kunnia/tta* **kuolee.**
He who grows up *without discipline* will die *without honour.*

The preposition **ilman** 'without' is usually used instead of the abessive; it
takes the partitive, e.g. **ilman raha/a** 'without money', **ilman passi/a**
'without a passport'.

The instructive ending is **-n**. It occurs almost exclusively in a few fixed
plural expressions.

om/*i*/n silm/*i*/n	with (one's) own eyes
kaik/*i*/n puol/*i*/n	in all respects
palja/*i*/n pä/*i*/n	with bare head
nä/*i*/llä ma/*i*/n	in these parts (areas)
kaks/*i*/n käs/*i*/n	with both hands

The comitative ending is **-ine-**, and this is always followed by a possessive suffix. Because the **-i-** of the ending is in fact a fossilized plural **-i-**
(cf. §26), there is no difference between the comitative singular and plural.
The meaning of the case is 'with, accompanied by'.

Läsnä oli Viljo Kohonen *vaimo/ine/en.*
Present was Viljo Kohonen *with his wife.*

Läsnä olivat Viljo Kohonen ja Esko Kallio *vaimo/ine/en.*
Present were Viljo Kohonen and Esko Kallio, *accompanied by their wives.*

Rauma on mukava kaupunki *vanho/ine talo/ine/en* **ja** *kape/ine katu/ine/en.*
Rauma is a pleasant town *with its old houses* and *narrow streets.*

12   NUMERALS

- *Cardinal numbers*
- *Ordinal numbers*

§52   CARDINAL NUMBERS

§52.1   INFLECTION OF CARDINAL NUMBERS

All cardinal numbers decline like nouns, adjectives and pronouns: they inflect for number and case. Several sound alternations occur in the inflected forms.

	Basic form	*Inflectional stem (no consonant gradation)*	*Inflectional stem (with consonant gradation)*	*Partitive singular*
1	yksi	yhte/en	yhde/n	yh/tä
2	kaksi	kahte/en	kahde/n	kah/ta
3	kolme	kolme/en		kolme/a
4	neljä	neljä/än		neljä/ä
5	viisi	viite/en	viide/n	viit/tä
6	kuusi	kuute/en	kuude/n	kuut/ta
7	seitsemän	seitsemä/än		seitsemä/ä
8	kahdeksan	kahdeksa/an		kahdeksa/a
9	yhdeksän	yhdeksä/än		yhdeksä/ä
10	kymmenen	kymmene/en		kymmen/tä

The cardinal numbers 11–19 are formed from the numbers 1–9 by the addition of the invariable form **toista** (cf. **toinen** '(an)other, second').

11   yksitoista
12   kaksitoista
13   kolmetoista
14   neljätoista
15   viisitoista
16   kuusitoista
17   seitsemäntoista
18   kahdeksantoista
19   yhdeksäntoista

Endings are added to the inflectional stem of the first part of the number.

yhde/<u>ssä</u>/toista	in 11
kolme/<u>n</u>/toista	of 13
viide/<u>stä</u>/toista	out of 15
seitsemä/<u>ä</u>/toista	17 (*partitive*)
yhdeksä/<u>lle</u>/toista	to 19

The tens from 20 upward are formed from the cardinal numbers two to nine followed by **kymmentä** (cf. **kymmenen** 'ten').

20	kaksikymmentä
30	kolmekymmentä
40	neljäkymmentä
50	viisikymmentä
60	kuusikymmentä
70	seitsemänkymmentä
80	kahdeksankymmentä
90	yhdeksänkymmentä
100	sata

27	kaksikymmentäseitsemän
39	kolmekymmentäyhdeksän
52	viisikymmentäkaksi
76	seitsemänkymmentäkuusi
99	yhdeksänkymmentäyhdeksän

Note that **kymmentä (kymmenen)** declines together with the other parts of the numeral.

kahde/<u>n</u>/kymmene/<u>n</u>	of 20
kolme/<u>lle</u>/kymmene/<u>lle</u>	to 30
viide/<u>stä</u>/kymmene/<u>stä</u>	out of 50
kuute/<u>na</u>/kymmene/<u>nä</u>	as 60
yhdeksä/<u>llä</u>/kymmene/<u>llä</u>	with 90
kahde/<u>lta</u>/kymmene/<u>ltä</u>/kolme/<u>lta</u>	from 23
seitsemä/<u>stä</u>/kymmene/<u>stä</u>/kahdeksa/<u>sta</u>	out of 78

The cardinal numbers continue in the same way. The hundreds and thousands are formed from the numbers two to nine followed by **sataa** '100', **tuhatta** '1,000', **miljoonaa** '1,000,000', which all inflect for number and case like the other parts of the numeral.

200	kaksisataa
300	kolmesataa
700	seitsemänsataa
1,000	tuhat (tuhante/en, tuhanne/n, tuhat/ta)
3,000	kolmetuhatta

9,000	yhdeksäntuhatta

238	kaksisataakolmekymmentäkahdeksan
902	yhdeksänsataakaksi
2,134	kaksituhatta satakolmekymmentäneljä
9,876	yhdeksäntuhatta kahdeksansataaseitsemänkymmentäkuusi
87,100	kahdeksankymmentäseitsemäntuhatta sata
456,302	neljäsataaviisikymmentäkuusituhatta kolmesataakaksi
1,000,000	miljoona
4,000,000	neljä miljoonaa

Case endings are added to all the parts of a cardinal number, but in long numerals the ending is often added to the last element only.

kahde/n/sada/n	of 200
kolme/lle/sada/lle	to 300
viide/stä/tuhanne/sta	out of 5,000
kolme/lla/tuhanne/lla sada/lla/kahde/lla	with 3,102
kolmetuhatta satakahde/lla	with 3,102

E.g. in sport the following colloquial numerals are often used: **ykkönen** (1), **kakkonen** (2), **kolmonen** (3), **nelonen** (4), **vitonen** (5), **kuutonen** (6), **seiska** (7), **kasi** (8), **ysi** (9), **kymppi** (10).

§52.2 USE OF CARDINAL NUMBERS

When a cardinal number is the subject, object or complement, i.e. when it occurs in the nominative or partitive, the rest of the phrase it modifies takes the partitive singular, e.g. **kolme talo/a** 'three houses'.

> When a cardinal number is the subject, object or complement the words it modifies take the partitive singular.

> When the numeral expression is the subject, the predicate verb is in the singular.

Kadulla seisoo *kolme mies/tä*.
There are *three men* standing in the street.

Minulla on *kaksi velje/ä*.
I have *two brothers*.

Neljä ministeri/ä **erosi hallituksesta**.
Four ministers resigned from the cabinet.

Kuusitoista ihmis/tä sai surmansa lento-onnettomuudessa.
Sixteen people died in the plane crash.

Ostan kolme pullo/a punaviiniä.
I will buy *three bottles* of red wine.

Eilen kirjoitin seitsemän sivu/a.
Yesterday I wrote *seven pages*.

En omista kah/ta auto/a.
I don't own *two cars*.

Opiskelen kolme/a kiel/tä.
I am studying *three languages*.

Viit/tä/kymmen/tä osanottaja/a emme voi hyväksyä.
Fifty participants we cannot accept.

Hän ei maksa kolme/a/tuhatta markka/a koneesta.
He/she will not pay *three thousand marks* for the machine.

Hinta on yhdeksän markka/a kilolta.
The price is *nine marks* per kilo.

When a cardinal number is an attribute or an adverbial, i.e. appears in cases other than nominative or partitive, its case is determined by that of the headword (the noun), and all the parts of a compound numeral are similarly inflected. With the exception of invariable plurals these expressions are always singular.

> Cardinal numbers agree with the headword in the genitive, all six local cases, the essive and the translative.

Matkallani käyn kolme/ssa maa/ssa.
On my trip I shall visit three countries ('*in three countries*').

Neljä/n litra/n hinta on seitsemän markkaa.
The price *of four litres* is seven marks.

En ole käynyt Suomessa viite/en/toista vuote/en.
I have not been to Finland *for 15 years*.

Hän on kahde/n piene/n lapse/n äiti.
She is the mother *of two small children*.

**Verotoimistot palauttavat rahaa seitsemä/lle/sada/lle/tuhanne/lle
suomalaise/lle.**
The tax offices (will) refund money *to 700,000 Finns*.

tuhanne/n ja yhde/n yö/n **tarinat**
a thousand and one nights ('*the stories of* . . .')

Yhte/nä päivä/nä **viikossa olen Helsingissä.**
I am in Helsinki *one day* a week.

Olen *kolme/n/kymmene/n/kahde/n vuode/n* **ikäinen.**
I am *32 years* old.

Kuude/ssa/toista tapaukse/ssa **sairas kuoli.**
In 16 cases the patient died.

Kirje tuli *kahde/lta ystävä/ltä/ni.*
The letter came *from two of my friends.*

Kahde/lla/tuhanne/lla marka/lla **pääsee jopa Afrikkaan.**
For 2,000 marks one can even get to Africa.

Minulla on *kahde/t sakse/t.*
I have *two pairs of scissors.*

Tänä lauantaina on vain *yhde/t hää/t.*
This Saturday there is only *one wedding.*

Tämä kangas pitää leikata *kaks/i/lla saks/i/lla.*
This cloth has to be cut *with two pairs of scissors.*

When the numeral expression is the subject, the verb, as was said above, is generally in the singular, e.g. **kolme tyttöä juokse/e** 'three girls run'. But when the numeral expression is preceded e.g. by the words **nämä** 'these' or **nuo** 'those' (which make the phrase definite), the verb is then in the plural.

Nämä kolme miestä *seiso/vat* **kadulla.**
These three men *are standing* in the street.

Nuo kaksi *o/vat* **naimisissa.**
Those two *are* married.

Nämä neljä ehdotusta *o/vat* **yhtä hyviä.**
These four proposals *are* equally good.

In other contexts too the verb may be in the plural when the subject is a definite numeral expression.

Kuusi paikallissijaa *tuli/vat* **esille luvussa 10.**
The six local cases *were discussed* in Chapter 10.

Kolmetoista maata *pääsi/vät* **eilen sopimukseen.**
The 13 countries *reached* an agreement yesterday.

§53 ORDINAL NUMBERS

The nominative of ordinal numbers is formed by adding the ending **-s** to the inflectional stem of the corresponding cardinal number (exceptions are **ensimmäinen** 'first' and **toinen** 'second'). In the ordinal inflectional stem **-s** is replaced by **-nte-**, which alternates with **-nne-** in accordance with the consonant gradation rules. The partitive singular has the ending **-ta ~ -tä**, and **-s** then changes to **-t-**. 1 = 1st, 2 = 2nd, 3 = 3rd, etc.

	Basic form	Inflectional stem (no consonant gradation)	Inflectional stem (with consonant gradation)	Partitive singular
1	ensimmäinen	ensimmäise/en		ensimmäis/tä
2	toinen	toise/en		tois/ta
3	kolma/s	kolma/**nte**/en	kolma/**nne**/n	kolma/**t**/ta
4	neljäs	neljänteen	neljännen	neljättä
5	viides	viidenteen	viidennen	viidettä
6	kuudes	kuudenteen	kuudennen	kuudetta
7	seitsemäs	seitsemänteen	seitsemännen	seitsemättä
8	kahdeksas	kahdeksanteen	kahdeksannen	kahdeksatta
9	yhdeksäs	yhdeksänteen	yhdeksännen	yhdeksättä
10	kymmenes	kymmenenteen	kymmenennen	kymmenettä
11	yhdestoista	yhdenteentoista	yhdennentoista	yhdettätoista
12	kahdestoista	kahdenteentoista	kahdennentoista	kahdettatoista
13	kolmastoista	kolmanteentoista	kolmannentoista	kolmattatoista
16	kuudestoista	kuudenteentoista	kuudennentoista	kuudettatoista
20	kahdes-kymmenes	kahdenteen-kymmenenteen	kahdennen-kymmenennen	kahdetta-kymmenettä
50	viides-kymmenes	viidenteen-kymmenenteen	viidennen-kymmenennen	viidettä-kymmenettä
100	sadas	sadanteen	sadannen	sadatta
300	kolmas-sadas	kolmanteen-sadanteen	kolmannen-sadannen	kolmatta-sadatta
1,000	tuhannes	tuhannenteen	tuhannennen	tuhannetta
9,000	yhdeksäs-tuhannes	yhdeksänteen-tuhannenteen	yhdeksännen-tuhannennen	yhdeksättä-tuhannetta

In long compound ordinal numbers often only the last element is given an ending.

3,134th   **kolmetuhatta satakolmekymmentäneljä/s**
(cf. **kolma/s/tuhanne/s sada/s/kolma/s/kymmene/s/neljä/s**)
kolmetuhatta satakolmekymmentäneljä/nne/n
(cf. **kolma/nne/n/tuhanne/nne/n sada/nne/n/kolma/nne/n/ kymmene/nne/n/neljä/nne/n**)

Ordinal numbers like 21st, 32nd have two alternative forms: **kahdeskymmenesyhdes** or **kahdeskymmenesensimmäinen, kolmaskymmeneskahdes** or **kolmaskymmenestoinen**. The words **eka** 'first' and **toka** 'second' are frequently used in colloquial speech.

> Ordinal numbers function like adjectives and agree with the head-word in case and number.

Miettusen *kolma/nne/ssa* **hallituksessa**
in Miettunen's *third* cabinet

Vasta *toinen* **yritys onnistui**.
Only the *second* attempt succeeded.

tammikuun *neljä/nte/nä* **päivänä**
(*on*) the *fourth* (day) of January

helmikuun *seitsemä/nte/nä/toista* **päivänä**
(*on*) the *17th* of February

Olen syntynyt joulukuun *kahde/nte/na/kymmene/nte/nä/kuude/nte/na*
päivänä.
I was born *on the 26th* of December.

Poikani on *ensimmäise/llä* **luokalla**.
My son is *in the first* class.

Hissi menee *viide/nte/en* **kerrokseen**.
The lift goes *to the fifth* floor.

Joka *seitsemä/nne/llä* **suomalaisella on liian pitkä työmatka**.
Every *seventh* Finn has too long a journey to work.

13 PRONOUNS

- *Personal pronouns*
- *Demonstrative pronouns*
- *Interrogative pronouns*
- *Indefinite pronouns*
- *Relative pronouns*

Finnish pronouns inflect for number and case. Some pronouns function like nouns, as independent words (a), while others are like adjectives and agree with their headword in the normal way (b).

(a) **Tämä on kirja.**   *This* is a book.
    Tuo ei ole totta.   *That* is not true.
    Hän on näyttelijä.   *He* is an actor.

(b) **Asun** *tä*/ssä *talo*/ssa.   I live *in this house.*
    Mi/ssä *talo*/ssa **asut?**   *In which house* do you live?
    Mi/nä *päivä*/nä **lähdette?**   *What day* are you leaving?

There often occur exceptional forms in the declension of pronouns: these are indicated below. Note in particular the pronouns **joka** 'who, which', **mikä** 'which, what' and **tämä** 'this', where the last syllable **-ka**, **-kä**, **-mä** occurs only in the nominative singular and plural and the genitive singular. In all other forms this syllable is dropped: cf. **tämä** 'this': **tämä/n** 'of this': **tä/ssä** 'in this': **tä/llä** 'with this', etc.

In the following sections the pronouns are presented in five groups. For each pronoun the most important case forms are given in the singular and plural (if they occur), together with examples of how they are used.

§54 PERSONAL PRONOUNS

	Singular			*Plural*		
Nom.	**minä** I	**sinä** you	**hän** he, she	**me** we	**te** you	**he** they
Gen.	minu/n	sinu/n	häne/n	me/i/dän	te/i/dän	he/i/dän
Acc.	minu/t	sinu/t	häne/t	me/i/dät	te/i/dät	he/i/dät
Part.	minu/a	sinu/a	hän/tä	me/i/tä	te/i/tä	he/i/tä
Iness.	minu/ssa	sinu/ssa	häne/ssä	me/i/ssä	te/i/ssä	he/i/ssä
Elat.	minu/sta	sinu/sta	häne/stä	me/i/stä	te/i/stä	he/i/stä
Illat.	minu/un	sinu/un	häne/en	me/i/hin	te/i/hin	he/i/hin
Adess.	minu/lla	sinu/lla	häne/llä	me/i/llä	te/i/llä	he/i/llä

Singular			*Plural*		
Ablat.	minu/lta	sinu/lta	häne/ltä	me/i/ltä	te/i/ltä	he/i/ltä
Allat.	minu/lle	sinu/lle	häne/lle	me/i/lle	te/i/lle	he/i/lle

Sinu/ssa ei ole mitään vikaa.	There is nothing wrong *with you.*
Minä rakastan *te/i/tä.*	I love *you* (pl. or polite sing.).
Anna kirje *häne/lle!*	Give the letter *to him/her!*
Minu/lla on kova nälkä.	*I* am very hungry.
He/i/hin ei voi luottaa.	One cannot trust *them.*
Minu/sta ehdotus on hyvä.	*In my opinion* the proposal is good.
Näin *häne/t* ravintolassa.	I saw *him/her* in the restaurant.
Tämä on *he/i/dän* kirjansa.	This is *their* book.
Saatte vastauksen *me/i/ltä* huomenna.	You will receive an answer *from us* tomorrow.
Saatamme *te/i/dät* kotiin.	We will see *you* home.
Ettekö enää tunne *minu/a?*	Don't you know *me* any longer?

For concord between personal pronouns and verbs see §24, and for the possessive forms and the possessive suffixes see §36.

The Finnish reflexive pronoun is **itse** 'self', which inflects for case and is followed by the appropriate possessive suffix. It has no separate plural forms.

Haen sen *itse.*	I will fetch it *myself.*
Ajan *itse* **partani.**	I shave ('my beard') *myself.*
Annan kirjeen hänelle *itse/lle/en.*	I will give the letter to him *himself.*
Saitko kirjeen häneltä *itse/ltä/än?*	Did you get a letter from him *himself?*
Pidätkö *itse/ä/si* **viisaana?**	Do you regard *yourself* as wise?
Pohdin asiaa *itse/kse/ni.*	I will consider the matter *by myself.*
Itse/e/nsä **ei voi luottaa.**	One cannot trust *oneself.*
Ole oma *itse/si!*	Be *yourself* ('your own self')!

The combination **toinen – toinen** 'one – the other/another' is used to express the reciprocal sense 'each other, one another'. The first word of the pair is indeclinable but the second occurs in the singular followed by the necessary case ending and possessive suffix. Another way of expressing reciprocity is to use only the one word **toinen**, in the plural and inflected for the appropriate case ending and possessive suffix.

Lähetämme kirjeitä *toinen toise/lle/mme* (~ **tois/i/lle/mme**).
We send letters *to each other.*

Rakastatteko *toinen tois/ta/nne* (~ **tois/i/a/nne**)?
Do you love *each other?*

Ajamme *toinen toise/mme* (~ **tois/te/mme**) **autoilla.**
We drive in *each other's* cars.

§55 DEMONSTRATIVE PRONOUNS

The main demonstrative pronouns are **tämä** 'this' and **tuo** 'that'. The pronoun **se** 'it' refers primarily to something previously mentioned. The plural forms of all these pronouns are irregular (the initial consonant changes, etc.). In the declension of **tämä** the syllable **-mä** occurs only in the nominative singular and plural and the genitive singular.

	Singular			*Plural*		
Nom.	**tämä** this	**tuo** that	**se** it	**nämä** these	**nuo** those	**ne** they
Gen.	tämä/n	tuo/n	se/n	nä/i/den	no/i/den	ni/i/den
Part.	tä/tä	tuo/ta	si/tä	nä/i/tä	no/i/ta	ni/i/tä
Iness.	tä/ssä	tuo/ssa	sii/nä	nä/i/ssä	no/i/ssa	ni/i/ssä
Elat.	tä/stä	tuo/sta	sii/tä	nä/i/stä	no/i/sta	ni/i/stä
Illat.	tä/hän	tuo/hon	sii/hen	nä/i/hin	no/i/hin	ni/i/hin
Adess.	tä/llä	tuo/lla	si/llä	nä/i/llä	no/i/lla	ni/i/llä
Ablat.	tä/ltä	tuo/lta	si/ltä	nä/i/ltä	no/i/lta	ni/i/ltä
Allat.	tä/lle	tuo/lle	si/lle	nä/i/lle	no/i/lle	ni/i/lle
Ess.	tä/nä	tuo/na	si/nä	nä/i/nä	no/i/na	ni/i/nä
Transl.	tä/ksi	tuo/ksi	si/ksi	nä/i/ksi	no/i/ksi	ni/i/ksi

Tämä kirja on minun.　　　　*This* book is mine.
Tämä on kirja.　　　　　　　*This* is a book.
Tuo nainen on Tyyne Nyrkiö.　*That* woman is Tyyne Nyrkiö.
Onko tuo sinun autosi?　　　　Is *that* your car?
Se on minun autoni.　　　　　*It* is my car.
Se auto on Tyynen.　　　　　 *That* car is Tyyne's.

Tä/ssä on leipää ja juustoa.
Here is (some) bread and (some) cheese.

Tä/ssä ravintolassa on hyvä ruoka.
This ('*in this*') restaurant has good food.

Hän meni tuo/hon taloon.
He/she went *into that* house.

Miksi puhut tuo/lla tavalla?
Why do you speak *in that* way?

Si/llä tavalla ei saa puhua!
One must not speak like that ('*in that* way').

Si/nä päivänä aurinko paistoi.
On *that* day the sun shone.

Sii/nä huoneessa ei voi olla.
One can't stay *in* (i.e. 'use') *that* room.

Tauno meni *sii/hen* huoneeseen missä Ristokin oli.
Tauno went *into the* room where Risto was too.

***Sii/tä* asia/sta en tiedä mitään.**
About that matter I know nothing.

Tunnetko *no/i/ta* miehiä?
Do you know *those* men?

En tunne *he/i/tä*.
I don't know *them*.

***He/i/llä* on uusi talo.**
They have a new house.

En kerro *he/i/lle* tästä.
I won't tell *them* about this.

***Nämä* kukat maksavat viisi markkaa.**
These flowers cost five marks.

Mitä *nuo* maksavat?
What do *those* cost?

***Ne/kin* maksavat viisi markkaa.**
They also cost five marks.

***Nä/i/den* kukkien hinta on kolme markkaa.**
The price *of these* flowers is three marks.

Entä *no/i/den*?
And *of those*?

***Ni/i/nä* aikoina asuin kotona.**
At that time ('*those* times') I was living at home.

Tällainen 'of this kind', **tuollainen** 'of that kind', **sellainen** 'such' and **semmoinen** 'such' all decline like **ihminen** nominals (§20.1).

***Tällaise/lla* autolla ei voi ajaa.**
One cannot drive in a car *like this*.

Paljonko *tuollainen* auto maksaa?
How much does *that kind* of car cost?

Oletko syönyt *tällais/ta* ruokaa ennen?
Have you eaten *this kind* of food before?

En ole syönyt *sellais/ta* ruokaa.
I have not eaten *such* food.

Sellais/i/a ihmisiä ei ole paljon.
There are not many *such* people.

Tällaise/ssa tilanteessa täytyy olla hiljaa.
In this kind of situation one must keep silent.

En lue *tuollais/i/a* kirjoja.
I don't read books *of that kind*.

§56 INTERROGATIVE PRONOUNS

Interrogative pronouns were briefly introduced in §30.2 above. Many of the question words are actually inflected forms of the interrogative pronouns **kuka** 'who' and **mikä** 'which, what'. The singular forms of **kuka** are based on the stem **kene-** (NB: partitive singular **ke/tä**), and the plural forms on the stem **ke-**. Note in particular the accusative singular **kene/t** and the nominative plural **ke/t/kä**. In the declension of **mikä** the syllable **-kä** is dropped in all cases except the nominative singular and plural and the genitive singular (**mikä**, **mi/n/kä**, **mi/t/kä**). Almost all the plural forms of **mikä** are the same as the singular.

	Singular		Plural	
Nom.	**kuka** who	**mikä** which, what	ke/t/kä	mi/t/kä
Gen.	kene/n	mi/n/kä	ke/i/den	mi/n/kä
Acc.	kene/t	mi/n/kä	ke/t/kä	mi/t/kä
Part.	ke/tä	mi/tä	ke/i/tä	(other forms
Iness.	kene/ssä	mi/ssä	ke/i/ssä	as singular)
Elat.	kene/stä	mi/stä	ke/i/stä	
Illat.	kene/en	mi/hin	ke/i/hin	
Adess.	kene/llä	mi/llä	ke/i/llä	
Ablat.	kene/ltä	mi/ltä	ke/i/ltä	
Allat.	kene/lle	mi/lle	ke/i/lle	
Ess.	kene/nä	mi/nä	ke/i/nä	
Transl.	kene/ksi	mi/ksi	ke/i/ksi	

Kuka tuo mies on?	*Who* is that man?
Kene/n kynä tämä on?	*Whose* pen is this?
Mi/ssä talossa asut?	*In which* house do you live?
Mi/tä kieltä opiskelemme?	*What* language are we studying?
Mi/hin ravintolaan mennään?	*Which* restaurant shall we go *to*?
Kene/ssä vika on?	*Whose* fault is it ('*in whom* is the fault')?
Mi/n/kä omenan valitset?	*Which* apple do you choose?
Ke/t/kä nuo ihmiset ovat?	*Who* are those people?
Kene/ltä voimme kysyä?	Whom ('*from whom*') could we ask?
Mi/hin kaupunkeihin matkustat?	*Which* towns are you travelling *to*?

Mi/tä **ihmisiä tapasit siellä?**	*What* people did you meet there?
Ke/i/lle **lähetämme kirjat?**	*Whom* shall we send the books *to?*
Mi/ltä **sää näyttää?**	*What* does the weather look *like?*
Mi/tä **tämä on?**	*What* is this?
Kene/t **näit?**	*Whom* did you see?
Mi/nä **päivänä he tulevat?**	*What* day are they coming?

Kumpi 'which of two' declines like the comparative forms of adjectives (see §85).

	Singular	*Plural*
Nom.	**kumpi** which (of two)	kumma/t
Gen.	kumm**a**/n	kump/i/en
Part.	kumpa/a	kump/i/a
Iness.	kumma/ssa	kumm/i/ssa
Elat.	kumma/sta	kumm/i/sta
Illat.	kumpa/an	kump/i/in
Adess.	kumma/lla	kumm/i/lla
Ablat.	kumma/lta	kumm/i/lta
Allat.	kumma/lle	kumm/i/lle
Ess.	kumpa/na	kump/i/na
Transl.	kumma/ksi	kumm/i/ksi

Kumma/lla puolella olet?
Which side are you *on?*

Kumma/ssa huoneessa Reino on?
In which room (of the two) is Reino?

Kumma/t kengät ostat?
Which shoes (of the two pairs) will you buy?

Kumpa/an kaupunkiin muutat?
Which town (of the two) are you moving *to?*

Kumma/lle annat lahjan?
To whom (of the two) will you give the present?

The interrogative pronouns **millainen** and **minkälainen** 'what kind of' decline like **ihminen** nominals (§20.1).

Millainen **sää on ulkona?**	*What is* the weather *like* outside?
Minkälais/ta **lihaa teillä on?**	*What kind of* meat do you have?
Millaise/n **palkan saat?**	*What kind of* salary do you get?

Minkälaise/ssa lentokoneessa pääministeri saapuu?
In what kind of aeroplane is the Prime Minister arriving?

Millais/i/a vieraita teille tulee?
What kind of guests are you having?

§57   INDEFINITE PRONOUNS

The most common indefinite pronouns are **joku** 'someone', **jokin** 'something', **(ei) kukaan** 'no one', **(ei) mikään** 'nothing', **jompikumpi** 'either', **kumpikin** 'each (of two)' and **kukin** 'each one, everyone'. **Joku** is a two-part pronoun: both **jo-** and **-ku** inflect for a given ending.

	Singular	*Plural*
Nom.	**joku** someone	jo/t/ku/t
Gen.	jo/**n**/ku/**n**	jo/i/**den**/ku/i/**den**
Part.	jo/ta/ku/ta	jo/i/ta/ku/i/ta
Iness.	jo/ssa/ku/ssa	jo/i/ssa/ku/i/ssa
Elat.	jo/sta/ku/sta	jo/i/sta/ku/i/sta
Illat.	jo/hon/ku/hun	jo/i/hin/ku/i/hin
Adess.	jo/lla/ku/lla	jo/i/lla/ku/i/lla
Ablat.	jo/lta/ku/lta	jo/i/lta/ku/i/lta
Allat.	jo/lle/ku/lle	jo/i/lle/ku/i/lle
Ess.	jo/na/ku/na	jo/i/na/ku/i/na
Transl.	jo/ksi/ku/ksi	jo/i/ksi/ku/i/ksi

Joku koputtaa oveen.
Someone is knocking at the door.

Olet saanut kirjeen *jo/lta/ku/lta*.
You have got a letter *from someone*.

Tunnetko *jo/ta/ku/ta* **hyvää lääkäriä?**
Do you know a (*'any'*) good doctor?

Jo/i/den/ku/i/den **mielestä meidän pitäisi lähteä jo nyt**.
In the opinion *of some* we ought to leave right now.

Jo/lla/ku/lla **on avaimet**.
Someone has the keys.

Jo/i/hin/ku/i/hin **ei voi luottaa**.
Some people cannot be trusted.

Pitäisin enemmän *jo/sta/ku/sta* **toisesta**.
I would prefer *someone* else.

In the pronoun **jokin** 'something', **-kin** is an enclitic particle, so that number and case endings are placed in the middle of the word. In case forms ending in **-a** (e.g. **-lla**, **-ta**, **-sta**) the **-k-** of this particle may be dropped, especially in the spoken language but also often in the written language.

	Singular		Plural	
Nom.	**jokin** something		jo/t/kin	
Gen.	jo/**n**/kin		jo/i/**den**/kin	
Part.	jo/ta/kin	(~ jotain)	jo/i/ta/kin	(~ joitain)
Iness.	jo/ssa/kin	(~ jossain)	jo/i/ssa/kin	(~ joissain)
Elat.	jo/sta/kin	(~ jostain)	jo/i/sta/kin	(~ joistain)
Illat.	jo/hon/kin		jo/i/hin/kin	
Adess.	jo/lla/kin	(~ jollain)	jo/i/lla/kin	(~ joillain)
Ablat.	jo/lta/kin	(~ joltain)	jo/i/lta/kin	(~ joiltain)
Allat.	jo/lle/kin		jo/i/lle/kin	
Ess.	jo/na/kin	(~ jonain)	jo/i/na/kin	(~ joinain)
Transl.	jo/ksi/kin		jo/i/ksi/kin	

Olohuonessa liikkuu *jokin*.
Something is moving in the living room.

***Jo/na/kin* sunnuntaina lähden hiihtämään.**
One Sunday I'll go skiing.

***Jo/lla/kin* tavalla aion myydä sen.**
Somehow ('in *some* way') I'm going to sell it.

Sinulla on aina *jo/i/ta/kin* esteitä.
There is always something that prevents you ('you always have *some*
     obstacles').

Söisin mielelläni *jo/ta/kin*.
I would like to eat *something*.

***Jo/t/kin* asiat ovat hyvin tärkeitä.**
Some things are very important.

Olen lukenut sen *jo/sta/kin*.
I have read it ('*from*') *somewhere*.

***Jo/i/hin/kin* ihmisiin ei voi uskoa.**
Some people cannot be believed.

***Jo/i/lle/kin* asioille ei voi mitään.**
There are *some* things one can't do anything about.

Olli on *jo/ssa/kin* ulkona.
Olli is *somewhere* outside.

As the examples show, **jokin** may sometimes be used to refer to people
as well, especially in the spoken language.
     The negative equivalent of **joku** is (**ei**) **kukaan** 'no one, anyone'; **-kaan**
~ **-kään** is an enclitic particle, and so the other endings appear before it.
Kukaan usually occurs together with the negation verb. The stem for most

of the singular forms is **kene-**, and for the plural forms **ke-**; cf. the declension of **kuka** above (§56). There are also some shorter alternative forms in the singular.

	Singular	*Plural*
Nom.	**(ei) kukaan** no one	(eivät) ke/t/kään
Gen.	(ei) kene/n/kään	(ei) ke/i/den/kään
Part.	(ei) ke/tä/än	(ei) ke/i/tään
Iness.	(ei) kene/ssä/kään (~ kessään)	(ei) ke/i/ssä/kään
Elat.	(ei) kene/stä/kään (~ kestään)	(ei) ke/i/stä/kään
Illat.	(ei) kene/en/kään (~ kehenkään)	(ei) ke/i/hin/kään
Adess.	(ei) kene/llä/kään (~ kellään)	(ei) ke/i/llä/kään
Ablat.	(ei) kene/ltä/kään (~ keltään)	(ei) ke/i/ltä/kään
Allat.	(ei) kene/lle/kään (~ kellekään)	(ei) ke/i/lle/kään

Kukaan ei usko minua.	*No one* believes me.
En usko ke/tä/än.	I don't believe *anyone*.
Kene/ssä/kään ei ole vikaa.	It's *no one's* fault.
Onko täällä ke/tä/än?	Is there *anybody* here?
Ke/i/tään ei ole näkynyt.	*No one* was to be seen.
Älä tee kene/lle/kään pahaa!	Do no harm *to anyone*.
Tämä ei ole kene/stä/kään hyvää.	*No one* thinks this is good ('This is not good *in anyone's opinion*').
Ke/t/kään eivät kannata ehdotusta.	*Nobody* supports the proposal.
En saa apua kene/ltä/kään.	I get no help *from anyone*.
Ke/i/llä/kään ei ole varaa tähän.	*No one* can afford this.

The declension of **(ei) mikään** 'nothing', the negative equivalent of **jokin**, is similar; cf. **mikä** (§56). For both **mikä** and **(ei) mikään** almost all the plural forms are the same as the corresponding singular ones.

	Singular	*Plural*
Nom.	**(ei) mikään** nothing	(eivät) mi/t/kään
Gen.	(ei) mi/n/kään	(other forms as singular)
Part.	(ei) mi/tä/än	
Iness.	(ei) mi/ssä/än	
Elat.	(ei) mi/stä/än	
Illat.	(ei) mi/hin/kään	
Adess.	(ei) mi/llä/än	
Ablat.	(ei) mi/ltä/än	
Allat.	(ei) mi/lle/kään	
Ess.	(ei) mi/nä/än	
Transl.	(ei) mi/ksi/kään	

Mikään ei auta.	*Nothing* helps.
En näe mi/tä/än.	I don't see *anything*.

Siellä ei ole *mi/tä/än*.   There is *nothing* there.
Hän ei välitä *mi/stä/än*.   He/she doesn't care *about anything*.
Tyynestä ei ole *mi/hin/kään*.   Tyyne is not good *for anything*.

En voi auttaa teitä *mi/llä/än* **tavalla**.
I cannot help you *in any* way.

Siitä ei ole *mi/tä/än* **hyötyä**.
That is *no* use.

Mi/t/kään **selitykset eivät auta**.
No explanations help.

Mi/stä/än **maasta ei tule enemmän edustajia kuin Suomesta**.
From *no* country are there coming more representatives than from
   Finland.

Mi/n/kään **koneen ominaisuudet eivät ole paremmat kuin tämän**.
No machine has better qualities than this one ('the qualities *of no*
   machine are ...').

Mi/ssä/än **tapauksessa en suostu tähän**.
On no account do I agree to this.

Mi/nä/än **vuonna ei ole satanut niin paljon kuin tänä vuonna**.
In no year has it rained as much as this year.

Jompikumpi 'either, one or the other' is similar to **joku** in that both **jompi**
and **kumpi** decline. In **kumpikin** 'each of two, both', the first part declines
exactly like the pronoun **kumpi** (§56) and the particle **-kin** is added.
Kumpikaan 'neither' declines like **kumpikin**.

	Singular	Plural
Nom.	**jompikumpi** either	jomma/t/kumma/t
Gen.	jomma/n/kumma/n	jomp/i/en/kump/i/en
Part.	jompa/a/kumpa/a	jomp/i/a/kump/i/a
Iness.	jomma/ssa/kumma/ssa	jomm/i/ssa/kumm/i/ssa
Elat.	jomma/sta/kumma/sta	jomm/i/sta/kumm/i/sta
Illat.	jompa/an/kumpa/an	jomp/i/in/kump/i/in
Adess.	jomma/lla/kumma/lla	jomm/i/lla/kumm/i/lla
Abl.	jomma/lta/kumma/lta	jomm/i/lta/kumm/i/lta
Allat.	jomma/lle/kumma/lle	jomm/i/lle/kumm/i/lle
Ess.	jompa/na/kumpa/na	jomp/i/na/kump/i/na
Transl.	jomma/ksi/kumma/ksi	jomm/i/ksi/kumm/i/ksi

	Singular	Plural
Nom.	**kumpikin** each of two	kumma/t/kin
Gen.	kumma/n/kin	kump/i/en/kin
Part.	kumpa/a/kin	kump/i/a/kin

	Singular	Plural
Iness.	kumma/ssa/kin	kumm/i/ssa/kin
Elat.	kumma/sta/kin	kumm/i/sta/kin
Illat.	kumpa/an/kin	kump/i/in/kin
Adess.	kumma/lla/kin	kumm/i/lla/kin
Ablat.	kumma/lta/kin	kumm/i/lta/kin
Allat.	kumma/lle/kin	kumm/i/lle/kin
Ess.	kumpa/na/kin	kump/i/na/kin
Transl.	kumma/ksi/kin	kumm/i/ksi/kin

Jompikumpi ehdotus voittaa.
One or the other proposal will win.

Kumpikaan ei voita.
Neither will win.

En tunne *kumpa/a/kaan* heistä.
I don't know either of them.

***jomma/ssa/kumma/ssa* tapauksessa**
in either case

Pidän *kumma/sta/kin*.
I like both of them.

Tulen *jompa/na/kumpa/na* pääsiäispäivänä.
I'll come on one of the Easter holidays (i.e. the Sunday or the Monday).

En tule *kumpa/na/kaan* päivänä.
I'm not coming on either day.

***Kumma/sta/kin* talosta tulee yksi mies.**
From each of the (two) houses comes one man.

***Kumpa/an/kin* perheeseen syntyi tyttö.**
Into both families a girl was born.

Voit ottaa *jomma/t/kumma/t* kengät.
You can take either pair of shoes.

***Kumma/t/kin* häät ovat ennen joulua.**
Both weddings are before Christmas.

En pidä *kumma/sta/kaan* kirjasta.
I don't like either of the books.

Sain kirjan *jomma/lta/kumma/lta*, en muista keneltä.
I got a letter from one of them, I don't remember which.

Hän ei osaa *kumpa/a/kaan* kieltä.
He/she does not speak *either* language.

***Kumma/n/kin* kengät ovat eteisessä.**
The shoes *of both* are in the hall.

Similarly, in the declension of **kukin** 'each, everyone' the case endings are placed before the particle **-kin**.

	Singular
Nom.	**kukin** each
Gen.	ku/**n**/kin
Part.	ku/ta/kin
Iness.	ku/ssa/kin
Elat.	ku/sta/kin
Illat.	ku/hun/kin
Adess.	ku/lla/kin
Ablat.	ku/lta/kin
Allat.	ku/lle/kin
Ess.	ku/na/kin
Transl.	ku/ksi/kin

***Kukin* saa yhden voileivän.**
Everyone gets one sandwich.

Annamme *ku/lle/kin* yhden voileivän.
We will give *everyone* one sandwich.

***Ku/lla/kin* on huolensa.**
Everyone has his/her worries.

***Ku/ssa/kin* talossa asuu neljä perhettä.**
In each house there live four families.

***Ku/n/kin* täytyy tehdä kaikkensa.**
Everyone must do his/her best ('his/her all').

Maksamme sata markkaa *ku/lta/kin* sivulta.
We pay 100 marks *for each* page.

Perehdymme *ku/hun/kin* tapaukseen erikseen.
We investigate *each* case separately.

Note further the following words which decline like the corresponding nouns and adjectives.

Basic form		Genitive	Partitive
eräs	a certain	erää/n	eräs/tä
jokainen	every, each one	jokaise/n	jokais/ta
kaikki	all, everything	kaike/n	kaikke/a

Basic form		Genitive	Partitive
molemma/t	both	molemp/i/en	molemp/i/a
moni	many (a)	mone/n	mon/ta
muutama	some, a few	muutama/n	muutama/a
muu	other, else	muu/n	muu/ta
toinen	another, other	toise/n	tois/ta
usea	many (a), several	usea/n	usea/a

Molemma/t, **muutama** and **usea** occur in both singular and plural.

Melkein *jokaise/lla* **perheellä on televisio**.
Almost *every* family has a television.

Kaikki **tulevat meille illalla**.
Everyone comes to us in the evening.

Kaik/i/lla **on hauskaa**.
Everyone has a nice time.

Molemma/t **lapset ovat koulussa**.
Both the children are at school.

Annan banaanin *molemm/i/lle*.
I (will) give a banana *to both*.

erää/nä **päivänä viime viikolla**
one/a certain day last week

Teos on *erää/llä* **tavalla hyvä**.
In one way the work is good.

Eräs **toinen tyttö tuli sisään**.
Another ('*a certain* other') girl came in.

Tiedän *kaike/n*.
I know *everything*.

Moni **yritys epäonnistuu**.
Many an attempt fails.

Tuli *mon/ta* **vierasta**.
There came *many* guests.

Olen ollut *mon/i/ssa* **maissa** (~ *mone/ssa* **maassa**).
I have been *in many* countries.

Mon/i/en **mielestä tämä on huono ehdotus**.
In many people's opinion this is a bad proposal.

Mone/lla **yrittäjällä on vaikeuksia**.
Many an entrepreneur has difficulties.

Tunnen *mon/i/a* **ihmisiä.**
I know *many* people.

Muu/t **ovat eri mieltä.**
The others/the rest are of a different opinion.

Olen käynyt *mu/i/ssa/kin* **Pohjoismaissa.**
I have also visited *the other* Nordic countries.

Ostin takin *muutama/lla* **markalla.**
I bought a coat *for a few* marks.

Muutama/t **ihmiset väittävät, että ...**
Some/a few people claim that ...

Työ on valmis *muutama/ssa* **minuutissa.**
The work will be ready *in a few* minutes.

muutam/i/a **vuosia sitten**
a few years ago

Selitän asian *muutama/lla* **sanalla.**
I will explain the matter *in a few* words.

Tämä on *toinen* **asia.**
This is *another* matter.

Usea/t **ihmiset sanovat, että ...**
Many/several people say that ...

use/i/ssa **tapauksissa**
in many/several cases

Use/i/den **mielestä hallitus on kelvoton.**
In many people's opinion the government is no good.

En ole nähnyt Osmoa *use/i/hin* **vuosiin.**
I haven't seen Osmo *for several* years.

§58   RELATIVE PRONOUNS

The most common relative pronoun is **joka** 'who, which', the final syllable
of which occurs only in the nominative singular and plural and the genitive
singular.

	Singular	Plural
Nom.	**joka** who, which, that	jo/t/ka
Gen.	jo/n/ka	jo/i/den
Part.	jo/ta	jo/i/ta
Iness.	jo/ssa	jo/i/ssa

	Singular	Plural
Elat.	jo/sta	jo/i/sta
Illat.	jo/hon	jo/i/hin
Adess.	jo/lla	jo/i/lla
Ablat.	jo/lta	jo/i/lta
Allat.	jo/lle	jo/i/lle
Ess.	jo/na	jo/i/na
Transl.	jo/ksi	jo/i/ksi

Mikä (mentioned above as an interrogative pronoun, §56) is also used as a relative pronoun. With the exception of the nominative and accusative the plural forms are the same as the corresponding singular ones; otherwise it declines like **joka**.

	Singular	Plural
Nom.	**mikä** which, that	mi/t/kä
Gen.	mi/n/kä	(other forms as singular)
Part.	mi/tä	
Iness.	mi/ssä	
Elat.	mi/stä	
Illat.	mi/hin	
Adess.	mi/llä	
Ablat.	mi/ltä	
Allat.	mi/lle	
Ess.	mi/nä	
Transl.	mi/ksi	

Joka is a more common relative pronoun than **mikä**, and it is mainly, but not always, used to refer to entities that are alive. **Mikä** is mostly used only for inanimate entities; it is also used when the reference is to a clause or to an expression containing a superlative.

Hän on mies, *joka* ei pelkää.
He is a man *who* does not fear.

Tämä on kirja, *jo/ta* en halua lukea.
This is a book *that* I don't want to read.

Talo *jo/ssa* asun on Vilhonkadulla.
The house *where* I live is in Vilho's Street.

Sain lahjan, *jo/sta* on hyötyä.
I got a present which is useful ('*of which* is use').

Ne olivat aikoja, *jo/t/ka* eivät palaa.
They were times *that* will never return.

Tapahtumat *jo/i/sta* **kuulin olivat kauheita**.
The events *which* I heard *about* were terrible.

Se on paras paikka *mi/n/kä* **tiedän**.
It is the best place *that* I know.

Tässä ovat kirjeet, *mi/t/kä* **lähetit minulle**.
Here are the letters *that* you sent to me.

Tuo on kertomus, *jo/hon* **en usko**.
That is a story *that* I don't believe.

Tuli sade, *mikä* **esti matkamme**.
It rained, *which* prevented our trip.

14 TENSES

- *Present*
- *Past*
- *Perfect*
- *Pluperfect*
- *Negative forms*

§59 PRESENT TENSE

Finnish has four tense forms: two simple (present and past) and two compound (perfect and pluperfect). Compare present **sano/n** 'I say', past **sano/i/n** 'I said', perfect **ole/n sano/nut** 'I have said' and pluperfect **ol/i/n sano nut** 'I had said'.

The present tense is used for non-past time: usually a time simultaneous with the moment of utterance, and sometimes also future time, i.e. later than the moment of utterance. It is also used for general eternal truths of the kind **leijona on eläin** 'the lion is an animal'; **leijonat ovat eläimiä** 'lions are animals'.

There is no separate ending for the present. But note that in the third person singular the short final vowel of the stem lengthens, i.e. doubles (§24). Otherwise only the normal personal endings are added to the inflectional stem (§23).

Kalle *on* **ulkona.**	Kalle *is* outside.
(Minä) *ole/n* **kotona.**	*I am* at home.
(Me) *lue/mme* **sanomalehteä.**	*We are reading* the newspaper.
Pertti *luke/e* **sanomalehteä.**	Pertti *is reading* the newspaper.
Mitä *sano/tte*?	What do *you say*?
Auto *seiso/o* **tallissa.**	The car *is standing* in the garage.
Ritva *halua/a* **olutta.**	Ritva *wants* some beer.
Tuula ja Leena *lähte/vät* **Espanjaan.**	Tuula and Leena *are going* to Spain.
Mattikin *lähte/e* **sinne.**	Matti *is going* there too.
Pekka *on kirjoitta/ma/ssa* **kirje/ttä.**	Pekka *is writing* a letter.

§60 PAST TENSE

The past tense is used for past time, to express an action which took place before the moment of utterance. The past tense ending is **-i**, which is added to the inflectional stem (§23) and is followed by the personal ending.

> The past tense ending is **-i**, which is added to the inflectional stem (§23).

The verbs **sano/a** 'say', **puhu/a** 'speak' and **anta/a** 'give' thus conjugate as follows in the past tense. For consonant gradation see §15.

First p. sing.	(**minä**)	**sano/i/n**	I said
		puhu/i/n	I spoke
		anno/i/n	I gave
Second p. sing.	(**sinä**)	**sano/i/t**	you said
		puhu/i/t	you spoke
		anno/i/t	you gave
Third p. sing.	**hän**	**sano/i**	he/she said
	äiti	**puhu/i**	mother spoke
	Kalle	**anto/i**	Kalle gave
First p. pl.	(**me**)	**sano/i/mme**	we said
		puhu/i/mme	we spoke
		anno/i/mme	we gave
Second p. pl.	(**te**)	**sano/i/tte**	you said
		puhu/i/tte	you spoke
		anno/i/tte	you gave
Third p. pl.	**he**	**sano/i/vat**	they said
	naiset	**puhu/i/vat**	the women spoke
	miehet	**anto/i/vat**	the men gave

Before the past tense **-i** the usual vowel change rules apply (§16); cf. above **anno/i/n**, etc. The table below gives first the basic form of the verb (first infinitive), then the third person singular of the present as an example of the inflectional stem, and the section number (§) explaining the vowel change in question, and finally the third person singular of the past tense (without consonant gradation) and the first person singular of the past tense (with consonant gradation).

Infinitive		*Third p. sing. present*	*Cf. §*	*Third p. sing. past*	*First p. sing. past*
kerto/a	tell	kerto/o	16(1)	kerto/**i**	kerro/**i**/n
asu/a	live	asu/u	"	asu/**i**	asu/**i**/n
pysy/ä	stay	pysy/y	"	pysy/**i**	pysy/**i**/n
luke/a	read	luke/e	16(5)	luk/**i**	lu/**i**/n
etsi/ä	look for	etsi/i	16(6)	ets/**i**	ets/**i**/n
oppi/a	learn	oppi/i	"	opp/**i**	op/**i**/n
vetä/ä	pull	vetä/ä	16(7)	vet/**i**	ved/**i**/n

Infinitive		Third p. sing. present	Cf. §	Third p. sing. past	First p. sing. past
yrittä/ä	try	yrittä/ä	16(7)	yritt/**i**	yrit/**i**/n
anta/a	give	anta/a	16(8)	**a**nt**o**/**i**	ann**o**/**i**/n
sata/a	rain	sata/a	"	s**ato**/**i**	
jaka/a	divide	jaka/a	"	j**ak****o**/**i**	ja**o**/**i**/n
muista/a	remember	muista/a	16(8)	m**u**ist/**i**	muist/**i**/n
otta/a	take	otta/a	"	**o**tt/**i**	ot/**i**/n
rakasta/a	love	rakasta/a	"	rakast/**i**	rakast/**i**/n
osta/a	buy	ost**a**/a	"	**o**st/**i**	ost/**i**/n
saa/da	get	saa	16(2)	sa/**i**	sa/**i**/n
myy/dä	sell	myy	"	my/**i**	my/**i**/n
voi/da	be able	vo**i**	16(4)	vo/**i**	vo/**i**/n
juo/da	drink	j**u**o	16(3)	jo/**i**	jo/**i**/n
pysäköi/dä	park	pysäkö**i**	16(4)	pysäkö/**i**	pysäkö/**i**/n
luennoi/da	lecture	luenno**i**	"	luenno/**i**	luenno/**i**/n
nous/ta	rise	nouse/e	16(5)	nous/**i**	nous/**i**/n
tul/la	come	tule/e	"	tul/**i**	tul/**i**/n
men/nä	go	mene/e	"	men/**i**	men/**i**/n
ajatel/la	think	ajattele/e	"	ajattel/**i**	ajattel/**i**/n
kierrel/lä	circle	kiertele/e	"	kiertel/**i**	kiertel/**i**/n
julkais/ta	publish	julkaise/e	"	julkais/**i**	julkais/**i**/n
tarvit/a	need	tarvitse/e	"	tarvits/**i**	tarvits/**i**/n
häirit/ä	disturb	häiritsee	"	häirits/**i**	häirits/**i**/n
paet/a	flee	pakene/e	"	paken/**i**	paken/**i**/n

In some verbs of the **anta/a** type, where because of the deletion of **-a** or **-ä** the short consonant **-t-** occurs immediately before the past tense ending, this **-t-** changes to **-s-**. This most often happens when the **-t-** occurs after two vowels or after **l**, **n** or **r**.

> **-t-** sometimes changes to **-s-** if, after the deletion of **-a** or **-ä**, it occurs immediately before the past tense ending.

Infinitive		Third p. sing. present	Third p. sing. past	First p. sing. past
tietä/ä	know	tie**t**ä/ä	tie**s**/**i**	tie**s**/**i**/n
löytä/ä	find	löy**t**ä/ä	löy**s**/**i**	löy**s**/**i**/n
huuta/a	shout	huu**t**a/a	huu**s**/**i**	huu**s**/**i**/n
piirtä/ä	draw	piir**t**ä/ä	piir**s**/**i**	piir**s**/**i**/n
työntä/ä	push	työn**t**ä/ä	työn**s**/**i**	työn**s**/**i**/n

Infinitive		Third p.	Third p.	First p.
		sing. present	sing. past	sing. past
lentä/ä	fly	lentä/ä	lens/i	lens/i/n
kiertä/ä	turn	kiertä/ä	kiers/i	kiers/i/n
pyytä/ä	ask	pyytä/ä	pyys/i	pyys/i/n
kiiltä/ä	shine	kiiltä/ä	kiils/i	kiils/i/n

Verbs to which this rule does not apply include **pitä/ä** 'keep', **vetä/ä** 'pull', **sietä/ä** 'bear', **hoita/a** 'take care of', cf. **hän pit/i** 'he/she kept', **pid/i/n** 'I held', **Reijo vet/i** 'Reijo pulled', **ved/i/n** 'I pulled', etc.

The important group of **huomat/a** verbs form their past tense according to the following special change.

The past tense of **huomat/a** verbs is formed by changing the last **-a** or **-ä** of the inflectional stem to **-s-**, and then adding the past tense **-i**.

Infinitive		Third p.	Third p.	First p.
		sing. present	sing. past	sing. past
huomat/a	notice	huomaa	huomas/i	huomas/i/n
osat/a	know how	osaa	osas/i	osas/i/n
hypät/ä	jump	hyppää	hyppäs/i	hyppäs/i/n
pelät/ä	fear	pelkää	pelkäs/i	pelkäs/i/n
maat/a	lie	makaa	makas/i	makas/i/n
tavat/a	meet	tapaa	tapas/i	tapas/i/n
määrät/ä	order	määrää	määräs/i	määräs/i/n
halut/a	want	halua/a	halus/i	halus/i/n
tarjot/a	offer	tarjoa/a	tarjos/i	tarjos/i/n

The examples below illustrate the use of the past tense.

Koira *makas/i* **lattialla.**	The dog *lay* on the floor.
Oskari *anto/i* **minulle suukon.**	Oskari *gave* me a kiss.
Poliisi *kysy/i* **nimeäni.**	The policeman *asked* me my name.
Kuka siellä *ol/i?*	Who *was* there?
Jo/i/t/ko **punaviiniä eilen?**	*Did you drink* red wine yesterday?
Mitä he *tek/i/vät* **illalla?**	What *did they do* in the evening?
Mitä *te/i/tte* **illalla?**	What *did you do* in the evening?
Niin me *ajattel/i/mme/kin.*	That's just what *we thought.*
Ajo/i/n **Turusta Helsinkiin kahdessa tunnissa.**	*I drove* from Turku to Helsinki in two hours.
Mitä *ost/i/t* **Kaleville lahjaksi?**	What *did you buy* as a present for Kalevi?

He *läht/i/vät* **jo aamulla.**   *They left* ('already') in the morning.
Ties/i/tte/kö **tämän?**   *Did you know* this?
Keijo *avas/i* **vieraille oven.**   Keijo *opened* the door for the guests.

Note that the verb **käy/dä** 'go' has an exceptional past tense: **käv/i**, cf. **käv/i/n** 'I went', **he käv/i/vät** 'they went'.

§61   PERFECT TENSE

The perfect tense is used for past actions whose influence is in some way still valid at the moment of utterance: the perfect is the tense of 'present relevance'. It is formed with the present tense of the auxiliary verb **ol/la** 'be' inflected for person, followed by the past participle in the singular or plural form according to the number of the subject. The participle ending is **-nut ~ -nyt**; e.g. (**minä**) **ole/n sanonut** 'I have said', (**sinä**) **ole/t luke/nut** 'you have read', **hän on syö/nyt** 'he/she has eaten'.

The past participle is formed by adding the ending **-nut ~ -nyt** to the infinitive stem (§23).

If the infinitive stem ends in a consonant

(a) which is **l**, **r** or **s**, the **n** of the participle changes to a second **l**, **r** or **s**;

(b) which is **t**, this **t** changes to **n**.

Infinitive		*Past participle*	*Cf. third p. sing. present*
osta/a	buy	osta/**nut**	osta/a
itke/ä	cry	itke/**nyt**	itke/e
seiso/a	stand	seiso/**nut**	seiso/o
tanssi/a	dance	tanssi/**nut**	tanssi/i
löytä/ä	find	löytä/**nyt**	löytä/ä
anta/a	give	anta/**nut**	anta/a
näyttä/ä	show	näyttä/**nyt**	näyttä/ä
synty/ä	be born	synty/**nyt**	synty/y
saa/da	get	saa/**nut**	saa
myy/dä	sell	myy/**nyt**	myy
juo/da	drink	juo/**nut**	juo
soi/da	ring	soi/**nut**	soi
vartioi/da	guard	vartioi/**nut**	vartioi
nou_s_/ta	rise	nou_s_/**sut**	nouse/e

pes/tä	wash	pes/**syt**	pese/e
tul/la	come	tul/**lut**	tule/e
ol/la	be	ol/**lut**	on
ajatel/la	think	ajatel/**lut**	ajattele/e
pur/ra	bite	pur/**rut**	pure/e
väitel/lä	dispute	väitel/**lyt**	väittele/e
huomat/a	notice	huoma**n**/**nut**	huomaa
osat/a	know how	osa**n**/**nut**	osaa
halut/a	want	halu**n**/**nut**	halua/a
veikat/a	bet	veika**n**/**nut**	veikkaa
pelät/ä	fear	pelä**n**/**nyt**	pelkää
hypät/ä	jump	hypä**n**/**nyt**	hyppää
kelvat/a	be good enough	kelva**n**/**nut**	kelpaa
tarvit/a	need	tarvi**n**/**nut**	tarvitse/e
paet/a	flee	pae**n**/**nut**	pakene/e
lämmet/ä	become warm	lämme**n**/**nyt**	lämpene/e
havait/a	observe	havai**n**/**nut**	havaitse/e

The inflectional stem of the past participle is formed by changing **-ut** ~ **-yt** to **-ee-**, e.g. sano/**nut** : sano/**nee-**, and any endings are added to this stem. The different persons of the perfect tense are thus as follows.

First p. sing.	(**minä**)	**ole/n sano/nut**	I have said
		ole/n ol/lut	I have been
		ole/n huoman/nut	I have noticed
Second p. sing.	(**sinä**)	**ole/t sano/nut**	you have said
		ole/t ol/lut	you have been
		ole/t huoman/nut	you have noticed
Third p. sing.	**hän**	**on sano/nut**	he/she has said
	hän	**on ol/lut**	he/she has been
	hän	**on huoman/nut**	he/she has noticed
First p. pl.	(**me**)	**ole/mme sano/neet**	we have said
		ole/mme ol/leet	we have been
		ole/mme huoman/neet	we have noticed
Second p. pl.	(**te**)	**ole/tte sano/neet**	you have said
		ole/tte ol/leet	you have been
		ole/tte huoman/neet	you have noticed
Third p. pl.	**he**	**ovat sano/neet**	they have said
	he	**ovat ol/leet**	they have been
	he	**ovat huoman/neet**	they have noticed

Below are some examples of the use of the perfect.

Keihänen *on matkusta/nut* **Espanjaan.**
Keihänen *has travelled* to Spain.

On/ko johtaja *men/nyt* **lounaalle?**
Has the manager *gone* to lunch?

Ole/tte/ko **ennen** *ol/leet* **Suomessa?**
Have you been in Finland before?

Kari ja Pertti *ovat lähte/neet* **pois.**
Kari and Pertti *have gone* away.

Ole/t/ko **jo** *syö/nyt?*
Have you already *eaten?*

Ole/n maan/nut **sängyssä koko päivän.**
I have lain in bed all day.

Ole/tte/ko luke/neet **Salaman uusimman kirjan?**
Have you read Salama's latest book?

The perfect can also occur in the conditional mood, when the ending **-isi-** is added to the auxiliary **olla**, and in the potential mood, which is formed from an exceptional stem of the verb **olla**, **liene-**, followed by a personal ending. After these forms of the auxiliary the past participle follows (see Chapter 15).

Ol/isi/n ol/lut **iloinen, jos** *ol/isi/t tul/lut.*
I would have been pleased if *you* had ('*would have*') *come.*

Ol/isi/mme lähte/neet **Espanjaan, jos meillä** *ol/isi ol/lut* **rahaa.**
We would have gone to Spain if we had ('*would have*') *had* money.

Ahtisaari *liene/e käy/nyt* **Marokossa.**
Ahtisaari *has probably been to* Morocco.

He *liene/vät hankki/neet* **auton.**
They (*have*) *probably obtained* a car.

§62   PLUPERFECT TENSE

The pluperfect is used for actions which have taken place before some point of time in the past. It is formed from the past tense of **ol/la** (**ol/i/n**, **ol/i/t**, **ol/i**, **ol/i/mme**, **ol/i/tte**, **ol/i/vat**), followed by the past participle (§61).

Ol/i/n **juuri** *tul/lut* **kotiin, kun soitit.**
I had just *come* home when you rang.

Ol/i/mme tul/leet **kotiin ...**
We had come home ...

Hän *ol/i opiskel/lut* **suomea ennen kuin hän tuli Suomeen.**
He *had studied* Finnish before he came to Finland.

Kalle *ol/i odotta/nut* **kymmenen minuuttia kun tulin.**
Kalle *had waited/been waiting* ten minutes when I came.

He *ol/i/vat odotta/neet* **...**
They *had waited* ...

§63 NEGATIVE FORMS

All negative forms are based on the negation verb **en**, **et**, **ei**, **emme**, **ette**, **eivät**. The present tense negative has been discussed earlier (§29); here the negation verb is followed by a minimal stem form of the main verb subject to consonant gradation.

Affirmative		*Negative*	
kerro/n	I tell	**en kerro**	I do not tell
kerro/t		**et kerro**	
hän kerto/o		**hän ei kerro**	
kerro/mme		**emme kerro**	
kerro/tte		**ette kerro**	
he kerto/vat		**he eivät kerro**	

> The negative of the past tense is formed differently: the negation verb is followed by the past participle (§61).

Affirmative		*Negative*	
kerro/i/n	I told	**en kerto/nut**	I did not tell
kerro/i/t		**et kerto/nut**	
hän kerto/i		**hän ei kerto/nut**	
kerro/i/mme		**emme kerto/neet**	
kerro/i/tte		**ette kerto/neet**	
he kerto/i/vat		**he eivät kerto/neet**	

Here are some further examples of the formation of the past tense negative.

Affirmative		*Negative*	
tanss/i/n	I danced	**en tanssi/nut**	I did not dance
tanss/i/tte	you (pl.) danced	**ette tanssi/neet**	
itk/i/t	you (sing.) cried	**et itke/nyt**	
hän näytt/i	he/she showed	**hän ei näyttä/nyt**	
he anto/i/vat	they gave	**he eivät anta/neet**	
lu/i/n	I read	**en luke/nut**	
ol/i/mme	we were	**emme ol/leet**	
ol/i/t	you (sing.) were	**et ol/lut**	

nous/i/n	I got up	**en nous/<u>sut</u>**
he nous/i/vat	they got up	**he <u>eivät</u> nous/<u>seet</u>**
ajattel/i/mme	we thought	**emme ajatel/<u>leet</u>**
Tuula sa/i	Tuula got	**Tuula <u>ei</u> saa/<u>nut</u>**
osas/i/mme	we knew how	**emme osan/<u>neet</u>**
osas/i/t	you (sing.) knew how	**et osan/<u>nut</u>**
hän pelkäs/i	he/she feared	**hän <u>ei</u> pelän/<u>nyt</u>**
pelkäs/i/tte	you (pl.) feared	**ette pelän/<u>neet</u>**
tarvits/i/n	I needed	**en tarvin/<u>nut</u>**
he häirits/i/vät	they disturbed	**he <u>eivät</u> häirin/<u>neet</u>**

The negative of the perfect tense is formed from the negation verb followed by **ole** (without a personal ending) and the past participle of the main verb (singular or plural).

Affirmative   *Negative*

ole/n osta/nut	I have bought	**en <u>ole</u> osta/<u>nut</u>**	I have not bought
ole/t osta/nut	you (sing.) have bought	**et <u>ole</u> osta/<u>nut</u>**	
hän on osta/nut	he/she has bought	**hän <u>ei</u> <u>ole</u> osta/<u>nut</u>**	
ole/mme osta/neet	we have bought	**emme <u>ole</u> osta/<u>neet</u>**	
ole/tte osta/neet	you (pl.) have bought	**ette <u>ole</u> osta/<u>neet</u>**	
he ovat ostaneet	they have bought	**he <u>eivät</u> <u>ole</u> osta/<u>neet</u>**	
ole/n ol/lut	I have been	**en <u>ole</u> ol/<u>lut</u>**	
ole/mme ol/leet	we have been	**emme <u>ole</u> ol/<u>leet</u>**	
ole/t näyttä/nyt	you (sing.) have shown	**et <u>ole</u> näyttä/<u>nyt</u>**	
he ovat anta/neet	they have given	**he <u>eivät</u> <u>ole</u> anta/<u>neet</u>**	
ole/mme saa/neet	we have got	**emme <u>ole</u> saa/<u>neet</u>**	
ole/n ajatel/lut	I have thought	**en <u>ole</u> ajatel/<u>lut</u>**	
hän on osan/nut	he/she has known how	**hän <u>ei</u> <u>ole</u> osan/<u>nut</u>**	
ole/mme pelän/neet	we have feared	**emme <u>ole</u> pelän/<u>neet</u>**	
ole/n tarvin/nut	I have needed	**en <u>ole</u> tarvin/<u>nut</u>**	
ol/isi/n osta/nut	I would have bought	**en ol/<u>isi</u> osta/<u>nut</u>**	
ol/isi/tte osta/neet	you (pl.) would have bought	**ette ol/<u>isi</u> osta/<u>neet</u>**	
he ol/isi/vat osta/neet	they would have bought	**he <u>eivät</u> ol/<u>isi</u> osta/<u>neet</u>**	
hän liene/e osta/nut	he/she has probably bought	**hän <u>ei</u> <u>liene</u> osta/<u>nut</u>**	

The negative of the pluperfect is formed from the negation verb followed by the past participle of **ol/la** – **ol/lut** ~ **ol/leet** – and the past participle of the main verb (singular or plural).

Affirmative		*Negative*	
ol/i/n osta/nut	I had bought	**en ol/lut osta/nut**	I had not bought
ol/i/t ostanut	you (sing.) had bought	**et ol/lut osta/nut**	
hän ol/i osta/nut	he/she had bought	**hän ei ol/lut osta/nut**	
ol/i/mme osta/neet	we had bought	**emme ol/leet osta/neet**	
ol/i/tte osta/neet	you (pl.) had bought	**ette ol/leet osta/neet**	
he ol/i/vat osta/neet	they had bought	**he eivät ol/leet osta/neet**	
ol/i/n ol/lut	I had been	**en ol/lut ol/lut**	
ol/i/mme ol/leet	we had been	**emme ol/leet ol/leet**	
ol/i/t näyttä/nyt	you (sing.) had shown	**et ol/lut näyttä/nyt**	
ol/i/mme osan/neet	we had known how	**emme ol/leet osan/neet**	
ol/i/t saa/nut	you (sing.) had got	**et ol/lut saa/nut**	
hän ol/i pelän/nyt	he/she had feared	**hän ei ol/lut pelän/nyt**	
ol/i/mme tul/leet	we had come	**emme ol/leet tul/leet**	
ol/i/n näh/nyt	I had seen	**en ol/lut näh/nyt**	

And note finally the following sentence examples.

***En osta* maitoa**.	*I do/will not buy* any milk.
***En osta/nut* maitoa**.	*I did not buy* any milk.
***En ole osta/nut* maitoa**.	*I have not bought* any milk.
***En ol/lut osta/nut* maitoa**.	*I had not bought* any milk.

15 MOODS

- *Indicative*
- *Conditional*
- *Imperative*
- *Potential*

§64 INDICATIVE

The term 'mood' refers to certain verb endings expressing the manner in which the speaker presents the action of the verb. There are four moods in Finnish: the indicative (which is not marked by a separate ending) is the most common, and expresses the action of the verb 'as such'. The conditional **-isi-** mostly indicates a hypothetical action; the imperative (several different endings according to person) indicates a command; and the potential **-ne-**, a rare mood, presents an action as probable or conceivable.

The indicative mood is thus the most common mood. It has no ending and presents an action as such, without any indication of the speaker's attitude. Tense and personal endings are added in the normal way.

Nyt *mene/n* kotiin.	Now *I'm going* home.
Lapsi *leikki/i* pihalla.	A/the child *plays* in the yard.
Vieraat *tule/vat* illalla.	The guests *are coming* in the evening.
Eilen *sa/i/n* kaksi kirjettä.	Yesterday *I got* two letters.
Koska *sairastu/i/t?*	When *did you fall* ill?
He *o/vat asu/neet* kymmenen vuotta Turussa.	They *have lived* in Turku for ten years.
Missä *ole/t synty/nyt?*	Where *were you born?*
Vuonna 1960 Paasikivi *ol/i* jo *kuol/lut.*	In the year 1960 Paasikivi *had* already *died.*

These verb forms contain no mood ending, then, only personal and (where necessary) tense endings.

§65 CONDITIONAL

The conditional **-isi-** mostly indicates an action that is presented as hypothetical, and occurs most commonly in conditional clauses after **jos** 'if' and in the accompanying main clause.

The conditional ending is **-isi-**, which is added to the inflectional stem (§23).

The conditional ending does not cause consonant gradation in the stem preceding it (§15.2), but many vowel change rules apply when **-isi-** follows the inflectional stem (§16). The conditional ending is followed by a personal ending, after which there may also be an enclitic particle.

The verbs **sano/a** 'say', **puhu/a** 'speak' and **anta/a** 'give' have the following conditional forms in the three singular persons.

First p. sing.	(**minä**)	**sano/isi/n**	I would say
		puhu/isi/n	I would speak
		anta/isi/n	I would give
Second p. sing.	(**sinä**)	**sano/isi/t**	you would say
		puhu/isi/t	you would speak
		anta/isi/t	you would give
Third p. sing.	**hän**	**sano/isi**	he/she would say
	Kalle	**puhu/isi**	Kalle would speak
	äiti	**anta/isi**	mother would give

Below are examples of the effect of vowel changes before the conditional ending. The table shows first the basic form of the verb, then the third person singular present indicative as an example of the inflectional stem, with the section number (§) explaining the change in the final vowel of the inflectional stem, and finally the first person singular of the conditional (the other persons only differ in the personal ending).

Infinitive		*Third p. sing. present indicative*	*Cf. §*	*First p. sing. conditional*
kerto/a	tell	kerto/o	16(1)	kerto/**isi**/n
asu/a	live	asu/u	"	asu/**isi**/n
pysy/ä	stay	pysy/y	"	pysy/**isi**/n
luke/a	read	luk**e**/e	16(5)	luk/**isi**/n
tunte/a	know, feel	tunt**e**/e	"	tunt/**isi**/n
oppi/a	learn	opp**i**/i	16(6)	opp/**isi**/n
salli/a	allow	sall**i**/i	"	sall/**isi**/n
näyttä/ä	show	näyttä/ä	16(7)	näyttä/**isi**/n
vetä/ä	pull	vetä/ä	"	vetä/**isi**/n
jaka/a	divide	jaka/a	16(8)	jaka/**isi**/n
otta/a	take	otta/a	"	otta/**isi**/n
rakasta/a	love	rakasta/a	"	rakasta/**isi**/n

Infinitive		*Third p. sing.* *present* *indicative*	*Cf. §*	*First p. sing.* *conditional*
huomat/a	notice	huom**aa**	16(2)	huoma/**isi**/n
hypät/ä	jump	hypp**ää**	"	hyppä/**isi**/n
pelät/ä	fear	pelk**ää**	"	pelkä/**isi**/n
tavat/a	meet	tap**aa**	"	tapa/**isi**/n
saa/da	get	s**aa**	16(2)	sa/**isi**/n
tuo/da	bring	t**u**o	16(3)	to/**isi**/n
vie/dä	take	v**i**e	"	ve/**isi**/n
syö/dä	eat	s**y**ö	"	sö/**isi**/n
voi/da	be able	vo**i**	16(4)	vo/**isi**/n
pysäköi/dä	park	pysakö**i**	"	pysäkö/**isi**/n
nous/ta	rise	nous**e**/e	16(5)	nous/**isi**/n
tul/la	come	tul**e**/e	"	tul/**isi**/n
men/nä	go	men**e**/e	"	men/**isi**/n
ajatel/la	think	ajattel**e**/e	"	ajattel/**isi**/n
hymyil/lä	smile	hymyil**e**/e	"	hymyil/**isi**/n
tarvit/a	need	tarvits**e**/e	"	tarvits/**isi**/n
vanhet/a	grow old	vanhen**e**/e	"	vanhen/**isi**/n

Below are some examples of the use of the conditional.

Ol/isi/n **iloinen, jos** *tul/isi/t.*
I would be pleased if you came.

Jo/isi/n **mielelläni kahvia.**
I would love some coffee ('I would drink with pleasure').

Jos vesi *ol/isi* **lämmintä,** *sa/isi/t* **uida.**
If the water were warm you could swim.

Väittä/isi/n, **että ...**
I would claim that ...

Muutta/isi/t/ko **pois Suomesta?**
Would you move away from Finland?

Tul/isi/vat/ko **he jos** *pyytä/isi/mme*?
Would they come if we asked (them)?

Kyllä Kantanen *voitta/isi* **jos** *halua/isi.*
Kantanen would certainly win if he wanted to.

The conditional is often used to show politeness.

Kaata/isi/t/ko **lisää teetä?**   Would you pour some more tea?
Kysy/isi/n, **onko teillä ...**   May I ask whether you have ...

Läht/isi/mme/kö jo kotiin?   *Shall we go home now?*
Ruoka ol/isi nyt valmista.   The meal *is* ready now (in the
                                    sense 'dinner is served').

As was mentioned above (§61), the conditional also occurs in the perfect. These structures consist of the forms **ol/isi/n ~ ol/isi/t**, etc. followed by the past participle of the main verb.

Ol/isi/n ol/lut iloinen, jos ...
I would have been pleased if ...

Ol/isi/n mielelläni lähte/nyt Ruotsiin, jos ol/isi/n voi/nut.
I would have gone to Sweden with pleasure if I had been able to.

Ol/isi/t/ko tul/lut meille?
Would you have come to us?

Ol/isi/vat/ko he suostu/neet tähän?
Would they have agreed to this?

Ol/isi/n sairastu/nut, ellei Martti ol/isi autta/nut minua.
I would have fallen ill if Martti had not helped me.

The negative forms of the conditional are constructed from the negation verb **en ~ et**, etc. and the main verb with the ending **-isi-** but without a personal ending.

Affirmative		*Negative*	
ol/isi/n	I would be	**en ol/isi**	I would not be
tul/isi/t	you would come	**et tul/isi**	
he anta/isi/vat	they would give	**he eivät anta/isi**	
kerto/isi/mme	we would tell	**emme kerto/isi**	
halua/isi/n	I would like	**en halua/isi**	
sata/isi	it would rain	**ei sata/isi**	
sö/isi/n	I would eat	**en sö/isi**	
luk/isi/mme	we would read	**emme luk/isi**	
he vetä/isi/vät	they would pull	**he eivät vetä/isi**	
ol/isi/n otta/nut	I would have taken	**en ol/isi otta/nut**	
ol/isi/tte syö/neet	you would have eaten	**ette ol/isi syö/neet**	
he ol/isi/vat lähte/neet	they would have left	**he eivät ol/isi lähte/neet**	

§66   IMPERATIVE

The imperative is primarily used for commands, requests and exhortations, and in the third person also wishes. There is no imperative form for the first person singular.

	Singular	Plural
First p.	–	**-kaamme ~ -käämme**
Second p.	(no ending)	**-kaa ~ -kää**
Third p.	**-koon ~ -köön**	**-koot ~ -kööt**

The second person singular and plural forms, e.g. **sano** and **sano/kaa**, are the most common. The third person forms occur mostly in the literary language.

> The second person singular of the imperative has the same form as the first person singular of the present indicative, without the final **-n**.

This form is also identical with that of the main verb in the present indicative negative (§63), cf. **sano/n** 'I say', **tule/n** 'I come', **pelkää/n** 'I fear' – **en sano** 'I do not say', **en tule** 'I do not come', **en pelkää** 'I do not fear' – **sano** 'say!', **tule** 'come!', **pelkää** 'fear!'.

> The other imperative forms are based on the infinitive stem (§22).

The imperative forms of the verbs **sano/a** 'say', **men/nä** 'go' and **kerto/a** 'tell' are thus as follows.

	Singular		Plural	
First p.	–		**sano/kaamme**	let us say
	–		**men/käämme**	let us go
	–		**kerto/kaamme**	let us tell
Second p.	**sano**	say!	**sano/kaa**	say!
	mene	go!	**men/kää**	go!
	kerro	tell!	**kerto/kaa**	tell!
Third p.	**sano/koon**	may he say	**sano/koot**	may they say
	men/köön	may he go	**men/kööt**	may they go
	kerto/koon	may he tell	**kerto/koot**	may they tell

The table below shows the infinitive, the first person singular present, and the second person singular and plural of the imperative.

Infinitive		First p. sing. present	Second p. sing. imperative	Second p. pl. imperative
anta/a	give	anna/n	anna	anta/**kaa**
osta/a	buy	osta/n	osta	osta/**kaa**
unohta/a	forget	unohda/n	unohda	unohta/**kaa**

Infinitive		*First p. sing.*	*Second p. sing.*	*Second p. pl.*
		present	*imperative*	*imperative*
luke/a	read	lue/n	lue	luke/**kaa**
vetä/ä	pull	vedä/n	vedä	vetä/**kää**
sulke/a	close	sulje/n	sulje	sulke/**kaa**
herättä/ä	wake	herätä/n	herätä	herättä/**kää**
avat/a	open	avaa/n	avaa	avat/**kaa**
maat/a	lie	makaa/n	makaa	maat/**kaa**
tavat/a	meet	tapaa/n	tapaa	tavat/**kaa**
määrät/ä	order	määrää/n	määrää	määrät/**kää**
hakat/a	hew	hakkaa/n	hakkaa	hakat/**kaa**
tarjot/a	offer	tarjoa/n	tarjoa	tarjot/**kaa**
myy/dä	sell	myy/n	myy	myy/**kää**
syö/dä	eat	syö/n	syö	syö/**kää**
ui/da	swim	ui/n	ui	ui/**kaa**
teh/dä	do	tee/n	tee	teh/**kää**
pysäköi/dä	park	pysäköi/n	pysäköi	pysäköi/**kää**
nous/ta	rise	nouse/n	nouse	nous/**kaa**
tul/la	come	tule/n	tule	tul/**kaa**
men/nä	go	mene/n	mene	men/**kää**
juos/ta	run	juokse/n	juokse	juos/**kaa**
ajatel/la	think	ajattele/n	ajattele	ajatel/**kaa**
harkit/a	consider	harkitse/n	harkitse	harkit/**kaa**
paet/a	flee	pakene/n	pakene	paet/**kaa**

The object of an imperative verb is in the partitive if any of the normal partitive rules apply (§33.2). The accusative object of an imperative takes no ending if the imperative is first or second person, but the ending **-n** if the imperative is third person, cf. §38.

The examples below illustrate the use of the imperative.

Mene **kotiin!**	*Go* home! (sing.)
Men/kää **kotiin!**	*Go* home! (pl.)
Tule **tänne!**	*Come* here! (sing.)
Tul/kaa **tänne!**	*Come* here! (pl.)
Osta **minulle kuppi kahvia!**	*Buy* me a cup of coffee!
Anta/kaa **meille vettä.**	*Give* us some water!
Anna **minulle lusikka!**	*Give* me a spoon!
Ol/kaa **hyvä!**	Please. (*lit.* 'Be good!') (pl.)
Ole **hyvä!**	Please. ('Be good!') (sing.)
Ole **hyvä ja** *avaa* **ovi!**	Please *open* the door. ('Be good and *open* . . .')
Teh/käämme **kuten hän sanoo.**	Let us *do* as he says.
Varat/kaa **meillekin pöytä!**	*Reserve* a table for us, too!

Elä/*köön* **Suomi!**	*Long* *live* Finland! ('*May* Finland *live*.')
Onneksi *ol*/*koon*!	Congratulations! ('*May it be* to (your) happiness.')
Puhu/*kaamme* **suomea.**	*Let us speak* Finnish.
Juo/*kaamme* **Lipposen malja!**	*Let us drink* a toast to Lipponen!
Tul/*koot* **he tänne.**	*Let* them *come* here.
Men/*kööt* **he sinne, me jäämme kotiin.**	*Let* them *go* there, we are staying at home.
Ajattele **asiaa!**	*Think* about the matter!
Nous/*kaa* **ylös!**	*Get* up!
Kukin *teh*/*köön* **kuten haluaa.**	*Let* everyone *do* as he/she likes.
Luke/*kaa* **läksynne kunnolla!**	*Do* ('*read*') your homework properly! (pl.)
Lue **läksysi kunnolla!**	*Do* your homework properly! (sing.)

In the spoken language the passive is always used instead of the first person plural imperative form, e.g. **sanotaan** 'one says' but often also 'let's say', **mennään** 'let's go', **tehdään** 'let's do' for **sanokaamme**, **menkäämme**, **tehkäämme**.

The negative forms of the imperative are constructed differently; here too the second person singular is unlike the other forms.

The second person singular imperative negative is formed from the word **älä**, placed before the imperative affirmative form.

Affirmative		*Negative*	
osta	buy!	**älä** osta	don't buy!
lue	read!	**älä** lue	
vedä	pull!	**älä** vedä	
avaa	open!	**älä** avaa	
makaa	lie!	**älä** makaa	
syö	eat!	**älä** syö	
tule	come!	**älä** tule	

The other imperative negative forms are based on the stem **äl-** with the appropriate imperative ending, followed by the infinitive stem of the main verb with the ending **-ko** ~ **-kö**.

The negation words are thus **älköön** (third person singular), **älkäämme** (first person plural), **älkää** (second person plural) and **älkööt** (third person plural).

Infinitive		*Imperative negative 2 pl.*	
sano/a	say	**älkää** sano/**ko**	don't say!
otta/a	take	**älkää** otta/**ko**	
pelät/ä	fear	**älkää** pelät/**kö**	
määrät/ä	order	**älkää** määrät/**kö**	
maat/a	lie	**älkää** maat/**ko**	
tuo/da	bring	**älkää** tuo/**ko**	
tul/la	come	**älkää** tul/**ko**	
men/nä	go	**älkää** men/**kö**	
ajatel/la	think	**älkää** ajatel/**ko**	

Examples of the imperative negative follow below. The object is in the partitive, in accordance with the normal rules (§33.2).

Älä pelkää **koiraa!**	*Don't be afraid of* the dog! (sing.)
Älkää syö/kö **niin nopeasti!**	*Don't eat* so quickly! (pl.)
Älä polta **täällä!**	*Don't smoke* here! (sing.)
Älkää poltta/ko **täällä!**	*Don't smoke* here! (pl.)
Älkää lähte/kö **kotiin vielä!**	*Don't go* home yet! (pl.)
Älä lyö **minua!**	*Don't hit* me! (sing.)
Älkää lyö/kö **minua!**	*Don't hit* me! (pl.)
Älkäämme ajatel/ko **sitä enää.**	*Let us not think* about it any longer. (pl.)
Älä tanssi **Uolevin kanssa!**	*Don't dance* with Uolevi! (sing.)
Älköön **kukaan** *usko/ko,* **että ...**	*Let* no one *believe* that . . . (sing.)
Älkää avat/ko **tuota ikkunaa!**	*Don't open* that window! (pl.)
Älä sylje **lattialle!**	*Don't spit* on the floor! (sing.)

§67   POTENTIAL

The potential, which has the ending **-ne-**, is a rare mood and thus of less importance. It indicates that the action of the verb is probable, possible or conceivable.[1]

> The basic ending of the potential is **-ne-**, which is added to the infinitive stem (§22).

The potential is thus formed in the same way as the past participle, which has the ending **-nut** ~ **-nyt** (§61). The sound alternations are also the same.

---

1 *Translator's note*: the potential is normally glossed 'may' in isolation (e.g. in the Appendix below); but in context the degree of probability implied is often more accurately rendered by 'probably'.

If the infinitive stem ends in a consonant

(a) which is **l, r, s**, the **n** of the **-ne-** ending changes to a second **l, r, s**;
(b) which is **t**, this **t** changes to **n**.

After the ending **-ne-** the personal ending follows.

Infinitive		*Third p. sing. potential*	*Cf. third p. sing. present indic.*
anta/a	give	anta/**ne**/e	anta/a
löytä/ä	find	löytä/**ne**/e	löytä/ä
luke/a	read	luke/**ne**/e	luke/e
saa/da	get	saa/**ne**/e	saa
voi/da	be able	voi/**ne**/e	voi
vartioi/da	guard	vartioi/**ne**/e	vartioi
nou<u>s</u>/ta	rise	nous/**se**/e	nouse/e
tu<u>l</u>/la	come	tul/**le**/e	tule/e
ajate<u>l</u>/la	think	ajatel/**le**/e	ajattele/e
huoma<u>t</u>/a	notice	huoma**n**/**ne**/e	huomaa
kohda<u>t</u>/a	meet	kohda**n**/**ne**/e	kohtaa
leika<u>t</u>/a	cut	leika**n**/**ne**/e	leikkaa
tarvi<u>t</u>/a	need	tarvi**n**/**ne**/e	tarvitse/e
vali<u>t</u>/a	choose	vali**n**/**ne**/e	valitse/e
häiri<u>t</u>/ä	disturb	häiri**n**/**ne**/e	häiritse/e

The potential forms of the verb **ol/la** 'be' are exceptional. They are based on the stem **liene-**, which is followed by the personal endings: **liene/n, liene/t, liene/e, liene/mme, liene/tte, liene/vät.**

The following examples illustrate the use of the potential.

Presidentti Havel *saapu/ne/e* **huomenna.**
President Havel *will probably arrive* tomorrow.

Eduskunta *valin/ne/e* **Riitta Uosukaisen puhemieheksi.**
Parliament *will probably elect* Riitta Uosukainen Speaker.

Ahtisaari *liene/e* **ulkomailla.**
Ahtisaari *may be/is probably* abroad.

Utsjoki *sijain/ne/e* **pohjoisessa.**
Utsjoki *is probably* ('situated') in the north.

He *liene/vät* **samaa mieltä kanssamme.**
They *are probably* of the same opinion as we are.

Hyväksy/ne/tte **päätöksemme.**
You will probably accept our decision.

The potential also occurs in the perfect, when the structure is **liene-** plus the past participle of the main verb (§61).

Ahtisaari *liene/e käy/nyt* **Brasiliassa.**
Ahtisaari *has probably been* to Brazil.

Hän *liene/e ol/lut* **myös Marokossa.**
He *has probably* also *been* to Morocco.

Liene/mme näh/neet **tämän elokuvan aikaisemmin.**
We may have seen/have probably seen this film before.

The negative forms of the potential are constructed in the normal way. In the present the negation verb **en**, **et**, etc. is followed by the potential form without a personal ending, e.g. **en osta/ne** 'I shall probably not buy'. The negative of the potential perfect follows the same pattern: negation verb + **liene** (without personal ending) + past participle, e.g. **en liene osta/nut** 'I have probably not bought'.

Virtanen *ei syö/ne* **tällaista ruokaa.**
Virtanen *probably does not eat* this kind of food.

Emme uskalta/ne **tehdä näin.**
We probably do not dare to do (it like) this.

Utsjoki *ei sijain/ne* **Pohjanmaalla.**
Utsjoki *is probably not* in Ostrobothnia.

He *eivät liene soitta/neet* **vielä.**
They *probably have not rung* yet.

16 THE PASSIVE

- *General*
- *Passive present*
- *Passive past*
- *Passive perfect and pluperfect*
- *Passive moods*

§68 GENERAL

The Finnish passive is a very common and important verb form. It indicates that the action of the verb is performed by an unspecified person, i.e. that the agent is impersonal (indefinite). It thus roughly corresponds to Swedish and German '*man*', French '*on*' and English 'one'. The passive has two endings: the passive marker itself, which is **-tta-** ~ **-ttä-** or **-ta-** ~ **-tä-**, and a special personal ending **-Vn**, e.g. **sano/ta/an** 'one says, it is said'.

Passive sentences should be distinguished from generic sentences expressing a general truth or law or state of affairs. The predicate verb of generic sentences appears in the third person singular active and there is no separate subject:

Usein *kuule/e*, että ...	*One* often *hears* that ...
Siellä *saa* hyvää kahvia.	*One gets* good coffee there.
Tästä *näke/e* hyvin.	*You/one can see* well from here.
Jos *juokse/e* joka aamu, *tule/e* terveeksi.	If *you run* every morning *you will become* healthy.

The passive occurs in all tenses (present, past, perfect and pluperfect) and also all moods (indicative, conditional, imperative and potential). The basic pattern of the passive forms is illustrated in the table below.

Root	Passive	Tense, mood	Person	Particle		
sano	ta		an		one says	(*pass. pres.*)
sano	tt	i	in		one said	(*pass. past*)
sano	tta	isi	in		one would say	(*pass. cond.*)
sano	tta	ne	en		one may say	(*pass. pot.*)
sano	tta	ko	on		let one say	(*pass. imp.*)
sano	ta		an	han	one does say	(*pass. pres.*)
sano	tt	i	in	ko	did one say?	(*pass. past*)

In this chapter, however, the formation of the passive will not be described as the addition of these endings: we do not need to say for instance that the passive present is formed by adding the endings **-ta-** and **-Vn**: **sano/ta/an** 'one says'. Instead, we shall make use of a number of 'short cuts' which are available because the passive happens to resemble several forms we have already discussed, in particular the infinitive. In this way many of the complex sound alternations in the passive can be derived automatically.

§69   PASSIVE PRESENT

With the exception of **anta/a** verbs, the passive present can be formed according to the following simple rule:

> The passive present is formed by adding the ending **-an** ~ **-än** to the first infinitive (does not apply to **anta/a** verbs).

This rule thus covers **huomat/a**, **saa/da**, **nous/ta**, **tul/la** and **lämmet/ä** verbs. The oblique lines in the examples below indicate the positions of the passive endings proper.

First infinitive	*Passive present*	
huomat/a	**huomat/a/an**	one notices
osat/a	**osat/a/an**	one knows how
hypät/ä	**hypät/ä/än**	one jumps
määrät/ä	**määrät/ä/än**	one orders
pelät/ä	**pelät/ä/än**	one fears
saa/da	**saa/da/an**	one gets
myy/dä	**myy/dä/än**	one sells
voi/da	**voi/da/an**	one can
teh/dä	**teh/dä/än**	one does
nous/ta	**nous/ta/an**	one rises
men/nä	**men/nä/än**	one goes
tul/la	**tul/la/an**	one comes
ajatel/la	**ajatel/la/an**	one thinks
julkais/ta	**julkais/ta/an**	one publishes
tarvit/a	**tarvit/a/an**	one needs
valit/a	**valit/a/an**	one chooses
paet/a	**paet/a/an**	one flees

The passive present of **anta/a** verbs is formed by adding the passive endings **-ta/an** ~ **-tä/än** to the first person singular stem of the active, e.g. **sano/n** :

sano/ta/an 'one says'; immediately before the passive endings the usual consonant gradation rules apply (cf. §15.2, rule B(a)). If the final vowel of the stem is **-a** or **-ä**, this changes to **-e** in the passive.

The passive present of **anta/a** verbs is formed

(a) by adding **-ta/an ~ -tä/än** to the first person singular stem and
(b) changing the final **-a** or **-ä** of the stem to **-e**.

Infinitive	*First person present*	*Passive present*	
sano/a	**sano/n**	**sano/<u>ta</u>/<u>an</u>**	one says
osta/a	**osta/n**	**oste/<u>ta</u>/<u>an</u>**	one buys
etsi/ä	**etsi/n**	**etsi/<u>tä</u>/<u>än</u>**	one looks for
kysy/ä	**kysy/n**	**kysy/<u>tä</u>/<u>än</u>**	one asks
nukku/a	**nuku/n**	**nuku/<u>ta</u>/<u>an</u>**	one sleeps
anta/a	**anna/n**	**anne/<u>ta</u>/<u>an</u>**	one gives
sulke/a	**sulje/n**	**sulje/<u>ta</u>/<u>an</u>**	one closes
lentä/ä	**lennä/n**	**lenne/<u>tä</u>/<u>än</u>**	one flies
unohta/a	**unohda/n**	**unohde/<u>ta</u>/<u>an</u>**	one forgets
otta/a	**ota/n**	**ote/<u>ta</u>/<u>an</u>**	one takes
luke/a	**lue/n**	**lue/<u>ta</u>/<u>an</u>**	one reads
pyytä/ä	**pyydä/n**	**pyyde/<u>tä</u>/<u>än</u>**	one requests

---

The negative forms of the passive present consist of the negation verb **ei** followed by the passive form without the personal ending **-an ~ -än**.

Affirmative	*Negative*	
huomat/a/an	**ei huomat/<u>a</u>**	one does not notice
osat/a/an	**ei osat/<u>a</u>**	one does not know how
saa/da/an	**ei saa/<u>da</u>**	one does not get
teh/dä/än	**ei teh/<u>dä</u>**	one does not do
men/nä/än	**ei men/<u>nä</u>**	one does not go
nous/ta/an	**ei nous/<u>ta</u>**	one does not get up
tarvit/a/an	**ei tarvit/<u>a</u>**	one does not need
sano/ta/an	**ei sano/<u>ta</u>**	one does not say
anne/ta/an	**ei anne/<u>ta</u>**	one does not give
pyyde/tä/än	**ei pyyde/<u>tä</u>**	one does not request
ote/ta/an	**ei ote/<u>ta</u>**	one does not take

The sentences below illustrate the use of the passive present.

Suomessa *juo/da/an* **sekä maitoa että olutta.**
In Finland *people drink* both milk and beer.

Ravintolassa *tanssi/ta/an* **kello yhteentoista.**
In the restaurant there is dancing (*'one dances'*) until 11 o'clock.

Tanskassa *puhu/ta/an* **tanskaa.**	In Denmark *they speak* Danish.
Ei/kö täällä *puhu/ta* **ruotsia?**	*Isn't* Swedish *spoken* here?
Nyt *näh/dä/än,* **että ...**	Now *one sees* that ...
Mitä täällä *teh/dä/än?*	What *is being done* here?
Täällä *ei tarjot/a* **olutta.**	Beer *is not served* here.
Pelät/ä/än, **että Suomi häviää.**	*It is feared* that Finland will lose.
Väite/tä/än, **että hän on sairas.**	*It is claimed/they claim* that he/she is ill.

The singular accusative object of a passive verb has no ending (§38).

Huomiseksi lue/ta/an *seuraava kappale.*
The next chapter will be read for tomorrow.

Kirja **pan/na/an pöydälle.**
The book is put on the table.

Ovi **sulje/ta/an avaimella.**
The door is closed with a key.

Auto **voi/da/an ajaa pihalle.**
The car can be driven into the yard.

In the spoken language it is very common for the passive forms to be used in place of the first person plural indicative and imperative.

Written language		*Spoken language (often)*
(me) juo/mme	we drink	**(me) juo/daan**
(me) kerro/mme	we tell	**(me) kerro/taan**
(me) halua/mme	we want	**(me) halut/aan**
(me) ajattele/mme	we think	**(me) ajatel/laan**
juo/kaamme!	let us drink!	**juo/daan!**
kerto/kaamme!	let us tell!	**kerro/taan!**
ajatel/kaamme!	let us think!	**ajatel/laan!**
lähte/käämme!	let us leave!	**lähde/tään!**

§70   PASSIVE PAST

The past tense of the passive is formed from one of the endings **-tta-** ~ **-ttä-** or **-ta-** ~ **-tä-**, with the final vowel then being dropped before the past tense **-i-** (§16). After the passive ending come the past tense **-i-** and the personal ending **-Vn**. To make the description simpler these combinations of endings will henceforth be given as **-ttiin** and **-tiin**. The passive past can be derived from the passive present by the following rule:

The passive past is formed by using

(a) **-ttiin** in place of the passive present **-taan** ~ **-tään** when occurring after a vowel;

(b) **-tiin** in place of all other instances of passive present endings.

Examples:

Infinitive	First p. sing.	Passive present	Passive past	Meaning
sano/a	**sano/n**	**sano/taan**	**sano/ttiin**	one said
osta/a	**osta/n**	**oste/taan**	**oste/ttiin**	one bought
vaati/a	**vaadi/n**	**vaadi/taan**	**vaadi/ttiin**	one demanded
anta/a	**anna/n**	**anne/taan**	**anne/ttiin**	one gave
pyytä/ä	**pyydä/n**	**pyyde/tään**	**pyyde/ttiin**	one requested
rakasta/a	**rakasta/n**	**rakaste/taan**	**rakaste/ttiin**	one loved
huomat/a	**huomaa/n**	**huomat/aan**	**huomat/tiin**	one noticed
osat/a	**osaa/n**	**osat/aan**	**osat/tiin**	one knew how
palat/a	**palaa/n**	**palat/aan**	**palat/tiin**	one returned
pelät/ä	**pelkää/n**	**pelät/ään**	**pelät/tiin**	one feared
saa/da	**saa/n**	**saa/daan**	**saa/tiin**	one got
vie/dä	**vie/n**	**vie/dään**	**vie/tiin**	one took
syö/dä	**syö/n**	**syö/dään**	**syö/tiin**	one ate
tuo/da	**tuo/n**	**tuo/daan**	**tuo/tiin**	one brought
nous/ta	**nouse/n**	**nous/taan**	**nous/tiin**	one rose
tul/la	**tule/n**	**tul/laan**	**tul/tiin**	one came
men/nä	**mene/n**	**men/nään**	**men/tiin**	one went
ajatetel/la	**ajattele/n**	**ajatel/laan**	**ajatel/tiin**	one thought
ol/la	**ole/n**	**ol/laan**	**ol/tiin**	one was
tarvit/a	**tarvitse/n**	**tarvit/aan**	**tarvit/tiin**	one needed
paet/a	**pakene/n**	**paet/aan**	**paet/tiin**	one fled
ansait/a	**ansaitse/n**	**ansait/aan**	**ansait/tiin**	one earned
harkit/a	**harkitse/n**	**harkit/aan**	**harkit/tiin**	one considered

The negative forms of the passive past have the following structure: **ei** + past participle passive (§71). The examples below illustrate the use of the passive past in the affirmative.

Viime vuonna Suomeen *tuo/tiin* **enemmän kuin Suomesta** *vie/tiin.*
Last year more *was imported* to Finland than *was exported* from
Finland.

Ol/tiin **sitä mieltä, että ...**
One was of the opinion that ...

Pian *havait/tiin,* **että Eero oli lähtenyt**.
One/we soon *noticed* that Eero had left. (*Or: It was* soon *noticed* ...)

Meille *anne/ttiin* **monta hyvää neuvoa**.
We *were given* much good advice.

Tul/tiin **Helsinkiin aamulla**.
We *came* to Helsinki in the morning.

Maahan *valit/tiin* **uusi presidentti**.
The country *elected* a new president.
('A new president *was elected* to the country.')

Tukholmasta *lenne/ttiin* **Osloon**.
From Stockholm *we flew* to Oslo.

Nuku/ttiin **eri huoneissa**.
One/we *slept* in different rooms.

It will be evident from these examples that the passive often has the
meaning 'we', especially in the spoken language.

§71   PASSIVE PERFECT AND PLUPERFECT

The passive perfect and pluperfect have the structure **on** (perfect) or **oli**
(pluperfect) + past participle passive (for the past participle active see §61).
The past participle passive can be formed most conveniently from the past
tense by the following rule:

The past participle passive is formed by changing the passive past
-iin to **-u** or **-y**.

Infinitive	First p. sing.	Passive past	Passive past participle	Meaning
osta/a	**osta/n**	**oste/ttiin**	**oste/ttu**	bought
anta/a	**anna/n**	**anne/ttiin**	**anne/ttu**	given
nukku/a	**nuku/n**	**nuku/ttiin**	**nuku/ttu**	slept
pyytä/ä	**pyydä/n**	**pyyde/ttiin**	**pyyde/tty**	requested
huomat/a	**huomaa/n**	**huomat/tiin**	**huomat/tu**	noticed

Infinitive	First p. sing.	Passive past	Passive past participle	Meaning
määrät/ä	määrää/n	määrät/tiin	määrät/ty	ordered
pelät/ä	pelkää/n	pelät/tiin	pelät/ty	feared
saa/da	saa/n	saa/tiin	saa/tu	got
syö/dä	syö/n	syö/tiin	syö/ty	eaten
myy/dä	myy/n	myy/tiin	myy/ty	sold
nous/ta	nouse/n	nous/tiin	nous/tu	risen
ol/la	ole/n	ol/tiin	ol/tu	been
men/nä	mene/n	men/tiin	men/ty	gone
tarvit/a	tarvitse/n	tarvit/tiin	tarvit/tu	needed

The use of these forms is illustrated below.

On sano/ttu, että Suomi on tuhansien järvien maa.
It has been said that Finland is the land of a thousand lakes.

Ol/i sano/ttu, että ...
It had been said that ...

On väite/tty, ettei hän eroa koskaan.
It has been stated that he will never resign.

Tähän on tul/tu.
One has come to this.

Ol/i anne/ttu sellainen neuvo, että ...
There had been given such advice that ...

Kouluissa on lue/ttu saksaa jo pitkään.
German *has* long *been studied* in the schools.

Ol/i huomat/tu, että laiva uppoaa.
It had been noticed that the ship was sinking.

Ol/i jo syö/ty, kun vieraat tulivat.
One/we had already *eaten* when the guests came.

On esite/tty kolme ehdotusta.
Three suggestions *have been put forward.*

Tätä on pelät/ty monta vuotta.
This *has been feared* for many years.

On ol/tu myös sitä mieltä, että ...
People *have* also *been* of the opinion that ...

On/ko nyt men/ty liian pitkälle?
Has one/have we now *gone* too far?

Auto *ol/i oste/ttu* **jo eilen.**
The car *had* already been *bought* yesterday.

Autot *ol/i oste/ttu* **...**
The cars *had been bought* ...

The form of the passive perfect negative is **ei ole** + the past participle passive of the main verb; the corresponding pluperfect is **ei ol/lut** + the same participle (cf. §63).

Affirmative	*Negative*	*Meaning*
on saa/tu	**ei ole saa/tu**	one has not got
ol/i saa/tu	**ei ol/lut saa/tu**	one had not got
on sano/ttu	**ei ole sano/ttu**	one has not said
ol/i sano/ttu	**ei ol/lut sano/ttu**	one had not said
on määrät/ty	**ei ole määrät/ty**	one has not ordered
ol/i määrät/ty	**ei ol/lut määrät/ty**	one had not ordered
on ol/tu	**ei ole ol/tu**	one has not been
ol/i ol/tu	**ei ol/lut ol/tu**	one had not been

Special attention should be given to the past tense passive negative, which consists of the negation verb **ei** followed by the past participle passive (cf. §70).

Affirmative	*Negative*	*Meaning*
sano/ttiin	**ei sano/ttu**	one did not say
oste/ttiin	**ei oste/ttu**	one did not buy
kysy/ttiin	**ei kysy/tty**	one did not ask
huomat/tiin	**ei huomat/tu**	one did not notice
osat/tiin	**ei osat/tu**	one did not know how
pelät/tiin	**ei pelät/ty**	one did not fear
saa/tiin	**ei saa/tu**	one did not get
syö/tiin	**ei syö/ty**	one did not eat
tul/tiin	**ei tul/tu**	one did not come
ol/tiin	**ei ol/tu**	one was not
men/tiin	**ei men/ty**	one did not go
tarvit/tiin	**ei tarvit/tu**	one did not need

The use of the passive negative is further illustrated below.

Tätä *ei ole tarvit/tu* **ennenkään.**
This *has not been needed* before, either.

Ei/kö ole oste/ttu **ruokaa?**
Has no food *been bought*?

Keneltäkään *ei kysy/tty* **neuvoa.**
No one *was asked* for advice.

50 vuotta sitten Suomen kouluissa *ei* paljon *opiskel/tu* englantia.
50 years ago English *was not* much *studied* in Finnish schools.

Virtasta *ei* *valit/tu* puheenjohtajaksi.
Virtanen *was not elected* chairman.

Häntä *ei* *ol/lut* *näh/ty* kaupungilla.
He/she *had not been seen* in town.

Lakon aikana *ei* *saa/tu* sähköä.
During the strike *we didn't get* any electricity.

Läksyä *ei* *osat/tu* hyvin.
The homework *was not known* well.

Paitaanne *ei* vielä *ole pes/ty*.
Your shirt *has not* yet *been washed*.

Seurauksia *ei* *ol/lut* *ote/ttu* huomioon.
The consequences *had not been taken* into consideration.

Ehdotusta *ei* *ymmärre/tty*.
The proposal *was not understood*.

Sotaa *ei* koskaan *unohde/ttu*.
The war *was* never *forgotten*.

§72   PASSIVE MOODS

There is no mood ending for the indicative: for these forms see §69, e.g. **sano/ta/an** 'one says', **kerro/ta/an** 'one tells', **tul/la/an** 'one comes'. The other moods, i.e. the conditional (the ending of which is **-isi-**), the imperative (**-ko- ~ -kö-**) and the potential (**-ne-**), are all formed from the passive past tense (cf. §70) as can be seen below.

Change the passive past tense **-iin** to **-a** or **-ä** and add the required mood ending and the personal ending **-Vn**.

From the passive past **sano/tt/i/in** 'one said' we can thus derive the conditional **sano/tta/isi/in** 'one would say', the imperative **sano/tta/ko/on** 'let one say' and the potential **sano/tta/ne/en** 'one may say'. The vowel **V** is a copy of the final vowel of the mood ending.

Infinitive	Passive past	Passive conditional	Passive potential	Passive imperative	Meaning
katso/a	katso/ttiin	katso/ttaisiin	katso/ttaneen	katso/ttakoon	look
tunte/a	tunne/ttiin	tunne/ttaisiin	tunne/ttaneen	tunne/ttakoon	feel
odotta/a	odote/ttiin	odote/ttaisiin	odote/ttaneen	odote/ttakoon	wait
avat/a	avat/tiin	avat/taisiin	avat/taneen	avat/takoon	open
lisät/ä	lisät/tiin	lisät/täisiin	lisät/täneen	lisät/täköön	add
juo/da	juo/tiin	juo/taisiin	juo/taneen	juo/takoon	drink
saa/da	saa/tiin	saa/taisiin	saa/taneen	saa/takoon	get
ol/la	ol/tiin	ol/taisiin	ol/taneen	ol/takoon	be
men/nä	men/tiin	men/täisiin	men/täneen	men/täköön	go
hävit/ä	hävit/tiin	hävit/täisiin	hävit/täneen	hävit/täköön	disappear

The corresponding negative forms are as follows: in the conditional and potential the negation verb **ei** is followed by the appropriate passive form without the personal ending **-Vn**; in the imperative, **älköön** is followed by the passive form without the personal ending (cf. §66).

Affirmative	Negative	Meaning
juo/ta/isi/in	ei juo/ta/isi	one would not drink
ol/ta/isi/in	ei ol/ta/isi	one would not be
men/tä/neen	ei men/tä/ne	one may not/probably will not go
sano/tta/koon	älköön sano/tta/ko	let one not say
teh/tä/isi/in	ei teh/tä/isi	one would not do
rakenne/tta/isi/in	ei rakenne/tta/isi	one would not build
todet/ta/ne/en	ei todet/ta/ne	one may not/probably will not verify

Examples:

Tätä *ei sano/tta/isi*, jos ei olisi aihetta.
This *would not be said* if there were no cause.

Voi/ta/isi/in/ko tehdä näin?
Could one do it this way?

Ei voi/ta/isi. — *One could not.*
Pääte/ttä/ne/en, että ... — *It may be decided that ...*
Mitä sano/tta/isi/in, jos ... — What *would people say if ...*
Ei kai sano/tta/isi mitään. — I suppose nothing *would be said.*

Lakko lopete/tta/isi/in, jos pääs/tä/isi/in sopimukseen.
The strike *would be ended* if an agreement *could be reached.*

Ovea älköön avat/ta/ko liian nopeasti.
Let the door *not be opened* too quickly.

Tätä päätöstä *ei siis teh/tä/ne.*
This decision *will* thus *probably not be made.*

17 INFINITIVES

- *General*
- *First infinitive*
- *Second infinitive*
- *Third infinitive*
- *Fourth infinitive*

§73 GENERAL

Infinitives and participles constitute the set of non-finite verb forms, which all lack personal endings. The basic structure of the infinitives has been presented above (§14). Each of the infinitives has its own marker, a functional ending without any actual meaning. Some infinitives occur also in the passive (particularly the second infinitive), and some may take several case endings (particularly the third infinitive). Under certain conditions the first and second infinitives may also be followed by possessive suffixes. All the infinitives can take enclitic particles. Infinitives are never marked for number.

The infinitives function in a sentence as nouns, being nominal forms of verbs; the participles function as adjectives. The examples below illustrate the similarities between infinitives and nouns proper.

Haluan *omena/n.*	I want *an apple.* (noun)
Haluan *ui/da.*	I want *to swim.* (first inf.)
Haluan *osta/a* **omenan.**	I want *to buy* an apple. (first inf.)
Nälkä katoaa *minuuti/ssa.*	Hunger disappears *in a minute.* (noun in inessive)
Nälkä katoaa *syö/de/ssä.*	Hunger disappears as one eats ('*in eating*'). (second inf. in inessive)
Menen *Helsinki/in.*	I'm going *to Helsinki.* (noun in illative)
Menen ulos *juokse/ma/an.*	I'm going out *to run.* (third inf. in illative)
Satamaan pääsee myös *linja-auto/lla.*	One can also get to the harbour *by bus.* (noun in adessive)
juokse/*ma/lla* **hankitut tulot**	income earned *by running* (third inf. in adessive)

§74 FIRST INFINITIVE

§74.1 BASIC FORM OF THE FIRST INFINITIVE

The first infinitive appears in two cases: the basic form, with only the infinitive ending (e.g. **sano/a** '(to) say', **saa/da** '(to) get'); and the translative case, where the infinitive ending is followed by the ending **-kse-** (cf. §50) and a possessive suffix.

The first infinitive endings have been given above (§22). This infinitive is the dictionary form of verbs, for example in the *Nykysuomen sanakirja* ('Dictionary of Modern Standard Finnish') and many Finnish language textbooks. There are four different endings: (1) **-a ~ -ä**, (2) **-da ~ -dä**, (3) **-ta ~ -tä**, (4) **-la ~ -lä, -ra ~ -rä, -na ~ -nä**. The forms and their use are illustrated below.

(1)	**osta/a**	buy	(2)	**tuo/da**	bring
	vetä/ä	pull		**jää/dä**	stay
	varat/a	reserve		**saa/da**	get
	levät/ä	rest		**kanavoi/da**	direct
(3)	**juos/ta**	run	(4)	**ol/la**	be
	nous/ta	rise		**kysel/lä**	ask
	valais/ta	light		**pur/ra**	bite
	väris/tä	shiver		**men/nä**	go

Aion *lähte/ä* **ulos.**	I intend *to go* out.
Yritämme *ymmärtä/ä.*	We try *to understand.*
Mitä haluat *syö/dä?*	What do you want *to eat*?
Saat *lainat/a* **tämän kirjan.**	You may *borrow* this book.
Teillä on oikeus *otta/a* **yksi kuva.**	You have the right *to take* one picture.
On aika vaikea *oppi/a* **suomea.**	It is quite difficult *to learn* Finnish.
Onko sinulla jo ollut mahdollisuus *tilat/a?*	Have you already had an opportunity *to order?*
Teidän täytyy *tul/la* **meille!**	You must *come* to us/our place.
Täytyy *aja/a* **varovasti.**	One must *drive* carefully.
Anna hänen *men/nä!*	Let him/her *go!*
Antakaa Kallen *men/nä!*	Let Kalle *go!*
Koneessa täytyy *ol/la* **vika.**	There must *be* some fault in the machine.
Vian täytyy *ol/la* **koneessa.**	The fault must *be* in the machine.

Minulla on ajatus *lähte/ä* **Unkariin ensi kesänä.**
I am thinking of *going* ('I have the thought *to go*') to Hungary next summer.

Pakolaisten sallittiin *poistu/a* **maasta.**
The refugees were allowed *to leave* the country.

Particular attention should be paid to the special verbs of obligation (**täytyy** 'must', **pitää** 'have to') and permission (**antaa** *x*/:**n tehdä jotakin** 'let *x* do something'; **sallia** 'allow'), which often co-occur with the genitive (**antakaa Kalle/n mennä; via/n täytyy olla koneessa** (see the examples above)) and are followed by the first infinitive (**antakaa Kallen men/nä; vian täytyy ol/la koneessa**).

§74.2   FIRST INFINITIVE TRANSLATIVE

The basic form of the first infinitive may be followed by the translative ending **-kse-** and a possessive suffix corresponding to the person of the subject. This structure usually expresses the idea of aim or purpose.

Root	First inf.	Transl. case	Poss. suff.	Enclitic particle	Meaning
sano	a	kse	ni		in order that I shall say
elä	ä	kse	mme		in order that we shall live
oppi	a	kse	en	han	in order to learn (third p.) + emphasis
tavat	a	kse	si		in order that you shall meet
juo	da	kse	en		in order to drink (third p.)
ol	la	kse	nne		in order that you shall be

Examples:

Lähdin Hollantiin *levät/ä/kse/ni*. I went to Holland *in order to rest*.
Ihminen syö *elä/ä/kse/en*. Man eats *in order to live*.
Elätkö *syö/dä/kse/si?* Do you live *in order to eat?*
Pyörähdin *men/nä/kse/ni*. I turned round *in order to go*.

Monet suomalaiset menevät Ruotsiin *saa/da/kse/en* **työtä**.
Many Finns go to Sweden *in order to find* ('get') work.

Otatko työn *teh/dä/kse/si?* Do you undertake *to do* the job?
Muista/a/kse/ni **asia on näin**. *As far as I remember* it's like this.

Tietä/ä/kse/mme **hän ei ole täällä**.
As far as we know he/she is not here.

Osku on hyvin voimakas *ol/la/kse/en* **niin pieni**.
Osku is very strong for such a small man ('*to be* so small').

§75   SECOND INFINITIVE

§75.1   SECOND INFINITIVE INESSIVE

The second infinitive has two cases: the inessive case **-ssa ~ -ssä** expressing time, and the instructive case **-n** expressing manner. The instructive form is rarer.

A possessive suffix is often used with the inessive to mark the subject, e.g. **sano/e/ssa/ni** 'when I say'. The inessive form also occurs in the passive, e.g. **sano/tta/e/ssa** 'when one says'. Generally speaking, the second infinitive inessive can be said to correspond to a temporal subordinate clause beginning with **kun** 'when, as'.

The simplest way to form the stem of the second infinitive is given by the following rule (see §14 for some of the different endings).

The second infinitive is formed by changing the **-a** ~ **-ä** of the first infinitive to **-e**.

First infinitive	Meaning	Second infinitive stem
sano/a	say	**sano/e-**
vetä/ä	pull	**vetä/e-**
herät/ä	wake	**herät/e-**
tilat/a	order	**tilat/e-**
saa/da	get	**saa/de-**
myy/dä	sell	**myy/de-**
ol/la	be	**ol/le-**
men/nä	go	**men/ne-**
havait/a	observe	**havait/e-**

If the first infinitive stem ends in **-e**, this changes to **-i** in the second infinitive.

First infinitive	Meaning	Second infinitive stem
luke/a	read	**luki/e-**
itke/ä	cry	**itki/e-**
tunte/a	feel	**tunti/e-**
koke/a	experience	**koki/e-**

The passive forms of the second infinitive can be derived most easily by adding **-e-** to the passive stem, which is arrived at according to the first rule given in §72 (change the passive past tense **-iin** to **-a** ~ **-ä**; the passive stem **sano/tta-** is thus derived from the form **sano/ttiin**). The forms of the second infinitive are shown in the following table.

Root	Pass.	Inf.	Case	Poss. suff.	Particle	Meaning
sano		e	ssa	ni		when I say
sano		e	ssa	nne		when you (pl.) say

Root	Pass.	Inf.	Case	Poss. suff.	Particle	Meaning
sano		e	n			saying
sano	tta	e	ssa			when one says
sano	tta	e	ssa		han	when one says + emphasis
sano		e	ssa	mme	kin	when we say too
ol		le	ssa	ni		when I am
ol	ta	e	ssa			when one is
juo		de	ssa	an		when he/she drinks
juo	ta	e	ssa			when one drinks
Pekan herät		e	ssä			when Pekka wakes
herät	tä	e	ssä			when one wakes
luki		e	ssa	nne		when you read
Kallen tunti		e	ssa			when Kalle feels

The second infinitive inessive thus corresponds to a temporal subordinate clause, particularly one in which the action referred to is simultaneous with the action of the verb in the main clause, e.g. **sano/e/ssa/ni tämän kaikki nousivat** '*as I was saying/when I said* this everyone stood up'.

The subject of the temporal clause appears in the inessive construction as follows:

The subject is expressed

(a) by a possessive suffix alone, if the subject is identical with that of the main clause;
(b) by an independent word in the genitive, if the subject is different from that of the main clause;
(c) by the genitive form of personal pronouns (**minun**, etc.), always followed by a possessive suffix on the infinitive inessive (unstressed first and second personal pronouns may be omitted).

Kun clause	*Second infinitive inessive*
Kun *oli/n* Ruotsissa, *tapasi/n* useita ystäviä.	***Ol/le/ssa/ni* Ruotsissa tapasin useita ystäviä.**

When *I* was in Sweden *I* met many friends.

Kun *Pekka* heräsi, *hän* oli sairas.	***Herät/e/ssä/än* Pekka oli sairas.**

When *Pekka* woke up *he* was ill.

Kun clause	*Second infinitive inessive*

Kun *aja/t, sinun* **pitää olla**   *Aja/e/ssa/si* **sinun pitää olla**
varovainen.   **varovainen.**
When *you* drive *you* must be careful.

Kalevi **ajattelee paremmin, kun**   **Kalevi ajattelee paremmin**
hän **juo kahvia.**   *juo/de/ssa/an* **kahvia.**
Kalevi thinks better when *he* drinks coffee.

Ihmiset **nauttivat, kun** *he* **lähtevät**   **Ihmiset nauttivat** *lähti/e/ssä/än*
lomalle.   **lomalle.**
People enjoy themselves when *they* go on holiday.

Kun *Pekka* **herää,** *Liisa* **lähtee**   *Peka/n herät/e/ssä* **Liisa lähtee töihin.**
töihin.
When *Pekka* wakes, *Liisa* goes to work.

Viren **tuli maaliin, kun** *Päivärinta*   **Viren tuli maaliin** *Päivärinna/n*
oli vielä loppusuoralle.   *ol/le/ssa* **vielä loppusuoralla.**
Viren arrived at the finish when *Päivärinta* was still on the final straight.

Muut **nukkuivat, kun** *hän* **heräsi.**   **Muut nukkuivat** *häne/n*
                                                 herät/e/ssä/än.
The others were sleeping when *he/she* woke.

Vaimoni **heräsi, kun** (*minä*)   **Vaimoni heräsi** (**minun**) *tul/le/ssa/ni*
tuli/n **kotiin.**   **kotiin.**
My wife woke up when *I* came home.

The following examples show the use of the passive form of the inessive structure.

Turkuun *tul/ta/e/ssa* **satoi.**
When *one* (*we*) came to Turku it was raining.

Musiikkia *kuunnel/ta/e/ssa* **pitää olla hiljaa.**
When listening to music *one* must be quiet.

Ikkunan pitää olla auki *nuku/tta/e/ssa.*
The window must be open when *one* sleeps.

Tästä setelistä Suomen Pankki maksaa *vaadi/tta/e/ssa* **sata mk.**
For this note the Bank of Finland will pay 100 marks on demand ('when *one* demands').

As has been said, this inessive structure is used to refer to an action simultaneous with that of the main clause. If the action of the **kun** clause has taken place before the action of the main clause a different structure is used, the partitive form of the past participle (§83):

Ile/n herät/ty/ä **Mia lähti töihin.**   When Ile had woken up Mia went
                                           off to work.

Jäät lähtivät *kevää/n tul/tu/a.*   The ice melted ('left') when spring
                                           came.

§75.2   SECOND INFINITIVE INSTRUCTIVE

This form is derived by adding the instructive ending **-n** to the infinitive
stem arrived at according to the basic rule (§75.1), e.g. **sano/e/n** 'saying',
naura/e/n 'laughing', **hymyil/le/n** 'smiling', **huomat/e/n** 'noticing'. This
structure mainly indicates manner, and most commonly occurs in a number
of fixed expressions.

Lapsi tuli *itki/e/n* **kotiin.**   The child came home *crying.*

He astuivat *naura/e/n* **sisään ovesta.** They stepped in through the door
                                           laughing.

Kyllä sinne *kävel/le/n/kin* **pääsee.**   One can also get there on foot
                                           ('*walking*') all right.

kaikesta *päättä/e/n*   by all accounts ('*deciding* from
                                           everything')

illan *tul/le/n*   in the evening/when the evening
                                           comes

Kalle nauroi kaikkien *näh/de/n.*   Kalle laughed in full view of
                                           everybody ('everybody *seeing*').

näin *ol/le/n*   this being the case ('so *being*')

§76   THIRD INFINITIVE

§76.1   FORMATION

The third infinitive, which has the ending **-ma- ~ -mä-**, is a common and
important form in both the written and spoken language. It occurs in five
cases: the inessive **-ssa ~ -ssä**, the elative **-sta ~ -stä**, the illative **-Vn**, the
adessive **-lla ~ -llä**, and the abessive **-tta ~ -ttä**.

The stem of the third infinitive is formed by adding **-ma- ~ -mä-** to
the inflectional stem of the verb (§23).

The inflectional stem can be derived from the third person singular of the
present indicative, by detaching the personal ending.

First inf.	Meaning	Third p. sing present	Third infinitive stem
vetä/ä	pull	vetä/ä	vetä/mä-
otta/a	take	otta/a	otta/ma-
rakenta/a	build	rakenta/a	rakenta/ma-
huomat/a	notice	huomaa	huomaa/ma-
kaivat/a	long for	kaipaa	kaipaa/ma-
levät/ä	rest	lepää	lepää/mä-
maat/a	lie	makaa	makaa/ma-
lyö/dä	hit	lyö	lyö/mä-
ol/la	be	on	ole/ma- (NB!)
tul/la	come	tule/e	tule/ma-
men/nä	go	mene/e	mene/mä-
valit/a	choose	valitse/e	valitse/ma-

The following table shows the forms of the third infinitive.

Root	Inf.	Case	Particle	Meaning
lepää	mä	ssä		resting
lepää	mä	än		to rest
lepää	mä	än	kö	to rest?
vetä	mä	llä		by pulling
vetä	mä	llä	kin	also by pulling
mainitse	ma	tta		without mentioning
mainitse	ma	tta	kaan	without mentioning, either
teke	mä	stä		from doing

§76.2   THIRD INFINITIVE INESSIVE

The inessive indicates present continuous, i.e. an ongoing action or process; it usually occurs together with the verb **ol/la** 'be', and occasionally also with other verbs expressing a state.

Ville on kirjastossa *luke/ma/ssa*.
Ville is in the library *reading*.

Veljeni on *opiskele/ma/ssa* **Tampereella**.
My brother is *studying at* Tampere.

Lapset ovat ulkona *leikki/mä/ssä*.
The children are outside *playing*.

Olitko jo *nukku/ma/ssa* **kun soitin?**
Were you already *sleeping/asleep* when I rang?

Kalle ja Pekka ovat olutta *osta/ma/ssa*.
Kalle and Pekka are *buying* some beer.

Huomenna käyn äitiäni *katso/ma/ssa.*
Tomorrow I'll *go and see* my mother.

Istumme juuri *syö/mä/ssä.*
Just now we are sitting *eating.*

Pyykki on *kuivu/ma/ssa.*
The washing is *drying.*

§76.3   THIRD INFINITIVE ELATIVE

The elative form co-occurs with verbs indicating concrete or abstract movement, e.g. **tul/la** 'come' and **palat/a** 'return', to express coming 'from doing something'. Note in addition the verbs below which are always followed by the third infinitive.

estä/ä	prevent	**pelasta/a**	save
esty/ä	be prevented	**pelastu/a**	be saved
kieltä/ä	forbid	**varo/a**	beware of
kieltäyty/ä	refuse	**varoitta/a**	warn
lakat/a	cease	**vältä/ä**	avoid

Tuula *tuli* **rannalta** *ui/ma/sta.*
Tuula *came* from the beach, where she had been swimming (*'from swimming'*).

Eva *palasi* **Turusta** *opiskele/ma/sta.*
Eva *returned from studying at* ('from') Turku.

Silja *lakkasi itke/mä/stä.*
Silja *stopped crying.*

Kieltäydyn poltta/ma/sta **savukkeita.**
I *refuse to smoke* cigarettes.

Älä *estä* **minua** *näke/mä/stä!*
Don't *prevent* me *from seeing!*

Hän *pelasti* **minut** *hukku/ma/sta.*
He/she *saved* me *from drowning.*

§76.4   THIRD INFINITIVE ILLATIVE

The illative form is used after verbs of movement and indicates an action which is about to begin. Note in particular the structure **tul/la** 'come' + third infinitive illative, which refers to future time, e.g. **Tule/n palaa/ma/an** 'I will return'. The most common verbs followed by the third infinitive illative are the following:

joutu/a	come, be made to	**pysty/ä**	be capable
jättä/ä	leave	**pyytä/ä**	request
jää/dä	stay	**pääs/tä**	get
kehotta/a	urge	**ruvet/a**	begin
kyet/ä	be able	**ryhty/ä**	set about
käske/ä	command	**sattu/a**	happen
pakotta/a	force		

Menen ulos *syö/mä/än*. I'm going out *to eat*.

Tanssi/ma/an/ko **te menette?** Are you really going *dancing*?

Matkustan maalle *lepää/mä/än*. I'm going into the country *to rest*.

Illalla tulen teille *sauno/ma/an*. In the evening I'll come to your house *to have a sauna*.

Lähden *hake/ma/an* **lapset koulusta**. I'll *go and fetch* the children from school.

Menetkö kotiin *nukku/ma/an?* Are you going home *to sleep*?

Tulen *lähte/mä/än* **pois.** I will *go away*.

Jätin Kallen kotiin *luke/ma/an*. I left Kalle at home *to read*.

Jään vielä *työskentele/mä/än*. I'll stay a bit longer *to do some work*.

Kehotan teitä *lopetta/ma/an* **tupakoimisen.** I urge you *to give up* smoking.

Poliisi käski meitä *poistu/ma/an*. The policeman ordered us *to leave*.

Pystytkö *aja/ma/an* **Helsinkiin?** Can you *drive* to Helsinki?

Tuija pyysi minua *tanssi/ma/an*. Tuija asked me *to dance*.

Illalla rupesi *sata/ma/an*. In the evening it began *to rain*.

Reijo sattui *ole/ma/an* **paikalla.** Reijo happened *to be* there.

The third infinitive illative also occurs after certain adjectives, of which the most frequent are: **halukas** 'willing', **innostunut** 'keen', **kiinnostunut** 'interested', **valmis** 'ready'.

Kuka on halukas *vastaa/ma/an?* Who is willing *to answer*?

En ole innokas *tule/ma/an*. I'm not keen *to come*.

Olen kyllä kiinnostunut *osta/ma/an* **pesukoneen.** Yes, I am interested *in buying a* washing-machine.

Karikin on valmis *lähte/mä/än syö/mä/än*. Kari too is ready *to go and eat*.

§76.5 THIRD INFINITIVE ADESSIVE AND ABESSIVE

The adessive indicates means, and sometimes manner.

Voitin miljoonan *veikkaa/ma/lla*.

I won a million *by betting*.

Sinne pääsee mukavasti *kävele/mä/llä*.

One can get there easily on foot ('*by walking*').

Hän elää *kirjoitta/ma/lla* **kirjoja.**
He/she lives *by writing* books.

Kieliä oppii parhaiten *puhu/ma/lla.*
One learns languages best *by talking.*

The meaning of the abessive is 'without'; the object takes the partitive (cf. §33.2). If there is a subject it takes the genitive, and if it is a personal pronoun the verb also takes a possessive suffix.

Sehän on *sano/ma/tta/kin* **selvää.**
That goes *without saying* ('is clear *without one saying*').

Syö/mä/ttä **ja** *juo/ma/tta* **ei elä.**
Without eating and *drinking* one cannot live.

Kalle teki sen (*meidän***)** *tietä/mä/ttä/mme.*
Kalle did it *without our knowing.*

Myyjä tuli sisään *Leenan huomaa/ma/tta* **mitään.**
The seller came in *without Leena noticing* anything.

Koira karkasi *hänen huomaa/ma/tta/an.*
The dog ran away *without his/her noticing.*

The forms in **-ma-** ~ **-mä-** are also used adjectivally in what is called the agent construction (§84). A few examples:

Kalle/n *osta/ma* **auto**
the car Kalle *bought/bought* by Kalle

Oletko istunut Kalle/n *osta/ma/ssa* **autossa?**
Have you sat in the car Kalle *bought?*

En ole nähnyt Kalle/n *osta/ma/a* **autoa.**
I have not seen the car Kalle *bought.*

§77   FOURTH INFINITIVE

The fourth infinitive has the ending **-minen**, which is added to the inflectional stem of the verb (cf. §23; §76.1). Examples:

First infinitive		*Third p. sing*	*Fourth infinitive*
tietä/ä	know	**tietä/ä**	**tietä/minen**
suoritta/a	perform	**suoritta/a**	**suoritta/minen**
halut/a	want	**halua/a**	**halua/minen**
todet/a	verify	**totea/a**	**totea/minen**
lakat/a	cease	**lakkaa**	**lakkaa/minen**
jää/dä	stay	**jää**	**jää/minen**
ol/la	be	**on**	**ole/minen**

First infinitive		Third p. sing	Fourth infinitive
juos/ta	run	**juokse/e**	**juokse/<u>minen</u>**
havait/a	observe	**havaitse/e**	**havaitse/<u>minen</u>**

The fourth infinitive has only two rare forms: the nominative, indicating obligation, and the corresponding partitive.

> **Sinne** *ei ole mene/mis/tä.* (part.)
> One *must not* go there.

Note that the genitive case is used for the person obliged to do something, i.e. **minu/n** 'I (gen.)' in the example above.

More common ways than the fourth infinitive of expressing this meaning of obligation are for example:

(a) **Minun** *täytyy mennä ~ pitää mennä ~ on mentävä* **sinne**.
(b) **Tämä tehtävä** *on suoritettava ~ pitää suorittaa.*
(c) **Sinne ei** *pidä* **mennä**.

The fourth infinitive is used also in a construction where it occurs in the partitive sg. after a form of itself:

Tilanne huononee *huonone/mis/ta/an.*   The situation is *getting worse and worse.*

A much more frequent **-minen** form is that used to mark nouns derived from verbs (deverbal nouns: see further §93.1). A few examples:

*Tupakoi/**minen*** **on täällä kielletty**. *Smoking* is forbidden here.
Auton *aja/**minen*** **on hankalaa**. *Driving* a car is difficult.
*Sauno/**minen*** **on mukavaa**. *Having a sauna* is nice.

18 PARTICIPLES

- *General*
- *Present participle active*
- *Present participle passive*
- *The past participles*
- *The participial construction*
- *The temporal construction*
- *The agent construction*

§78 GENERAL

Like infinitives, participles are non-finite verb forms: they are not inflected for person. Finnish has two participles, the present and the past. Both have active and passive forms; cf. §14, where all the non-finite forms were introduced. The four participle forms of the verb **sano/a** 'say' are:

	Active		*Passive*	
Present	**sano/va**	saying	**sano/tta/va**	which is to be said
Past	**sano/nut**	said	**sano/ttu**	said

The participles function partly as verbs, e.g. (**olen**) **sano/nut** '(I have) said' (§61) and (**on**) **sano/ttu** '(one has) said' (§71), and partly as adjectives. In this latter function participles inflect in the normal adjectival way for number and case:

pitkä **mies**	a *tall* man
syö/vä mies	an *eating* man
syö/nyt mies	a man *who has eaten*
lyö/tä/vä mies	a man *who is to be hit*
lyö/ty mies	a man *who was hit*/a *beaten* man
pitkä/t **miehe/t**	the *tall* men
syö/vä/t miehe/t	the *eating* men
syö/nee/t miehe/t	the men *who have eaten*
lyö/tä/vä/t miehe/t	the men *who are to be hit*
lyö/dy/t miehe/t	the men *who were hit*

As premodifiers, participles are thus subject to the normal rules of concord for attributes (§31).

Participles also have other uses. For instance, all the participles (inflected in the genitive) can be used in what is called the participial construction, which corresponds to an **että** 'that' clause (§82):

Näen, että Pekka tulee. ~ **Näen Peka/n** *tule/va/n*.
I see that Pekka is coming. I see Pekka *coming*.

Näen, että Pekka on tullut. ~ **Näen Peka/n** *tul/lee/n*.
I see that Pekka has come. I see that Pekka *has come*.

The past participle passive, inflected in the partitive, may be used to replace a temporal subordinate clause indicating an action previous to that of the main clause (§83; cf. also §75.1):

Nukahdin, kun Pekka oli tullut. **Nukahdin Peka/n** *tul/tu/a*.
I fell asleep when Pekka had come. I fell asleep 'Pekka *having come*'/
when Pekka *had come*.

The third infinitive stem (**-ma-** ~ **-mä-**, see §76.1) is used in the agent construction to replace a relative clause:

Peka/n *osta/ma* **auto** **auto, jonka Pekka oli ostanut**
the car *bought* by Pekka the car which Pekka had bought

§79 PRESENT PARTICIPLE ACTIVE

This form has the ending **-va-** ~ **-vä-**, which is added to the inflectional stem of the verb (§23). It indicates a continuing action or process.

First infinitive	Third p. sing.	Present participle	Meaning
kerto/a	**kerto/o**	**kerto/va**	telling
kylpe/ä	**kylpe/e**	**kylpe/vä**	bathing
luvat/a	**lupaa**	**lupaa/va**	promising
kadot/a	**katoa/a**	**katoa/va**	disappearing
määrät/ä	**määrää**	**määrää/vä**	ordering
soi/da	**soi**	**soi/va**	ringing
men/nä	**mene/e**	**mene/vä**	going
ol/la	**on**	**ole/va**	being
härit/ä	**häiritse/e**	**häiritse/vä**	disturbing
ratkais/ta	**ratkaise/e**	**ratkaise/va**	deciding

The present participle often corresponds to a relative clause with a present tense verb:

Pihalla *seiso/va* **auto on sininen.** **Auto,** *joka seisoo* **pihalla, on sininen.**
The car *standing/which is standing* in the yard is blue.

Oletko nähnyt pihalla *seiso/va/n* **Oletko nähnyt auton,** *joka seisoo*
auton? **pihalla?**
Have you seen the car *standing/which is standing* in the yard?

työtä *teke/vä* **luokka**   **luokka,** *joka tekee* **työtä**
the *working* class

Pihalla on *huuta/v/i/a* **lapsia.**   **Pihalla on lapsia,** *jotka huutavat.*
In the yard there are children *shouting/who are shouting.*

Ratkaise/va/t **päätökset tehdään** **Päätökset,** *jotka ovat ratkaisevia,*
  nyt.   **tehdään nyt.**
The final decisions/decisions *which are final* are made now.

hyvää musiikkia *soitta/va* **yhtye** **yhtye,** *joka soittaa* **hyvää musiikkia**
a band *playing/which plays* good music

The examples also show that where a participle functioning as an attribute takes an object or adverbial, these appear before the participle: *musiikkia* **soittava yhtye** (object); *pihalla* **seisova auto** (adverbial).

§80 PRESENT PARTICIPLE PASSIVE

This form is most conveniently derived from the past tense passive (cf. §80) by the following rule (which is the same as that for the derivation of the passive moods, §72).

Change the passive past tense **-iin** to **-a** or **-ä** and add **-va- ~ -vä-**.

Example: **sano/ttiin** 'one said' → **sano/tta/va**. These participles have various special meanings. Usually they correspond to the following types of relative clause:

sano/tta/va asia   (1) a thing that *must/has to be/is to be said*
               (2) a thing that *can be said*
               (3) a thing that *will be said*
               (4) a thing that *is said*

First infinitive	Past tense passive	Present participle passive	Meaning
kerto/a	**kerro/ttiin**	**kerro/tta/va**	which is to be told
luke/a	**lue/ttiin**	**lue/tta/va**	" read
johta/a	**johde/ttiin**	**johde/tta/va**	" led
huomat/a	**huomat/tiin**	**huomat/ta/va**	" noticed
pelät/ä	**pelät/tiin**	**pelät/tä/vä**	" feared
rakenta/a	**rakennet/tiin**	**rakenne/tta/va**	" built
juo/da	**juo/tiin**	**juo/ta/va**	" drunk
ajatel/la	**ajatel/tiin**	**ajatel/ta/va**	" thought
hävit/ä	**hävit/tiin**	**hävit/tä/vä**	" lost

The use of these participles will become clearer from the following examples. All the meanings (1)–(4) are possible, depending on the context.

syö/tä/vä **sieni**
an *edible* mushroom ('that *can be eaten*')

Tämä ei ole *suositel/ta/va* **kirja.**
This is not a book *that can be recommended.*

Nämä eivät ole *suositel/ta/v/i/a* **kirjoja.**
These are not books *that can be recommended.*

Onko teillä *ilmoite/tta/v/i/a* **tuloja?**
Do you have any income *to be declared*?

Onko jääkaapissa jotain *juo/ta/va/a*?
Is there anything *to drink* in the fridge?

Ei tämä ole mikään *pelät/tä/vä* **koira!**
This is no dog *to be feared*/there is no need to be afraid of this dog!

Onko teillä *tarvit/ta/va* **pääoma?**
Do you have the *necessary* capital?

Ratkais/ta/va/t **kysymykset ovat ...**
The questions *to be solved* are ...

Onko vielä jotain *lisät/tä/vä/ä*?
Is there still something *to be added*?

Minulla ei ole muuta *sano/tta/va/a*.
I have nothing else *to say.*

Lainat/ta/va/t **kirjat ovat oikealla.**
The books *that can be borrowed* are on the right.

Viimeinen *suorite/tta/v/i/sta* **töistä oli vaikein.**
The last of the tasks *to be done* was the most difficult.

The present participle passive is also used in a number of special ways, for instance to express obligation in structures such as the following:

---

subject in the genitive case + **on, oli, olisi, lienee** + present participle passive

---

Minu/n *on sano/tta/va* **tämä.**   I *must say* this.
Mies/ten *oli lähde/ttä/vä*.   The men *had to leave.*
Nyt minun *on syö/tä/vä*.   Now I *must eat.*

On/ko sinun *lähde/ttä/vä* jo?   *Do* you *have to leave* already?
Meidän *oli* *tilat/ta/va* taksi.   We *had to order* a taxi.
Kaikkien *on* *men/tä/vä* ulos.   Everyone *must go* out.
Pekan *on* *usko/tta/va*, että . . .   Pekka *must believe* that . . .
Heidän *oli* *matkuste/tta/va*   They *had to go* to Helsinki.
   Helsinkiin.

The present participle passive inflected in the inessive plural, combined
with **ol/la**, indicates that something can(not) be done.

Onko Bill *tavat/ta/v/i/ssa*?   Is Bill *in/available/'to be met with'*?
Eikö johtaja ole *tavat/ta/v/i/ssa*? Isn't the manager *available*?
Päätös on *teh/tä/v/i/ssä*.   The decision *can be made*.
Tämä asia ei ole *muute/tta/v/i/ssa*. This matter *cannot be altered*.

This participle also occurs in certain fixed expressions.

Onko teillä huoneita *vuokrat/ta/va/na*?
Do you have rooms *to let*?

autoja *myy/tä/vä/nä*
cars *for sale*

Virka on julistettu *hae/tta/va/ksi*.
Applications are invited for the post. ('The post is declared *to be
   applied for*.')

Paavo on sairaalassa *tutki/tta/va/na*.
Paavo is in hospital for a check-up/*to be examined*.

§81   THE PAST PARTICIPLES

The past participles occur primarily in the compound tenses, i.e. the perfect
and pluperfect, for example **on sano/nut** 'has said', **on sano/ttu** 'one has
said'; **oli sano/nut** 'had said', **oli sano/ttu** 'one had said'. For the formation
of these participles see §61, §71. By way of recapitulation, here are a few
examples of this usage:

Past participle (perfect tense active)
(**minä**) **olen anta/<u>nut</u>**   I have given
(**sinä**) **olet anta/<u>nut</u>**   you have given (sing.)
Pekka on anta/<u>nut</u>   Pekka has given
(**me**) **olemme anta/<u>neet</u>**   we have given
(**te**) **olette anta/<u>neet</u>**   you have given (pl.)
he ovat anta/<u>neet</u>   they have given
on anne/<u>ttu</u>   one has given

The corresponding pluperfect forms are (**minä**) **olin anta/nut** 'I had given', **he olivat anta/neet** 'they had given', **oli anne/ttu** 'one had given', etc.

The past participles indicate completed action (**anta/nut, anne/ttu**), whereas the present participles indicate incomplete action (cf. §79, §80).

The past participles also occur as adjectivals, particularly as pre-modifiers, e.g. **lahjan anta/nut mies** 'the man who gave the present' and **anne/ttu lahja** 'a present that has been/was given'. If a participle has its own objects or adverbials these are placed before the participle (cf. §79).

Examples follow, first of the use of the active participle (**-nut ~ -nyt**). The inflectional stem is **-nee-**.

paljon *matkusta/nut* **ihminen**
a much *travelled* person

koke/nut **lääkäri**
an *experienced* doctor

Tunnen *koke/nee/n* **lääkärin.**
I know an *experienced* doctor.

En tunne *koke/nut/ta* **lääkäriä.**
I don't know an *experienced* doctor.

pois *juos/sut* **koira**
a dog *that has run* away

Vietnamissa *ol/lee/t* **ihmiset sanovat, että ...**
People *who have been* in Vietnam say that ...

Eilen *saapu/nee/t* **matkustajat ovat jo lähteneet.**
The travellers *who arrived* yesterday have already left.

Viime syksynä *ilmesty/nee/t* **kirjat ovat hyviä.**
The books *which were published* last autumn are good.

Pommin *löytä/nyt* **koira kuoli.**
The dog *which (had) found* the bomb died.

Pommin *löytä/nee/lle* **koiralle annettiin mitali.**
The dog *which (had) found* the bomb was given a medal.

Näin *pala/nee/n* **talon.**
I saw a *burnt/burned-down* house.

Pala/nee/ssa **talossa oli ollut ihmisiä.**
There had been people in the *burned-down* house.

Oletteko *väsy/ne/i/tä*?
Are you *tired*?

He ovat hyvin *koke/ne/i/ta*.
They are very *experienced*.

In the same way, the past participle passive **-(t)tu** ~ **-(t)ty** indicates a completed action performed by an unspecified agent.

kaupasta *oste/ttu* **kirja**
a book *bought* in a shop

syksyllä *rakenne/ttu* **talo**
a house *built* in the autumn

He asuvat syksyllä *rakenne/tu/ssa* **talossaan.**
They live in their house *which was built* in the autumn.

hyväksy/tty **ehdotus**
an *accepted* proposal

Hyväksy/ty/t **opiskelijat voivat jatkaa.**
Students *accepted* may continue.

syö/ty **piirakka**
a pie *that has been/was eaten*

Eilen *syö/dy/t* **piirakat olivat hyviä.**
The pies *that were eaten* yesterday were good.

anne/ttu **lahja**
a present *that has been/was given*

Anne/ttu/j/a **lahjoja ei voi ottaa takaisin.**
Presents *that have been given* cannot be taken back.

pelaste/ttu **merimies**
a *rescued* sailor

Pelaste/tu/t **merimiehet olivat hyvässä kunnossa.**
The *rescued* sailors were in good shape.

maalat/tu **seinä**
a *painted* wall

Seinät eivät ole *maala/tu/t*.
The walls are not *painted*.

§82   THE PARTICIPIAL CONSTRUCTION

The participial construction can be used to contract an affirmative **että** ('that') clause functioning as the object of certain verbs, e.g. **näh/dä** 'see', **kuul/la** 'hear', **usko/a** 'believe', **sano/a** 'say'. Both present and past participles appear in the participial construction, in both active and passive. The participle in the construction is always in the genitive (**-n**). The following forms occurring in the participial construction can thus be derived from the verb **itke/ä** 'cry':

		Basic form	*Genitive*
Present participle	*(active)*	itke/**vä**	itke/**vä/n**
	(passive)	itke/**ttä/vä**	itke/**ttä/vän**
Past participle	*(active)*	itke/**nyt**	itke/**nee/n**
	(passive)	itke/**tty**	itke/**ty/n**

These forms are used in context as follows:

Että clause	*Participial construction*

Näen, että Kalle itke/e.   **Näen Kalle/n** *itke/vä/n.*
I see that Kalle is crying/I see Kalle *crying.*

Näen, että Kalle on itkenyt.   **Näen Kalle/n** *itke/nee/n.*
I see that Kalle *has been crying.*

Näen, että täällä itke/tään.   **Näen täällä** *itke/ttä/vä/n.*
I see that people *are crying* here.

Näen, että täällä on itke/tty.   **Näen täällä** *itke/ty/n.*
I see that people *have been crying* here.

The use of the present or past participle is determined by the temporal relation between the **että** clause and the main clause. The following rule is an important one:

The present participles are used if the action of the **että** clause takes place at the same time as, or later than, that of the main clause; the past participles are used if the action of the **että** clause is earlier than that of the main clause.

The nominative subject of an **että** clause is expressed in the participial construction according to the following rule (which concerns active sentences only, since passive sentences have no subject!). Cf. the subject rule for the inessive structure (§75.1).

The nominative subject of the **että** clause is expressed

(a) by a possessive suffix alone, if the subject is the same as that of the main clause;
(b) by a genitive form preceding the participle, if the subject is different from that of the main clause (also applies to personal pronouns!).

The examples that follow illustrate first the most common structure, i.e. with the present participle active (**-va/n** ~ **-vä/n**). This is used when the action of the **että** clause is simultaneous with or later than the action of the main clause. When part (a) of the above subject rule is applied, the genitive **-n** is dropped (§36).

Että clause   *Participial construction*

Usko/n, **että** *nuku/n*.   **Uskon** *nukku/va/ni*.
I believe that *I shall sleep.*

Usko/t/ko, **että** *nuku/t?*   **Uskotko** *nukku/va/si?*
Do *you* believe that *you will sleep?*

Tiedä/n, **että** *ole/n* **vanha**.   **Tiedän** *ole/va/ni* **vanha**.
I know that *I am* old.

Pekka **luuli, että** *hän* **oli Lipponen.** **Pekka luuli** *ole/va/nsa* **Lipponen**.
Pekka thought *he was* Lipponen.

He **sanoivat, että** *he* **tulisivat**   **He sanoivat** *tule/va/nsa* **huomenna**.
    huomenna.
They said that *they would come* tomorrow.

Hän **väittää, että** *hän* **on sairas.**   **Hän väittää** *ole/va/nsa* **sairas**.
He claims that *he is* ill.

Tuula **huomasi, että** *hän* **itki**.   **Tuula huomasi** *itke/vä/nsä*.
Tuula noticed that *she was crying.*

Hallitus **tietää, että** *se* **tulee**   **Hallitus tietää** *eroa/va/nsa*.
    eroamaan.
The *government* knows that *it will resign.*

Luule/mme, **että** *lähde/mme*   **Luulemme** *lähte/vä/mme*
    huomenna.   **huomenna**.
We think that *we shall leave* tomorrow.

Tiedä/n, **että** *hän* **on ulkomailla.** **Tiedän** *häne/n* *ole/va/n* **ulkomailla**.
I know that *he is* abroad.

Luule/t/ko, **että** *tiedä/n* **tämän?** **Luuletko** *minu/n* *tietä/vä/n* **tämän?**
Do *you* think that *I know* this?

Näi/mme, **että** *he* **lähtivät.**   **Näimme** *heidä/n* *lähte/vä/n*.
We saw that *they left*/saw *them leave.*

Kuuli/mme, **että** *lapsi* **huusi**.   **Kuulimme** *lapse/n* *huuta/va/n*.
We heard that *the child was shouting*/heard *the child shout.*

Pekka **kuuli, että** *juna* **saapui.**   **Pekka kuuli** *juna/n* *saapu/va/n*.
Pekka heard that *the train was arriving*/heard *the train arrive.*

He luule/vat, että *suostu/t*   He luulevat *sinu/n suostu/va/n*
ehdotukseen.   ehdotukseen.
They think that *you will agree* to the proposal.

Note in particular that the personal pronoun subject of an **että** clause is
expressed in the participial construction as a genitive form alone, e.g.
... minu/n ole/va/n ... 'me being'. By contrast, the personal pronoun
subject of a **kun** ('when') clause is expressed in the temporal construction
both as a personal pronoun (optionally) and as a possessive suffix, e.g.
... (minu/n) ol/le/ssa/ni ... 'when being' (first p. sing.). Cf. §83.
    The following examples illustrate the use of the past participle active,
which is used when the action of the **että** clause precedes that of the main
clause.

Että clause   *Participial construction*
Luule/n, että *ole/n* **nukkunut.** **Luulen** *nukku/nee/ni.*
I think *I* have slept.

Usko/t/ko, että *nukui/t?*   **Uskotko** *nukku/nee/si?*
Do *you* think that *you* slept?

Tiedä/n, että *oli/n* **sairas.**   **Tiedän** *ol/lee/ni* **sairas.**
I know that *I* was ill.

Huomasi/mme, että *oli/mme*   **Huomasimme** *myöhästy/nee/mme.*
myöhästyneet.
We noticed that *we* were late.

He **sanoivat,** että *he* **olivat** **He sanoivat** *tul/lee/nsa* **jo eilen.**
tulleet jo eilen.
They said that *they* had already come yesterday.

Tuula **huomasi,** että *hän* **oli** **Tuula huomasi** *itke/nee/nsä.*
itkenyt.
Tuula noticed that *she* had cried.

TPS **tajusi,** että *se* **oli hävinnyt.**   **TPS tajusi** *hävin/nee/nsä.*
TPS (a sports team) realised that *it* had lost.

Tiedä/n, että *hän* **on ollut**   **Tiedän** *häne/n ol/lee/n* **ulkomailla.**
ulkomailla.
I know that *he* has been abroad.

Luule/t/ko, että *minä* **tiesin tämän?** **Luuletko** *minu/n tietä/nee/n* **tämän?**
Do *you* think that *I* knew this?

Ymmärsi/mme, että *he* **olivat**   **Ymmärsimme** *heidä/n lähte/nee/n.*
lähteneet.
We understood that *they* had left/understood *them* to have left.

Pekka kuuli, että *juna* oli   **Pekka kuuli *juna/n saapu/nee/n*.**
saapunut.
Pekka heard that *the train* had arrived.

He luule/vat, että suostui/t   **He luulevat *sinu/n suostu/nee/n***
ehdotukseen.   ehdotukseen.
They think that *you* agreed to the proposal.

Kerrotti/in, että *Virtanen* oli   **Kerrottiin *Virtase/n kuol/lee/n*.**
kuollut.
It was said that *Virtanen* had died/*Virtanen* was said to have died.

The participial construction is particularly common with the following verbs: **näky/ä** 'be seen', **näyttä/ä** 'seem', **kuulu/a** 'be heard', **tuntu/a** 'feel, seem'. The subject of the **että** clause becomes the subject of the main clause, and thus affects the concord of the verb (cf. **Näyttää (siltä), että auto on rikki** 'It seems that the car is broken' → **Auto näyttää olevan rikki** 'The car seems to be broken'). Examples:

Auto näyttää *ole/va/n* rikki.	The car seems *to be* broken.
Sinä näytät *ole/va/n* sairas.	You seem *to be* ill.
Auto näyttää *ol/lee/n* rikki.	The car seems *to have been* broken.
Sinä näytät *ol/lee/n* sairas.	You seem *to have been* ill.
Ahtisaari näyttää *sano/va/n*, että ...	Ahtisaari seems *to be saying* that ...
Ahtisaari näyttää *sano/nee/n*, että ...	Ahtisaari seems *to have said* that ...
Tilanne tuntuu *vaikeutu/va/n*.	The situation seems *to be getting more difficult*.
Tilanne tuntui *vaikeutu/nee/n*.	The situation seemed *to have got more difficult*.
Tilanne ei tunnu *vaikeutu/va/n*.	The situation does not seem *to be getting more difficult*.
Tilanne ei tuntunut *vaikeutu/va/n*.	The situation did not seem *to be getting more difficult*.
Tilanne ei tuntunut *vaikeutu/nee/n*.	The situation did not seem *to have got more difficult*.

The next examples illustrate passive **että** clauses. If the action expressed by the verb in the subordinate clause is simultaneous with or later than the action expressed by the main clause, the form **-(t)ta/va/n ~ -(t)tä/vä/n** is used, and if the **että** clause action is earlier the form **-tu/n ~ -ty/n** is used.

Että clause   *Participial construction*
Tiedän, että Ruotsissa *puhu/taan*   **Tiedän Ruotsissa *puhu/tta/va/n* myös**
myös suomea.   **suomea.**
I know that in Sweden Finnish *is* also *spoken*.

Kuulin, että *sano/ttiin,* **että ...**   **Kuulin** *sano/tta/va/n,* **että ...**
I heard that *it was said* that . . ./I heard it *said* that . . .

Kalle kuuli, että huoneessa   **Kalle kuuli huoneessa** *siivot/ta/va/n.*
siivot/tiin.
Kalle heard that *someone was cleaning* in the room/heard *someone cleaning* . . .

Huomasin, että alakerrassa   **Huomasin alakerrassa** *riidel/tä/vä/n.*
riidel/lään.
I noticed that *there is quarrelling* downstairs.

Tiedän, että *ol/laan* **sitä mieltä**   **Tiedän** *ol/ta/va/n* **sitä mieltä, että ...**
että ...
I know that *people are* of the opinion that . . .

Tiedän, että Virossa *on puhu/ttu*   **Tiedän Virossa** *puhu/tu/n* **myös**
myös ruotsia.   **ruotsia.**
I know that in Estonia Swedish *has* also *been spoken.*

Kuulin, että *oli sano/ttu* **että ...**   **Kuulin** *sano/tu/n,* **että ...**
I heard that *it had been said* that . . .

Huomasin, että *oli esite/tty*   **Huomasin** *esite/ty/n,* **että ...**
että ...
I noticed that *it had been proposed* that . . .

Kalle kertoi, että *oli rakenne/ttu*   **Kalle kertoi** *rakenne/tu/n* **talo.**
talo.
Kalle said that a house *had been built.*

Kalle kertoi, että talo *oli*   **Kalle kertoi** *talo/n rakenne/tu/n.*
rakenne/ttu.
Kalle said that the house *had been built.*

Note that in the last example above the fact that the object of the passive sentence is definite can be indicated by moving the object before the participle (i.e. to the beginning of its clause) and inflecting it in the genitive.

§83 THE TEMPORAL CONSTRUCTION

The temporal construction can be used to contract a **kun** ('when') clause. If the action of the **kun** clause is simultaneous with or later than that of the main clause, the form of the verb is the second infinitive inessive, e.g. **sano/e/ssa/ni** 'when I say' (cf. §75.1).

Kun clause   *Temporal construction*
Kun Kalle tuli, Pekka lähti.   ***Kalle/n tul/le/ssa* Pekka lähti.**
When Kalle *came* Pekka left.

Kun tulin, kompastuin.   *Tul/le/ssa/ni* **kompastuin.**
As I came I stumbled.

If the action of the **kun** clause is earlier than that of the main clause, the verb form in the temporal construction is the past participle passive inflected in the partitive, e.g. **sano/ttu/a** 'having said', **syö/ty/ä** 'having eaten' (cf. §71). The participle does not carry its normal passive meaning here.

Kun Kalle oli tullut, Pekka lähti.   **Kalle/n** *tul/tu/a* **Pekka lähti.**
When Kalle *had come*/Kalle *having come*, Pekka left.

Kun olin tullut, kompastuin.   *Tul/tu/a/ni* **kompastuin.**
When I had come I stumbled.

The table below is a reminder of the formation of the past participle passive.

Infinitive		*Past tense passive*	*Past participle passive*	*Partitive case*
sano/a	say	sano/ttiin	sano/ttu	sano/**ttu/a**
anta/a	give	anne/ttiin	anne/ttu	anne/**ttu/a**
juo/da	drink	juo/tiin	juo/tu	juo/**tu/a**
ol/la	be	ol/tiin	ol/tu	ol/**tu/a**
huomat/a	notice	huomat/tiin	huomat/tu	huomat/**tu/a**
pelät/ä	fear	pelät/tiin	pelät/ty	pelät/**ty/ä**
ansait/a	earn	ansait/tiin	ansait/tu	ansait/**tu/a**

The subject of the **kun** clause is indicated in the temporal construction according to the same rules as for the second infinitive inessive (§75.1).

The subject is expressed

(a) by a possessive suffix alone, if the subject is identical with that of the main clause;
(b) by an independent word in the genitive, if the subject is different from that of the main clause;
(c) by the genitive forms of personal pronouns (**minun**, etc.), always followed by a possessive suffix on the participle (unstressed first and second personal pronouns may be omitted).

Kun clause   *Past participle passive, partitive*
Kun *Pekka* **oli herännyt,** *hän*   *Herät/ty/ä/än* **Pekka lähti töihin.**
   lähti töihin.
When Pekka had woken up *he* went off to work.

Kun *oli/n* **herännyt,** *lähdi/n* **töihin.** *Herät/ty/ä/ni* **lähdin töihin.**
When *I* had woken up *I* went off to work.

Tule/t/ko **ulos,** *kun* *ole/t* **juonut   Tuletko ulos** *juo/tu/a/si* **kahvia?**
kahvia?
Will *you* come out when *you* have had some coffee?

Kun *oli/mme* **syöneet,** *lähdi/*   *Syö/ty/ä/mme* **lähdimme kävelylle.**
mme **kävelylle.**
When *we* had eaten *we* went for a walk.

Monet ihmiset ajattelevat   Monet ihmiset ajattelevat
paremmin, kun *he* **ovat   paremmin** *juo/tu/a/an* **kahvia.**
juoneet kahvia.
Many people think better when *they* have had some coffee.

Kun *Pekka* **oli herännyt,** *Liisa*   *Peka/n* **herät/ty/ä** *Liisa* **lähti töihin.**
lähti töihin.
When *Pekka* had woken up *Liisa* went off to work.

Kun *Viren* **oli tullut maaliin,**   *Vireni/n* *tul/tu/a* **maaliin Päivärinta**
Päivärinta **oli vielä   oli vielä loppusuoralla.**
loppusuoralla.
When *Viren* had arrived at the finish *Päivärinta* was still on the final
straight.

Kaikki **hämmästyivät, kun   Kaikki hämmästyivät** *Lippose/n*
Lipponen **oli sanonut tämän.**   *sano/ttu/a* **tämän.**
Everyone was surprised when *Lipponen* had said this.

Vaimoni **heräsi, kun** (*minä*)   **Vaimoni heräsi** (**minun**) *tul/tu/a/ni*
olin tullut kotiin.   kotiin.
My wife woke up when *I* had come home.

Kun *oli/mme* **olleet vuoden   (Meidän)** *ol/tu/a/mme* **vuoden**
Ruotsissa, *ajat* **huononivat.   Ruotsissa** *ajat* **huononivat.**
When *we* had been a year in Sweden *times* got worse.

§84   THE AGENT CONSTRUCTION

The agent construction is a way of contracting relative clauses, i.e. those
beginning with **joka**, **mikä** 'who, which'; in most cases these clauses then
become premodifiers, with the verb functioning as an adjective and the
subject (the agent) appearing e.g. in the genitive.

Relative clause   *Agent construction*
auto, jonka Kalle osti   *Kalle/n* *osta/ma* **auto**
the car that Kalle bought   the car bought by Kalle

auto, jonka (minä) ostin	**(minu/n)** *osta/ma/ni* **auto**
the car that I bought	the car bought by me

The following rule applies to the verb of the agent construction.

The verb of the agent construction

(a) usually indicates past time;
(b) is formed from the ending **-ma** ~ **-mä**, added to the inflectional stem (§76.1);
(c) functions like a normal adjective, inflecting for number and all cases (§31).

Point (a) of the rule means that the verb of the construction may correspond to any of the tenses indicating past time (past tense, perfect, pluperfect).

Kalle/n osta/ma **auto**	(a) the car which Kalle *bought*
	(b) the car which Kalle *has bought*
	(c) the car which Kalle *had bought*

Point (b) means that the verb is formed in the same way as the stem of the third infinitive (cf. §76.1).

Infinitive		*Third person singular*	*Verb form in -ma ~ -mä*
anta/a	give	anta/a	anta/**ma**
vetä/ä	pull	vetä/ä	vetä/**mä**
kaivat/a	long for	kaipaa	kaipaa/**ma**
määrät/ä	order	määrää	määrää/**mä**
syö/dä	eat	syö	syö/**mä**
valit/a	choose	valitse/e	valitse/**ma**
mainit/a	mention	mainitse/e	mainitse/**ma**

Point (c) means that the forms in **-ma** ~ **-mä** behave in the sentence like adjectives and are subject to the rules of concord (§31).

sininen **auto**	the *blue* car
Kallen *osta/ma* **auto**	the car Kalle *bought*
sinise/n auto/n	of the *blue* car
Kallen *osta/ma/n auto/n*	of the car Kalle *bought*
sinise/ssä auto/ssa	in the *blue* car
Kallen *osta/ma/ssa auto/ssa*	in the car Kalle *bought*

sinise/t auto/t	the *blue* cars
Kallen *osta/ma/t auto/t*	the cars Kalle *bought*
sinis/i/llä auto/i/lla	with the *blue* cars
Kallen *osta/m/i/lla auto/i/lla*	with the cars Kalle *bought*

The agent in this construction corresponds to the subject of the relative clause (i.e. **Kalle** in the examples above), and is expressed according to the same rules that apply to the subject in the temporal construction (§83).

The agent is expressed:

(a) by a possessive suffix alone, if it is the same as the corresponding constituent in the main clause (generally the subject);
(b) by an independent word in the genitive, if it is different from the corresponding constituent in the main clause;
(c) by the genitive forms of personal pronouns (**minun**, etc.), always followed by a possessive suffix (unstressed first and second personal pronouns may be omitted).

Tuula/n hankki/ma **vene maksoi 1 000 mk**.
The boat *Tuula got* cost 1,000 marks.

(Minun) hankki/ma/ni **vene maksoi 1 000 mk**.
The boat *I got* cost 1,000 marks.

Tuula istuu *hankki/ma/ssa/an* **veneessä**.
Tuula is sitting in the boat *she got*.

Istun *hankki/ma/ssa/ni* **veneessä**.
I am sitting in the boat *I got*.

Miksi ette aja *hankki/ma/lla/nne* **veneellä?**
Why don't you go ('drive') in the boat *you got*?

Hankki/ma/mme **veneet eivät maksaneet paljon**.
The boats *we got* didn't cost much.

Poik/i/en hankki/ma/t **veneet ovat mukavia**.
The boats *the boys got* are nice.

Hän ajaa *Tuula/n hankki/ma/lla* **veneellä**.
He is going in the boat *Tuula got*.

Particular attention should be paid to expressions such as the following, where the agent construction does not correspond directly to a relative clause.

Ehdotus on *Virtase/n esittä/mä.*
The proposal was *put forward by Virtanen.*

Tämä runo on *Saarikoske/n kirjoitta/ma.*
This poem was *written by Saarikoski.*

Nämä runot ovat *Saarikoske/n kirjoitta/ma/t ~ kirjoitta/m/i/a.*
These poems were *written by Saarikoski.*

Kene/n kirjoitta/m/i/a **nämä runot ovat?**
By whom were these poems *written?*

19 COMPARISON OF ADJECTIVES

- *Comparative*
- *Superlative*

§85 COMPARATIVE

The comparative ending is **-mpi**, which is added to the inflectional stem (see Chapter 5), e.g. **hullu** 'mad' : **hullu/mpi** 'madder'. The following sound change occurs before the comparative ending:

> The short **-a** ~ **-ä** of disyllabic adjectives changes to **-e** before the comparative ending.

Cf. **vahva** 'strong' : **vahve/mpi** 'stronger'; **selvä** 'clear' : **selve/mpi** 'clearer'. The rules of consonant gradation also apply before the comparative ending (§15.6), cf. **helppo** 'easy' : **helpo/mpi** 'easier'.

Basic form		*Comparative*	*Inflectional stem §*
paksu	thick	**paksu/mpi** thicker	–
iso	big	**iso/mpi**	–
kiltti	good-natured	**kilti/mpi**	–
vanha	old	**vanhe/mpi**	–
selvä	clear	**selve/mpi**	–
kova	hard	**kove/mpi**	–
paha	bad	**pahe/mpi**	–
jyrkkä	steep	**jyrke/mpi**	–
tarkka	exact	**tarke/mpi**	–
nopea	fast	**nopea/mpi**	–
vakava	serious	**vakava/mpi**	–
suuri	great	**suure/mpi**	18.3 (suure-)
pieni	small	**piene/mpi**	18.3 (piene-)
uusi	new	**uude/mpi**	18.4 (uute-)
terve	healthy	**tervee/mpi**	19 (tervee-)
tuore	fresh	**tuoree/mpi**	19 (tuoree-)
tavallinen	usual	**tavallise/mpi**	20.1 (tavallise-)

Basic form		*Comparative*	*Inflectional stem §*
punainen	red	**punaise/mpi**	20.1 (punaise-)
kaunis	beautiful	**kaunii/mpi**	20.3 (kaunii-)
puhdas	clean	**puhtaa/mpi**	20.3 (puhtaa-)
raitis	sober	**raittii/mpi**	20.3 (raittii-)
voimakas	powerful	**voimakkaa/mpi**	20.3 (voimakkaa-)
lyhyt	short	**lyhye/mpi**	20.8 (lyhye-)
kevyt	light	**kevye/mpi**	20.8 (kevye-)

The declension of the comparative forms has one special feature. In the inflectional stem the final part **-mpi** changes to **-mpa- ~ -mpä-**, and the consonant gradation rules then change this to **-mma- ~ -mmä-**. Before the plural **-i-** the final **-a ~ -ä** of these endings is dropped (cf. §16).

Comparative basic form			*Singular*	*Plural*
paksu/mpi	thicker	*Illat.*	paksu/**mpa**/an	paksu/**mp**/i/in
		Ess.	paksu/**mpa**/na	paksu/**mp**/i/na
		Part.	paksu/**mpa**/a	paksu/**mp**/i/a
		Gen.	paksu/**mma**/n	paksu/**mp**/i/en
		Iness.	paksu/**mma**/ssa	paksu/**mm**/i/ssa
		Elat.	paksu/**mma**/sta	paksu/**mm**/i/sta
		Adess.	paksu/**mma**/lla	paksu/**mm**/i/lla
		Ablat.	paksu/**mma**/lta	paksu/**mm**/i/lta
		Allat.	paksu/**mma**/lle	paksu/**mm**/i/lle
		Transl.	paksu/**mma**/ksi	paksu/**mm**/i/ksi

Similarly, the comparative basic form **selve/mpi** 'clearer' declines as follows: **selve/mpä/än** (illative), **selve/mmä/n** (genitive), **selve/mm/i/ssä** (inessive plural), etc.

The comparative forms of the adjectives **hyvä** 'good' and **pitkä** 'long' are exceptional: **hyvä : pare/mpi** 'better', and **pitkä : pite/mpi** 'longer'. **Pare/mpi** inflects e.g. **pare/mpa/an** (illative), **pare/mma/ssa** (inessive) and **pare/mm/i/lla** (adessive plural).

In context the comparative forms often co-occur with the word **kuin** 'than'; otherwise they behave like ordinary adjectives.

Minun autoni on *iso/mpi* **kuin sinun.**
My car is *bigger* than yours.

Ostan *iso/mma/n* **auton.**
I'll buy a *bigger* car.

Ei *iso/mma/lla* **autolla mitään tee!**
One can't do anything with a *bigger* car!

Sinä olet *nuore/mpi* **kuin minä.**
You are *younger* than me.

Mutta minä taas olen *vanhe/mpi* **kuin Lauri.**
But on the other hand I am *older* than Lauri.

Suomessa on monta *suure/mpa/a* **kaupunkia kuin Salo.**
In Finland there are many *bigger* towns than Salo.

Uskomme *pare/mpa/an* **tulevaisuuteen.**
We believe in a *better* future.

Näytät *tervee/mmä/ltä* **kuin eilen.**
You look *healthier* than yesterday.

Olenkin *tervee/mpi!*
I am *healthier!*

Pitäisi elää *tervee/mpä/ä* **elämää.**
One ought to lead a *healthier* life.

Pekka hankki *pare/mma/n* **asunnon.**
Pekka got a *better* flat.

Etkö pysty hankkimaan *pare/mpa/a* **asuntoa?**
Can't you get a *better* flat?

Kaupunki rakentaa *pare/mp/i/a* **asuntoja.**
The town is building *better* flats.

Appelsiinit ovat *kallii/mp/i/a* **kuin omenat.**
Oranges are *more expensive* than apples.

Keltaise/mma/t **appelsiinit ovat** *kypse/mp/i/ä.*
The *yellower* oranges are *riper.*

Ostan nuo *keltaise/mma/t* **appelsiinit.**
I'll buy those *yellower* oranges.

En osta noita *vihreä/mp/i/ä* **appelsiineja.**
I shan't buy those *greener* oranges.

Tämä on *lue/tu/mpi* **kirja.**
This book is *more* (widely) *read.*

The structure **kuin** + nominative can sometimes be replaced by a word in the partitive alone, placed before the comparative form. This structure is used mainly in the written language.

Olet vanhe/<u>mpi</u> *kuin minä.* **= Olet minu/<u>a</u> vanhe/<u>mpi</u>.**
You are *older* than me.

Tämä auto on kallii/mpi *kuin tuo.* = **Tämä auto on tuo/ta kallii/mpi.**
This car is *more expensive* than that one.

§86   SUPERLATIVE

The superlative ending is **-in**; like the comparative ending, it is added to the inflectional stem, e.g. **hullu** 'mad' : **hullu/in** 'maddest'. Consonant grada-tion occurs before the superlative ending (§15.6), e.g. **helppo** 'easy' : **helpo/in** 'easiest'.

> Before the superlative ending the vowel change rules also apply (§16): a long vowel shortens, short **-a**, **-ä** and **-e** are dropped, and **-i** and **-ii** change to **-e**.

Examples:

Basic form		Superlative	Inflectional stem §
paksu	thick	**paksu/in**	–
iso	big	**iso/in**	–
kiltti	good-natured	**kilte/in**	–
vanha	old	**vanh/in**	–
selvä	clear	**selv/in**	–
kova	hard	**kov/in**	–
jyrkkä	steep	**jyrk/in**	–
tarkka	exact	**tark/in**	–
nopea	fast	**nope/in**	–
tärkeä	important	**tärke/in**	–
matala	low	**matal/in**	–
suuri	great	**suur/in**	18.3 (suure-)
pieni	small	**pien/in**	18.3 (piene-)
uusi	new	**uus/in**	18.4 (uute-)
tavallinen	usual	**tavallis/in**	20.1 (tavallise-)
punainen	red	**punais/in**	20.1 (punaise-)
kaunis	beautiful	**kaune/in**	20.3 (kaunii-)
raitis	sober	**raitte/in**	20.3 (raittii-)
vapaa	free	**vapa/in**	–
vakaa	firm	**vaka/in**	–
terve	healthy	**terve/in**	19 (tervee-)
tuore	fresh	**tuore/in**	19 (tuoree-)
puhdas	clean	**puhta/in**	20.3 (puhtaa-)
voimakas	powerful	**voimakka/in**	20.3 (voimakkaa-)
runsas	abundant	**runsa/in**	20.3 (runsaa-)

Basic form		Superlative	Inflectional stem §
lyhyt	short	**lyh(y)/in**	20.8 (lyhy<u>e</u>-)
ohut	thin	**ohu/in**	20.8 (ohu<u>e</u>-)

The superlative forms also have an unusual declension, which partly resembles that of the comparative (§85). In the inflectional stem **-in** changes to **-impa-** ~ **-impä-**, which after consonant gradation becomes **-imma-** ~ **-immä-**. Before the plural **-i-** the final **-a** ~ **-ä** is dropped.

Superlative basic form			Singular	Plural
paksu/in	thickest	*Illat.*	**paksu/impa/an**	**paksu/imp/i/in**
		Ess.	**paksu/impa/na**	**paksu/imp/i/na**
		Part.	**paksu/in/ta/**	**paksu/imp/i/a**
		Gen.	**paksu/imma/n**	**paksu/imp/i/en**
		Iness.	**paksu/imma/ssa**	**paksu/imm/i/ssa**
		Elat.	**paksu/imma/sta**	**paksu/imm/i/sta**
		Adess.	**paksu/imma/lla**	**paksu/imm/i/lla**
		Ablat.	**paksu/imma/lta**	**paksu/imm/i/lta**
		Allat.	**paksu/imma/lle**	**paksu/imm/i/lle**
		Transl.	**paksu/imma/ksi**	**paksu/imm/i/ksi**

In the same way, the adjective **selvä** 'clear' has the superlative basic form **selv/in** 'clearest', and declines as, for example, **selv/impä/än** (illative), **selv/immä/stä** (elative), **selv/imp/i/in** (illative plural) and **selv/imm/i/llä** (adessive plural).

The partitive singular is normally formed directly from the basic form, by adding the ending **-ta** ~ **-tä**, e.g. **paksu/in/ta**, **selv/in/tä**, **vanh/in/ta** and **voimakka/in/ta**. The superlatives of **hyvä** and **pitkä** are exceptional.

Basic form	Comparative	Superlative	
hyvä	**pare/mpi**	**paras** ~ **parha/in**	(gen. **parhaa/n** ~
good	better	best	**parha/imma/n**,
			illat. **parha/impa/an**,
			illat. pl. **parha/imp/i/in**)
pitkä	**pite/mpi**	**pis/in**	(gen. **pis/immä/n**)
long	longer	longest	

The partitive singular forms here are **paras/ta** or **parha/in/ta**, and **pis/in/tä**, respectively.

In context the superlative forms function like ordinary adjectives.

Helsinki on Suomen *suur/in* kaupunki.
Helsinki is Finland's *biggest* town.

Oletko käynyt Suomen *suur/imma/ssa* kaupungissa?
Have you been to Finland's *biggest* town?

Helsinki on kehittynyt Suomen *suur/imma/ksi* kaupungiksi.
Helsinki has developed into Finland's *biggest* town.

Mikä on Suomen *vanh/in* kaupunki?
Which is Finland's *oldest* town?

Rauma kuuluu Suomen *vanh/imp/i/in* kaupunkeihin.
Rauma is one of Finland's *oldest* towns.

Asun kaupungin *vanh/imma/ssa* osassa.
I live in the *oldest* part of the town.

Aion muuttaa kaupungin *vanh/impa/an* osaan.
I'll move to the *oldest* part of the town.

Mitkä ovat kirjan *vaike/imma/t* luvut?
Which are the *most difficult* chapters of the book?

Viren oli kaikkein *nope/in*, Virtanen taas *hita/in*.
Viren was the *fastest* of all, and Virtanen the *slowest*.

Kuka pojista on *pisin*?
Which of the boys is the *tallest*?

Suomi on yksi maailman *pohjois/imm/i/sta* maista.
Finland is one of the *northernmost* countries in the world.

Suomi on maailman *pohjois/imp/i/a* maita.
Finland is one of the *northernmost* countries in the world.

Viren on Suomen *nope/imp/i/a* juoksijoita.
Viren is one of Finland's *fastest* runners.

Annan *parhaa/n* (*parhaimma/n*) palan sinulle.
I'll give the *best* bit to you.

Liha maistuu *parhaa/lta* (*parhaimma/lta*) paistettuna.
Meat tastes *best* when it is roasted.

Kalle on *parha/i/ta* ystäviäni.
Kalle is one of my *best* friends.

On *halv/in/ta* syödä puuroa.
It is *cheapest* to eat porridge.

Ostan *halv/imma/t* kengät.
I'll buy the *cheapest* shoes.

Onko Juhannustanssit Suomen *luetu/in* kirja?
Is Midsummer Dance the *most* (widely) *read* book in Finland?

Heikki Kinnunen on Suomen *pidety/imp/i/ä* **näyttelijöitä.**
Heikki Kinnunen is one of Finland's *most popular* actors.

The structure for the absolute superlative (meaning 'most *X*' or 'very *X*')
is **mitä** + superlative, e.g. **mitä hullu/in** 'very mad'.

Ehdotus on *mitä parhain.*	The proposal is *extremely good.*
Näytät *mitä terve/immä/ltä.*	You look *most healthy.*
Hän teki *mitä syv/immä/n* **vaikutuksen kuulijoihin.**	He/she exerted a *most profound* impression on the listeners.

20 OTHER WORD CLASSES

- *Adverbs*
- *Prepositions*
- *Postpositions*
- *Conjunctions*
- *Particles*

§87 ADVERBS

The most common type of adverb expresses manner, and is formed by adding the ending **-sti** to the inflectional stem of an adjective, e.g. **hauska** 'nice' : **hauska/sti** 'nicely'. This ending causes consonant gradation, e.g. **helppo** 'easy' : **helpo/sti** 'easily' (§15.6).

Basic form	*Adverb in -sti*	
paksu	**paksu/sti**	thickly
kiltti	**kilti/sti**	good-naturedly
nopea	**nopea/sti**	fast
suuri	**suure/sti**	greatly
tavallinen	**tavallise/sti**	usually
kaunis	**kaunii/sti**	beautifully
puhdas	**puhtaa/sti**	purely
voimakas	**voimakkaa/sti**	powerfully

Jussi laulaa *kaunii/sti*.	Jussi sings *beautifully*.
Panen *runsaa/sti* voita leivän päälle.	I put *plenty of* ('*abundantly*') butter on the bread.
Puhukaa aivan *vapaa/sti*!	Speak quite *freely*!
Nyt täytyy puhua *lyhye/sti*.	Now one must speak *briefly*.
Tavallise/sti menen sänkyyn klo 23.	*Usually* I go to bed at 11 o'clock.
Teen työtä *tehokkaa/sti*.	I work *efficiently*.
En pidä tästä *erityise/sti*.	I don't *particularly* like this.

The corresponding comparative and superlative expressions are derived by changing the endings **-mpi** and **-in** to **-mmin** (comparative) and **-immin** (superlative).

Adjective basic form		Comparative adjective basic form	Superlative adjective basic form	Comparative adverb in -mmin	Superlative adverb in -immin
helppo	easy	helpo/**mpi**	helpo/**in**	helpo/**mmin**	helpo/**immin**
selvä	clear	selve/mpi	selv/in	selve/mmin	selv/immin
kova	hard	kove/mpi	kov/in	kove/mmin	kov/immin
matala	low	matala/mpi	matal/in	matala/mmin	matal/immin
tarkka	exact	tarke/mpi	tark/in	tarke/mmin	tark/immin
suuri	great	suure/mpi	suur/in	suure/mmin	suur/immin
tavallinen	usual	tavallise/mpi	tavallis/in	tavallise/mmin	tavallis/immin
kaunis	beautiful	kaunii/mpi	kaune/in	kaunii/mmin	kaune/immin
puhdas	clean	puhtaa/mpi	puhta/in	puhtaa/mmin	puhta/immin
runsas	abundant	runsaa/mpi	runsa/in	runsaa/mmin	runsa/immin
terve	healthy	tervee/mpi	terve/in	tervee/mmin	terve/immin

Yrjö juoksee *nopea/mmin* kuin Lauri.
Yrjö runs *faster* than Lauri.

Aja *hitaa/mmin*!
Drive *more slowly*!

Tuo mies ajaa kaikkein *hita/immin*.
That man drives *the slowest* of all.

Yritä opiskella *ahkera/mmin*.
Try to study *more diligently*.

***Tavallis/immin* herään klo 7.**
Most commonly I wake at 7 o'clock.

Elä *tervee/mmin*!
Live *more healthily*!

Siellä oli *runsaa/mmin* ihmisiä kuin oli odotettu.
There were *more* people there than had been expected.

Kyllä Johanna laulaa *kaune/immin*, ainakin *kaunii/mmin* kuin Aune.
Johanna certainly sings *the most beautifully*, at least *more beautifully* than Aune.

The comparative and superlative of **paljon** 'much, many' are exceptional: **enemmän** 'more' and **eniten** 'most'. In the same way: **vähän** 'little' – **vähemmän** 'less' – **vähiten** 'least', and **hyvin** 'well' – **paremmin** 'better' – **parhaiten** 'best'.

Another common group of adverbs are those expressing place or direction, such as **alas** 'down', **pois** 'away'. These adverbs often inflect in the three external locative cases (§40) in accordance with the direction of the action of the verb.

alas	down
alhaa/lla, -lta, -lle	down, below
ede/ssä, -stä, eteen	in front, before
kaikkia/lla, -lta, -lle	everywhere
kaukana, kaukaa, kauas	far
kotona, kotoa, kotiin	at home
oikea/lla, -lta, -lle	on the right
poissa, pois	away
sie/llä, -ltä, sinne	there (unspecified place)
tuo/lla, -lta, -nne	there (place pointed to)
tää/llä, -ltä, tänne	here
ulkona, ulkoa, ulos	outside
vasemma/lla, -lta, -lle	on the left
ylös	up

Many common adverbs indicate time.

aikaisin	early	**joskus**	sometimes
aina	always	**kauan**	for a long time
eilen	yesterday	**kerran**	once
ennen	before	**kohta**	soon
harvoin	rarely	**myöhään**	late
heti	immediately	**nyt**	now
huomenna	tomorrow	**silloin**	then, at that time
tänään	today	**sitten**	then, after that
usein	often		

Another major group are those of degree, measure or quantity.

aika	quite, rather	**kovin**	very
aivan	quite, completely	**kyllin**	enough
erittäin	extremely	**liian**	too
hieman	slightly	**melko**	quite, considerably
hiukan	a little	**niin**	so
varsin	exceedingly, quite		

In addition to those mentioned above there are also other adverbs of manner.

hiljaa	quiet(ly)	**näin**	in this way
hyvin	well	**oikein**	right
ilmaiseksi	free of charge	**samoin**	in the same way
itsestään	of itself	**siten**	in that way
mielellään	with pleasure	**yksin**	alone

Also important are the modal adverbs, which indicate in a variety of subjective ways the speaker's attitude to what he or she is saying.

ainakin	at least	**muun muassa**	among other things
ehkä	perhaps	**myös**	also
jopa	even	**päinvastoin**	on the contrary
juuri	just	**tietenkin**	of course
kai	probably	**tietysti**	of course
kenties	perhaps	**tosin**	to be sure
kyllä	certainly, indeed; yes	**tosiaan**	really
mieluummin	rather	**vain**	only

§88 PREPOSITIONS

Prepositions and postpositions (§89) take either the genitive or the partitive. There are many more postpositions than prepositions in Finnish.

Prepositions precede the words whose case they determine, e.g. **ilman** 'without' (**ilman raha/a** 'without money'). The following prepositions take the partitive case:

ennen	before	**lähe/llä, -ltä, -lle**	near
ilman	without	**paitsi**	besides; except
keske/llä, -ltä, -lle	in the middle of	**pitkin**	along
kohti	towards	**päin**	towards
vasten	against		

ennen **tois/ta maailmansota/a**.	*before* the Second World War
Oletko *ilman* **raha/a?**	Don't you have any money? ('Are you *without* money?')
Koira makaa *keskellä* **lattia/a**.	The dog lies *in the middle of* the floor.
Ajan *kohti* **Kuopio/ta**.	I drive *towards* Kuopio.
Paitsi **viini/ä tarvitsemme oluttakin**.	*Besides* wine we need beer, too.
Varas juoksi *pitkin* **Eerikinkatu/a**.	The thief ran *along* Eric's Street.
Kaikki menee *päin* **helvetti/ä**.	Everything is going bloody badly ('*to* hell').
Nojasin *vasten* **seinä/ä**.	I leaned *against* the wall.

The following prepositions take the genitive case; there are not many of these.

alle	under (not in locative sense)	**läpi**	through (temporal)
halki	through (locative)	**sitten**	since
kautta	throughout		
kesken	in the middle of (temporal sense)		

Mies painaa *alle* sada/n kilon.	The man weighs *under* 100 kilos.
Kuljen *halki* metsä/n.	I walk *through* the wood.
Hänet tunnetaan *kautta* maa/n.	He/she is known *throughout* the country.
Kesken tunni/n Pekka lähti ulos.	*In the middle of* the lesson Pekka went out.
läpi vuotisato/j/en	*through* the centuries
Sitten viime syksy/n en ole käynyt ulkomailla.	*Since* last autumn I have not been abroad.

§89   POSTPOSITIONS

Postpositions occur after the words whose case they determine, e.g. **yli** 'over, across' (**kadu/n yli** 'across the street'). Postpositions taking the genitive case are very common, and the most important ones are given in the list below. Some of them inflect in three local cases.

aikana	during
alitse	below
a/lla, -lta, -lle	under (place)
ansiosta	thanks to
ede/llä, -ltä, -lle	in front of
ede/ssä, -stä, eteen	in front of
eduksi	to the advantage of
halki	through
hallu/ssa, -sta, haltuun	in the possession of
hyväksi	for (the benefit of)
johdosta	because of
jäljessä	after, behind
jälkeen	after, behind
kanssa	with
kautta	by means of, via
keskellä	in the middle of
kesken	between, among
keskuude/ssa, -sta, keskuuteen	among
kohda/lla, -lta, -lle	at, at the point of
luo, luokse	to
luona	near, at the house of
luota	from
lähe/llä, -ltä, -lle	near
läpi	through
lävitse	through
mielestä	in the opinion of
mukaan	according to

mukana	with
ohi	past
ohitse	past
osalta	as regards
perusteella	on the basis of
perässä	behind, after
poikki	across
puole/lla, -lta, -lle	on the side of
puolesta	on behalf of
pää/llä, -ltä, -lle	on (top of)
päässä	at a distance of
rinnalla	at the side of
sisällä	in, inside
sisään	in, into
taakse	behind (direction towards)
takaa	from behind
takana	behind, at the back of
takia	for the sake of, because of
tähden	for the sake of, because of
viere/llä, -ltä, -lle	beside
viere/ssä, -stä, -en	beside
vuoksi	for the sake of, because of
yli	over, across
ylitse	over, across
ympäri, -llä, -lle	around

Soda/n *aikana* Ryti oli presidenttinä.	*During* the war Ryti was president.
Koira on pöydä/n *alla*.	The dog is *under* the table.
Koira ryömi pöydä/n *alle*.	The dog crawled *under* the table.
Tule esiin pöydä/n *alta*!	Come out *from under* the table!
Sinu/n *ansiosta/si* olen nyt täällä.	*Thanks to* you I am here now.
Talo/n *edessä* on koivu.	*In front of* the house is a birch tree.
Pysäytän auton talo/n *eteen*.	I will park the car *in front of* the house.
Ajammeko kaupungi/n *halki*?	Shall we drive *through* the town?
Auto on Peka/n *hallussa*.	The car is *in* Pekka's *possession*.
Auto joutui Peka/n *haltuun*.	The car fell *into* Pekka's *possession*.
Auto on (minu/n) *hallussa/ni*.	The car is *in my possession*.
Tee jotain Chile/n *hyväksi*.	Do something *for* Chile.
Se/n *johdosta*, että . . .	*Because of* the fact that . . .
Tunni/n *jälkeen* menen kapakkaan.	*After* the lesson I'm going to the pub.

Menen tanssimaan Tuula/n *kanssa*.	I'm going dancing *with* Tuula.
Tuletko tanssimaan (minu/n *kanssa/ni?*	Will you come dancing *with* me?
Salo/n *kautta* **pääsee Hankoon.**	*Via* Salo one gets to Hanko.
Näin meidä/n *kesken* ...	Just *between* ourselves ...
Tori on kaupungi/n *keskellä.*	The market place is *in the centre of* the town.
Ruotsalais/ten *keskuudessa* **ollaan sitä mieltä, että** ...	*Among* the Swedes there is ('one is of') the opinion that ...
Pekka on Tuula/n *luona*.	Pekka is *at* Tuula's.
Seija on meidä/n *luona/mme*.	Seija is *at our place*.
Tulen Elisa/n *luota.*	I'm coming *from* Elisa's.
Lähdetkö Merja/n *luokse?*	Are you going *to* Merja's?
Naantali on Turu/n *lähellä.*	Naantali is *near* Turku.
Aion muuttaa Salo/n *lähelle.*	I intend to move *near* Salo.
Aurinko paistaa ikkuna/n *läpi.*	The sun shines *through* the window.
Kalle/n *mielestä* **tämä ei kannata.**	In Kalle's *opinion* this is not worth it.
Ukkose/n *mukana* **tuli sadetta.**	*With* the thunder came rain.
Menen poik/i/en *mukaan*.	I'm going *with* the boys.
Ajoimme kaupa/n *ohi*.	We drove *past* the shop.
Tämä/n asia/n *osalta* **olen eri mieltä.**	*As regards* this matter I am of a different opinion.
Sanotu/n *perusteella* **väitän, että** ...	*On the basis of* what has been said I claim that ...
Koira juoksi tie/n *poikki.*	The dog ran *across* the road.
Kene/n *puolella* **sinä olet?**	Whose *side* are you *on*?
Taistelemme isänmaa/n *puolesta.*	We are fighting *for* the fatherland.
Kukkulo/i/den *päällä* **kasvoi metsää.**	*On top of* the hills there were woods ('there grew forest').
Kilometri/n *päässä* **on kioski.**	A kilometre *away* there is a kiosk.
Talo/n *sisällä* **oli lämmintä.**	*Inside* the house it was warm.
Lapsi menee ove/n *taakse.*	The child goes *behind* the door.
Lapsi on ove/n *takana.*	The child is *behind* the door.
Lapsi tuli esille ove/n *takaa.*	The child came out *from behind* the door.
Häne/n *takia/an* **teen mitä vain.**	*For* his/her *sake* I will do anything.
Kirjasto on yliopisto/n *vieressä.*	The library is *next to* the university.
Saanko istua neidi/n *viereen?*	May I sit *next to* you, Miss? ('next to Miss')
Tällaise/n asia/n *vuoksi* **ei pidä riidellä.**	One should not quarrel *because of* this sort of thing.
Nyt mennään kadu/n *yli*.	Now let's go *across* the street.
Talo/j/en *ympärillä* **oli metsää.**	*Around* the houses there was forest.

Hän oli purjehtinut maailma/n   He/she had sailed *round* the world.
ympäri.

When a postposition occurs with a personal pronoun in the genitive a possessive suffix must be added to the postposition, but first and second person pronouns themselves may be omitted (§36).

(*minu/n*) **kanssa/ni**	with *me*
(*sinu/n*) **kanssa/si**	with *you*
häne/n **kanssa/an**	with *him/her*
(*me/i/dän*) **kanssa/mme**	with *us*, etc.

The most common postpositions taking the partitive case are the following:

alas	down	**päin**	towards
kohtaan	towards, to (abstract)	**varten**	for
kohti	towards, to (concrete)	**vastaan**	against
myöten	along	**vastapäätä**	opposite
pitkin	along	**ylös**	up

Johtaja on hyvin ystävällinen minu/a kohtaan.
The manager is very friendly *to* me.

Nyt lähdetään Turku/a kohti.
Now let's go *towards* Turku.

Hän kävelee katu/j/a myöten ~ pitkin.
He walks *along* the streets.

Sinu/a vartenhan se hankittiin.
We got it *for* you.

Leena tuli minu/a vastaan rautatieasemalle.
Leena came to *meet* me at the railway station ('*against* me').

Onko joku sinu/a vastassa?
Is there anyone *meeting* you?

Kirkko/a vastapäätä on Elanto.
Opposite the church is the Elanto shop.

Nyt täytyy kävellä mäke/ä ylös.
Now we have to walk *up* the hill.

The postpositions **asti** 'until, as far as' and **päin** 'towards' take the illative.

Opetus jatkuu ilta/an asti.	The teaching continues *until* the evening.
Juna kulkee Helsinki/in päin.	The train is going *towards* Helsinki.

§90   CONJUNCTIONS

Conjunctions are words that link sentences and parts of sentences together, such as **ja** 'and', **kun** 'when'. A list of the most common conjunctions follows below; the most common of all are marked with an arrow. Some are combinations of a conjunction and the negation verb, e.g. **etten** = **että en**, **ettet** = **että et**, **ettei** = **että ei**, and so on: i.e. they inflect for person.

ei – eikä (**en** – **enkä**, etc.)	neither – nor (inflects for person)
eli	or, i.e.
ellei (**ellen**, etc.)	if not, unless (inflects for person)
ennen kuin	before
ettei (**etten**, etc.)	that . . . not (inflects for person)
→ että	that
ikään kuin	as though
→ ja	and
joko – tai	either – or
jollei (**jollen**, etc.)	if not, unless (inflects for person)
→ jos	if
joskin	even if, even though
jotta	in order that, so that
→ koska	because, since
→ kuin	than
→ kun	when, as
kunnes	until
kuten	as, like
mikäli	as far as, in so far as; if
→ mutta	but
muttei (**mutten**, etc.)	but . . . not (inflects for person)
→ niin	so
niin että	so that
niin kuin	as, like
niin – kuin -kin	both – and
niin pian kuin	as soon as
nimittäin	namely, you see
näet	namely, you see
paitsi	except, besides
paitsi – myös	not only – but also
samoin kuin	in the same way as
sekä	and (more formal)
→ sekä – että	both – and
sen tähden että	because
→ sillä	for, because
→ tai (~ taikka)	or (not in questions, cf. **vai**)
toisin kuin	otherwise than

→ **vaan**	but (after a negative)
→ **vai**	or (in questions)
→ **vaikka**	although

Pentti *ja* Pirkko olivat naimisissa. Pentti *and* Pirkko were married.

Ei Pentti *eikä* Pirkko ole tullut vielä. *Neither* Pentti *nor* Pirkko have come yet.

Ellet ole hiljaa, menen ulos. *Unless* you are quiet I shall go out.

Ellemme yritä, emme onnistu. *If* we do *not* try we shall not succeed.

Ellei sää parane, jäämme kotiin. *Unless* the weather improves we shall stay at home.

Eniten *eli* 450 kappaletta myytiin autoja. The highest sales, *viz.* 450 units, were of cars.

Kesti pitkään *ennen kuin* nukahdin. It took a long time *before* I fell asleep.

Ei kestänyt kauan *ennen kuin* sää kirkastui. It didn't take long *before* the weather brightened up.

Huomaan, *että* kello on neljä. I notice *that* it is four o'clock.

Tiedän, *että* Pirkko on täällä. I know *that* Pirkko is here.

Väitätkö, *ettei* kello ole neljä? Are you claiming *that* it is *not* four o'clock?

Väitätkö, *että* kello *ei* ole neljä? Are you claiming *that* it is *not* four o'clock?

Väitätkö, *etten* tiedä tätä? Are you claiming *that* I *don't* know this?

Väitätkö, *että* en tiedä tätä? Are you claiming *that* I *don't* know this?

Kalle on pitkä *ja* komea. Kalle is tall *and* handsome.

Matkustan *joko* junalla *tai* autolla. I travel *either* by train *or* by car.

En matkusta autolla *enkä* junalla. I travel *neither* by car *nor* by train.

Tulen *jos* voin. I'll come *if* I can.

Tulen, *joskin* saatan myöhästyä hiukan. I'll come, *although* I might be a bit late.

Hölkkään *jotta* kunto paranisi. I go jogging *in order to* get into better condition.

En tule, *koska* olen sairastunut. I'm not coming, *because* I have fallen ill.

Tulen, *kun* olen terve. I'll come *when* I'm healthy.

Odotan, *kunnes* hän tulee. I will wait *until* he/she comes.

Kuten olen sanonut monta kertaa ... *As* I have said many times ...

Mikäli Yrjö tulee, lähden kotiin. *If* Yrjö comes I'm going home.

Teuvo on pitempi *kuin* minä. Teuvo is taller *than* me.

Teuvo on pitkä *mutta* laiha. Teuvo is tall *but* thin.

Mutta **sinähän sanoit, että ...**	*But* you did say that ...
Tulen, *mutten* **viivy kauan.**	I'll come, *but* I won't stay long.
Jos **et tule,** *niin* **rupean itkemään.**	*If* you don't come, *then* ('*so*') I shall start crying.
Niin **Karjalainen** *kuin* **Virolainen/kin pyrkivät presidentiksi.**	*Both* Karjalainen *and* Virolainen are seeking to become president.
Viren on *sekä* **nopea** *että* **kestävä.**	Viren is *not only* fast *but also* has stamina.
Tulen, *sillä* **en halua olla yksin kotona.**	I'll come, *because* I don't want to be alone at home.
Otan viiniä *tai* **olutta.**	I'll take wine *or* beer.
Otatko viiniä *vai* **olutta?**	Will you take wine *or* beer?
Otamme *joko* **viiniä** *tai* **vichyä.**	We'll take *either* wine *or* Vichy water.
Tulen, *vaikka* **olen sairas.**	I'll come, *although* I am ill.
En tule, *vaan* **jään kotiin.**	I'm not coming, (*but*) I'll stay at home.

§91   PARTICLES

There are five common enclitic particles appended after all other types of endings: **-ko ~ -kö**, **-kin**, **-kaan ~ -kään**, **-han ~ -hän** and **-pa ~ -pä**. Less common ones are **-ka ~ -kä** and **-s**. As has been said above, enclitic particles always occur last in the word, see the diagrams in sections 12–14.

The ending **-ko ~ -kö** is used to form direct questions (§30.1).

Tule/t/ko?	Are you *coming*?
Et/kö **tule?**	*Aren't* you coming?
Auto/lla/ko **tulet?**	Are you coming *by car*?
Kemi/in/kö **menet?**	Are you going *to Kemi*?
Sa/isi/n/ko **sipulipihvin?**	*Could I have* steak and onions?
Muutta/isi/t/ko **Ruotsiin jos voisit?**	*Would you move* to Sweden if you could?
Men/nä/än/kö **ulos?**	*Shall we go* out?
Sinä/kö **sen teit?**	Was it *you* who did it?
Jo/ko **olet korjannut autosi?**	Have you repaired your car *already*?

The particle **-kin** indicates stress and is often equivalent to 'also' or 'too'. The following examples illustrate its use with nouns:

Olen hankkinut *auto/n/kin.*	I have got *a car, too.*
Minä/kin **olen hankkinut auton.**	*I, too,* have got a car.
Oli hauskaa, että *sinä/kin* **tulit.**	It was nice that *you* came *too.*
Juotko *kahvi/a/kin?*	Do you drink *coffee as well*?
Olen ollut *Espanja/ssa/kin.*	I have been *to Spain, too.*

The particle **-kin** is also used with verbs, and then it is difficult to say precisely what meaning it has. It may for instance indicate that some expectation has been fulfilled, or mark a sense of surprise, or strengthen an exclamation.

Odotin häntä ja hän *tul/i/kin*.	I waited for him and he *really did come*.
Olen ollut *ui/ma/ssa/kin*.	I've been *swimming, too*.
Eikö hän *ole/kin* **ihana!**	*Isn't* he wonderful!
Kalle *on/kin* **täällä**.	Kalle *is in fact* here.
Etkö *lupaa/kin* **apuasi!**	*Surely you will promise* your help, *won't you?*
Men/i/n/kin **kotiin**.	I *did go* home.

The particle **-kaan** ~ **-kään** generally corresponds to **-kin** in negative sentences.

En ole hankkinut *auto/a/kaan*.	I haven't got *a car, either*.
Minä/kään **en ole hankkinut autoa**.	*Neither* have *I* got a car.
Etkö juo *kahvi/a/kaan?*	Don't/won't you drink *coffee, either?*
En ole ollut *Espanja/ssa/kaan*.	I *haven't* been to *Spain, either*.
Odotin häntä, mutta hän ei *tul/lut/kaan*.	I waited for him but he *didn't come*.
Kalle ei *ole/kaan* **täällä**.	Kalle *is not* here, *after all*.
Etkö *lupaa/kaan* **apuasi?**	Won't you *promise* your help *after all?*

The particle **-han** ~ **-hän** generally indicates that the sentence expresses something that is familiar or known. It may also be used simply to stress the speaker's message. It can only be added to the first element of the sentence.

Tämä/hän **on skandaali!**	*This really* is a scandal!
Ruotsi/han **on kuningaskunta**.	*As we know, Sweden* is a monarchy.
Minä/hän RAKASTAN **sinua!**	I LOVE you!
Rakasta/n/han **minä sinua**.	*Of course I love* you.
Sinu/a/han **minä rakastan**.	*You are the one* I love.
Huomenna/han **lähdemme lomalle**.	*Tomorrow* we're going on holiday, *aren't we?*
Viime sunnuntai/na/han **Kalle syntyi**.	*It was last Sunday that* Kalle was born.
Ole/n/han **minä käynyt Venäjälläkin**.	*Of course*, I've been to Russia as well.

The particle **-han** ~ **-hän** is also used in questions to make them more polite, and to soften commands.

On/ko/han **Pentti kotona?**	I *wonder if* Pentti is at home?
Paljon/ko/han **pieni kahvi maksaa?**	How much *might* a small coffee cost?
Sa/isi/n/ko/han **laskun?**	*Could* I have the bill, *please*?
Ota/han **vähän lisää!**	*Please take* a little more!
Astu/kaa/han **sisään!**	*Please come* in!
Ole/han **hiljaa!**	*Please be* quiet, *will you*?
Vie/hän **astiat keittiöön!**	*Take* the dishes into the kitchen, *could you*?

The particle **-pa** ~ **-pä** indicates emphasis. In the spoken language it is often followed by **-s**.

On/pa **hän pitkä!**	He really *is* tall!
Kyllä/pä **sinä olet ahkera!**	You ARE hard-working, *aren't you*?
Anna/pa **minullekin vähän kahvia!**	*Give* me a little coffee too!
En/pä **anna!**	*No* I won't ('give')!
On/pa(s) **täällä kuuma!**	It *really is* hot here!
Tuo/ssa/pa **on iso joukko!**	There's a *really* big group!

The ending **-ka** ~ **-kä** is fairly rare. It is mainly used with the negation verb to indicate emphasis.

En tiedä *en/kä* **halua tietää**.
I don't know, *and I don't* want to know *either*.

Mormonit eivät käytä kahvia *eivät/kä* **myöskään alkoholia**.
The Mormons don't drink coffee, *nor* alcohol *either*.

Älä heitä paperia *älä/kä* **sylje lattialle**.
Don't throw paper about *and don't* spit on the floor.

More than one particle may occasionally be attached to the same word.

On/ko/han **Sylvi kotona?**	I *wonder if* Sylvi is at home?
On/pa/han **täällä kuuma!**	It *really is* hot here, *isn't it*!
Tule/pa/han **vähän lähemmäs!**	*Come* a bit closer, *will you*?
Olutta/kin/ko **vielä otat?**	Will you *really* have some more beer, *too*?
Mene/pä/s **vähän sivummalle!**	*Move* over a bit, *will you*?

21 WORD FORMATION

- *General*
- *Derivation*
- *Compounding*

§92 GENERAL

There are two ways of forming new words from existing words and stems: derivation and compounding. In derivation, new words (word stems) are made by adding derivative endings or suffixes to the root or to another stem. To the adjective **kaunis : kaunii-** 'beautiful', for instance, we can add the ending **-ta** to form the derived verb stem **kaunis/ta-** 'beautify' (first infinitive **kaunis/ta/a**). In the same way we can take the verb stem **aja-** 'drive', and add the ending **-o** to form the derived noun **aj/o** 'drive, chase, hunt', or the ending **-ele-** to form the verb stem **aj/ele-** 'drive around' (first infinitive **aj/el/la**).

Derivative suffixes occur immediately after the root but before the inflectional endings, i.e. before number and case endings in nominals, before passive, tense, mood and personal endings in finite verb forms, and before the infinitive and participle endings in non-finite verb forms. (See the diagrams in Chapter 3.)

Derived nominals and verbs inflect just like non-derived ones. Derived words are subject to the same sound alternations as other words, in particular consonant gradation (§15) and the vowel changes (§16).

Adding derivative suffixes may cause sound alternations in the root: e.g. **kaunii-** : **kaune/us** and **aja-** : **aj/ele-**. In what follows these alternations will be evident from the examples, and separate rules will not be given. There may also be alternations in the derivative suffixes themselves when further suffixes are added.

It is characteristic of Finnish that a given word form may contain many derivative suffixes, one after the other. Below are some examples. The (non-derived) root is given on the left, the derived word in the middle, and the 'basic' or full forms of the derivative suffixes on the right.

Stem	Derived word		Derivative suffixes (basic forms)
aja-	aj/ele/minen	driving about	ele-minen
asee-	asee/llis/ta-	arm (verb)	llinen-ta
asee-	asee/llis/ta/minen	arming (noun)	llinen-ta-minen
aja-	aj/ele/hti-	drift	ele-hti
aja-	aj/ele/hti/va	drifting (adj.)	ele-hti-va
lika-	lika/is/uus	dirtiness	inen-uus
koti-	kodi/ttom/uus	homelessness	ton(ttoma)-uus
kuole-	kuole/ma/ttom/uus	immortality	ma-ton(ttoma)-uus
etsi-	etsi/skel/y	search (noun)	skele-y
haukkaa-	hauka/hd/us	yelp (noun)	hta-us
haukkaa-	hauka/ht/el/u	yelping (noun)	hta-ele-u
asu-	asu/nno/ttom/uus	without a house	nto-ton(ttoma)-uus
tuo-	tuo/tta/ma/ttom/uus	unproductiveness	tta-ma-ton(ttoma)-uus

Not all derivative suffixes are equally productive. Some are extremely productive, which means they can be added to practically all roots that belong to a given type. Examples are the suffixes **-ja** ~ **-jä** 'agent', **-minen** 'verbal noun' and **-ma/ton** ~ **-mä/tön** 'not', cf. **aja/ja** 'driver', **aja/minen** 'driving', **aja/ma/ton** 'undriven'; **tuli/ja** 'comer', **tule/minen** 'coming', **tule/ma/ton** 'not coming, not come'; **meni/jä** 'goer', **mene/minen** 'going', **mene/mä/tön** 'not going, not gone', etc.

Other suffixes occur primarily or exclusively with certain roots, and are thus more or less unproductive.

§93   DERIVATION

§93.1   NOMINAL SUFFIXES

Part A of this section deals with denominal suffixes forming new nominals, and Part B deals with deverbal suffixes forming new nominals.

PART A

Root (nom.)		Derived word	

-hko ~ **-hkö** (adjective, indicates 'somewhat')

kylmä	cold	**kylmähkö**	rather cold
kova	hard	**kovahko**	fairly hard
pieni	small	**pienehkö** (§18.3)	rather small
iloinen	glad	**iloisehko** (§20.1)	fairly glad

Root (nom.)		Derived word	

-inen (adjective)

aika	time	aikainen	early
hiki	sweat	hikinen	sweaty
jää	ice	jäinen	icy
lika	dirt	likainen	dirty
luu	bone	luinen	of bone
puu	wood	puinen	wooden

-isa ~ -isä (adjective)

kala	fish	kalaisa	abounding in fish
leikki	play	leikkisä	playful
raivo	fury	raivoisa	furious

-kko ~ -kkö (collective noun)

aalto	wave	aallokko	the waves, swell
koivu	birch	koivikko	birch grove
kuusi	spruce	kuusikko	spruce grove
pensas	bush	pensaikko	thicket, shrubbery

-la ~ -lä (noun, indicates location)

kahvi	coffee	kahvila	café
kylpy	bath	kylpylä	baths
neuvo	advice	neuvola	child health centre
pappi	clergyman, vicar	pappila	vicarage
ravinto	food	ravintola	restaurant
sairas	ill	sairaala	hospital

-lainen ~ -läinen (noun, or noun and adjective, indicates a person)

apu	help	apulainen	assistant
pako	flight	pakolainen	refugee
koulu	school	koululainen	school pupil
kansa	people	kansalainen	citizen
suku	family	sukulainen	relative
työ	work	työläinen	worker
kaupunki	town	kaupunkilainen	town-dweller
Turku	Turku	turkulainen	resident of Turku
Helsinki	Helsinki	helsinkiläinen	resident of Helsinki
Ruotsi	Sweden	ruotsalainen	Swede, Swedish
Suomi	Finland	suomalainen	Finn, Finnish
Saksa	Germany	saksalainen	German
Norja	Norway	norjalainen	Norwegian

Root (nom.)		*Derived word*	
-lainen ~ -läinen (adjective)			
eri	separate	erilainen	different
kaikki	all, everything	kaikenlainen	all kinds of
tuo	that	tuollainen	that kind of
tämä	this	tällainen	this kind of
heikko	weak	heikonlainen	rather weak
suuri	great	suurenlainen	rather great
-llinen (adjective)			
ase	weapon	aseellinen	armed
hetki	moment	hetkellinen	momentary
yö	night	yöllinen	nocturnal
onni	happiness	onnellinen	happy
perhe	family	perheellinen	with a family
isä	father	isällinen	fatherly
kieli	language	kielellinen	linguistic
kunta	commune, local council	kunnallinen	municipal, communal
nainen	woman	naisellinen	womanly, feminine
-mainen ~ -mäinen (adjective)			
poika	boy	poikamainen	boyish
tyttö	girl	tyttömäinen	girlish
ukko	old man	ukkomainen	senile
sika	pig	sikamainen	swinish, beastly
-nainen ~ -näinen (adjective)			
koko	whole	kokonainen	whole, total
eri	separate	erinäinen	particular, certain
itse	self	itsenäinen	independent
moni	many	moninainen	various
-nen (diminutive noun)			
kala	fish	kalanen	little fish
kirja	book	kirjanen	booklet
poika	boy	poikanen	little boy, offspring
kukka	flower	kukkanen	little flower

Root (nom.)		Derived word	

-sto ~ -stö (collective noun)

lähe-	near	**lähistö**	neighbourhood
saari	island	**saaristo**	archipelago
enempi	more	**enemmistö**	majority
vähempi	less	**vähemmistö**	minority
elin	organ	**elimistö**	organism
kasvi	plant	**kasvisto**	flora
maa	earth, country, land	**maasto**	terrain
laiva	ship	**laivasto**	fleet

-tar ~ -tär (feminine noun)

kuningas	king	**kuningatar**	queen
Pariisi	Paris	**pariisitar**	Parisian woman
laulaja	singer	**laulajatar**	female singer
myyjä	salesman	**myyjätär**	saleswoman

-ton ~ -tön (adjective, indicating 'without')

koti	home	**koditon**	homeless
nimi	name	**nimetön**	nameless
onni	happiness	**onneton**	unhappy
työ	work	**työtön**	unemployed
lapsi	child	**lapseton**	childless
tunne	feeling	**tunteeton**	unfeeling

-(u)us ~ -(y)ys (abstract noun)

heikko	weak	**heikkous**	weakness
vahva	strong	**vahvuus**	strength
terve	healthy	**terveys**	health
suuri	great	**suuruus**	greatness
korkea	high	**korkeus**	height
kaunis	beautiful	**kauneus**	beauty
isä	father	**isyys**	fatherhood, paternity
nuori	young	**nuoruus**	youth
ystävä	friend	**ystävyys**	friendship
yksinäinen	lonely	**yksinäisyys**	loneliness
syytön	innocent	**syyttömyys**	innocence
varovainen	cautious	**varovaisuus**	caution
lihava	fat	**lihavuus**	corpulence

PART B

First infinitive		Derived word	

-e (noun)

loista/a	shine	loiste	lustre
katso/a	look	katse	look
kasta/a	wet, dip	kaste	dew
puhu/a	speak	puhe	speech
sata/a	rain	sade	rain
toivo/a	hope	toive	hope, wish, expectation

-i (noun)

syöttä/ä	feed	syötti	bait
kasva/a	grow	kasvi	plant
paista/a	roast	paisti	roast meat
kasvatta/a	bring up, educate	kasvatti	foster child
muista/a	remember	muisti	memory

-in (noun, indicates instrument)

avat/a	open	avain	key
puhel/la	talk, chat	puhelin	telephone
soitta/a	play	soitin	(musical) instrument
pakasta/a	freeze	pakastin	freezer

-ja ~ -jä (noun, indicates agent)

myy/dä	sell	myyjä	seller
saa/da	get	saaja	receiver
anta/a	give	antaja	giver
kalasta/a	fish	kalastaja	angler
laula/a	sing	laulaja	singer
teh/dä	do	tekijä	doer, maker, author
palvel/la	serve	palvelija	servant
ol/la	be	olija	one who is
tunte/a	know	tuntija	connoisseur

-maton ~ -mätön (negative adjective)

kuol/la	die	kuolematon	immortal
ol/la	be	olematon	non-existent
asu/a	live	asumaton	uninhabited
koke/a	experience	kokematon	unexperienced
lyö/dä	hit, beat	lyömätön	unbeaten, unbeatable
näh/dä	see	näkemätön	unseeing, unseen

First infinitive		*Derived word*	
-nta ~ -ntä (noun)			
hankki/a	get, obtain	**hankinta**	acquisition
etsi/ä	look for	**etsintä**	search
kysy/ä	ask	**kysyntä**	demand
ampu/a	shoot	**ammunta**	shooting
-nti (noun)			
saa/da	get	**saanti**	catch
tuo/da	bring, import	**tuonti**	import
vie/dä	take, export	**vienti**	export
myy/dä	sell	**myynti**	sale
tupakoi/da	smoke	**tupakointi**	smoking
-nto ~ -ntö (noun)			
asu/a	live	**asunto**	residence
käyttä/ä	use	**käytäntö**	practice
luo/da	create	**luonto**	nature
-o ~ -ö (noun)			
jaka/a	divide	**jako**	division
huuta/a	shout	**huuto**	shout
lentä/ä	fly	**lento**	flight
levät/ä	rest	**lepo**	rest
lähte/ä	leave	**lähtö**	departure
teh/dä	do	**teko**	a deed, act
pelät/ä	fear	**pelko**	fear
tietä/ä	know	**tieto**	knowledge
näh/dä	see	**näkö**	sight
kuul/la	hear	**kuulo**	hearing
-os ~ -ös (noun, often indicates result of an action)			
kiittä/ä	thank	**kiitos**	thanks
osta/a	buy	**ostos**	purchase
tul/la	come	**tulos**	result
pettä/ä	deceive	**petos**	deceit
kääntä/ä	turn; translate	**käännös**	turn; translation
piirtä/ä	draw	**piirros**	drawing

First infinitive   *Derived word*

-ri (noun, indicates agent)

leipo/a	bake	**leipuri**	baker
aja/a	drive	**ajuri**	driver, cabby
kulke/a	go, walk	**kulkuri**	tramp
taiko/a	conjure, use magic	**taikuri**	conjurer, magician

-u ~ -y (noun)

alka/a	begin	**alku**	beginning
iske/ä	strike	**isku**	blow, stroke
itke/ä	cry	**itku**	crying
kylpe/ä	bathe	**kylpy**	bath
maksa/a	pay	**maksu**	payment
laula/a	sing	**laulu**	song
käske/ä	command	**käsky**	command
sur/ra	grieve	**suru**	sorrow, grief

-us ~ -ys (noun)

avat/a	open	**avaus**	opening
hengittä/ä	breathe	**hengitys**	breathing
kuljetta/a	transport	**kuljetus**	transportation
metsästä/ä	hunt	**metsästys**	hunting
kirjoitta/a	write	**kirjoitus**	writing, article
kalasta/a	fish	**kalastus**	fishing
puolusta/a	defend	**puolustus**	defence

-uu (noun)

palat/a	return	**paluu**	return
taat/a	guarantee	**takuu**	guarantee
kerjät/ä	beg	**kerjuu**	begging
kaivat/a	long for	**kaipuu**	longing
kehrät/ä	spin	**kehruu**	spinning

-vainen ~ -väinen (adjective)

opetta/a	teach, instruct	**opettavainen**	instructive
tyyty/ä	be satisfied	**tyytyväinen**	satisfied
kuol/la	die	**kuolevainen**	mortal
säästä/ä	save	**säästäväinen**	economical, thrifty
usko/a	believe	**uskovainen**	religious

§93.2 VERBAL SUFFIXES

New verbs can be derived from both verbs and nominals. Deverbal verbs are much more common than denominal ones. The abundance of deverbal verbal suffixes is in fact one of the distinguishing features of Finnish, compared to the Indo-European languages.

First infinitive   *Derived word*

-ahta- ~ -ähtä- (momentary verb)

haukku/a	bark	**haukahtaa**	give a bark
laula/a	sing	**laulahtaa**	sing for a moment
horju/a	stagger	**horjahtaa**	stagger ('once')
istu/a	sit	**istahtaa**	sit down

-aise- ~ -äise- (momentary verb)

kysy/ä	ask	**kysäistä**	pop a question
niel/lä	swallow	**nielaista**	gulp down
vetä/ä	pull	**vetäistä**	give a pull

-ele- ~ -ile- (frequentative verb)

aja/a	drive	**ajella**	drive around
astu/a	step	**astella**	step, walk around
kysy/ä	ask	**kysellä**	ask repeatedly
katso/a	look	**katsella**	look, watch
kalasta/a	fish	**kalastella**	be fishing
kiistä/ä	deny, contest	**kiistellä**	dispute, quarrel

-ksi- (frequentative verb)

ime/ä	suck	**imeksiä**	be sucking
kulke/a	go	**kuljeksia**	stroll
tunke/a	press, shove	**tungeksia**	be crowding

-skele- (frequentative verb)

etsi/ä	look for	**etsiskellä**	be searching
ime/ä	suck	**imeskellä**	be sucking
ol/la	be	**oleskella**	stay, be staying
oppi/a	learn	**opiskella**	study

-skentele- (frequentative verb)

myy/dä	sell	**myyskennellä**	be selling
käy/dä	go	**käyskennellä**	stroll about

First infinitive   *Derived word*

-tta- ~ **-ttä-** (causative verb)

teh/dä	do	**teettää**	have ... done
pes/tä	wash	**pesettää**	have ... washed
kasva/a	grow (up)	**kasvattaa**	grow, bring up
elä/ä	live	**elättää**	support, provide for

-u- ~ **-y-** (reflexive verb)

löytä/ä	find	**löytyä**	be found
siirtä/ä	move, transfer	**siirtyä**	move, be transferred
tunte/a	feel, know	**tuntua**	feel, be felt, seem
vaihta/a	change	**vaihtua**	change, be changed
tyhjentä/ä	empty	**tyhjentyä**	empty
rakasta/a	love	**rakastua**	fall in love
pelasta/a	save	**pelastua**	be saved
muutta/a	move, change	**muuttua**	be changed

-utu- ~ **-yty-** (reflexive verb)

kerät/ä	collect	**keräytyä**	collect, be collected
elä/ä	live	**eläytyä**	enter into the spirit of
vaivat/a	trouble	**vaivautua**	bother, take the trouble
jättä/ä	leave	**jättäytyä**	surrender
peri/ä	inherit	**periytyä**	be inherited
tunke/a	press, shove	**tunkeutua**	force one's way

-ile- (expresses continuity)

aika	time	**aikailla**	delay
pyörä	wheel	**pyöräillä**	cycle
nyrkki	fist	**nyrkkeillä**	box
teltta	tent	**telttailla**	go camping
pallo	ball	**palloilla**	play ball

-oi- ~ **-öi-** (expresses continuity)

tupakka	cigarette	**tupakoida**	smoke
elämä	life	**elämöidä**	make a noise
ikävä	longing	**ikävöidä**	long for, miss
hedelmä	fruit	**hedelmöidä**	bear fruit
isäntä	master, host	**isännöidä**	be in charge, act as host

-t-: **-ne-** (expresses change)

halpa	cheap	**halvet/a** **halpene-**	become cheaper

First infinitive		Derived word	
huono	bad	**huono<u>t</u>/a**	become worse
		huono<u>ne</u>-	
lyhyt	short	**lyhe<u>t</u>/ä**	become shorter
		lyhe<u>ne</u>-	
kylmä	cold	**kylme<u>t</u>/ä**	become colder
		kylme<u>ne</u>-	
tumma	dark	**tumme<u>t</u>a**	become darker
		tumme<u>ne</u>-	

-ta- ~ -tä-

mitta	measure	**mitata**	measure
naula	nail	**naulata**	nail
höylä	plane	**höylätä**	plane
kuva	picture	**kuvata**	describe
hauta	grave	**haudata**	bury

-tta- ~ -ttä-

koulu	school	**kouluttaa**	educate, train
lippu	flag	**liputtaa**	put out flags
vero	tax	**verottaa**	tax
puukko	sheath knife	**puukottaa**	stab

-u- ~ -y- (reflexive verb)

kuiva	dry	**kuivua**	(become) dry
tippa	drop	**tippua**	drip
ruoste	rust	**ruostua**	rust
kostea	damp	**kostua**	get damp

§94 COMPOUNDING

The most common type of compound word is made up of two non-derived nouns. In the following examples, the = symbol indicates internal word boundaries. Typical compounds are written without spaces.

kirja=kauppa	bookshop
vesi=pullo	water-bottle
pallo=peli	ball game
kirje=kuori	envelope ('letter=cover')
kivi=katu	paved street ('stone=street')
kivi=kausi	stone age
kirves=varsi	axe handle
keittiö=kone	kitchen machine, appliance

The first noun of these compounds is often in the genitive, e.g.:

meren=ranta	seashore (cf. **meri** 'sea')
kirjan=kansi	book cover (cf. **kirja** 'book')
auton=ikkuna	car window (cf. **auto** 'car')
avaimen=reikä	keyhole (cf. **avain** 'key')

The components of a compound may also be derived words themselves:

kaiv/in=kone	excavator, digging machine
lävist/ys=kone	punching-machine
pes/u=kone	washing-machine
kone=apu/lainen	machine operator
te/o/llis/uus=tuo/ta/nto	industrial ('industry') production

Also fairly common are compounds with more than two elements, such as:

maa=talo/us=tuo/ta/nto	agricultural production
el/o=kuva=te/o/llis/uus	film industry
huone=kalu=tehdas	furniture factory
koti=tarve=myynti	household sale
kauppa=tase=vaja/us	deficit in the balance of trade
täyde/nn/ys=koulu/t/us=kys/el/y	further training inquiry
el/in=keino=tulo=vero=laki	law concerning the taxation of earned income

Structurally rather complex compounds are formed when one of the elements is a deverbal noun and/or a word inflecting in a local case:

työn=saa/nti=mahdollis/uus	chance of finding work
tode/llis/uuden=hahmo/tta/mis=kyky	ability to give shape to reality
oman=voiton=pyy/nti	self-interest
jäsen=hanki/nta=kampanja	campaign to recruit members
nuoteista=laulu=taito	ability to sing at sight
hallituksessa=ol/o=aika	period ('being') in the government
pysä/hty/mis=merkin=ant/o=nappi	button giving the stop signal

Structures of this type are quite common and productive, particularly in the written language; compare also this example:

prahassa=käy/mä/ttöm/yys=kompleksi
complex about not having been to Prague

Such complex compounds often correspond to complete sentences. There are also many compound adjectives, especially with a derived adjective as the second element:

asian=muka/inen	appropriate
saman=koko/inen	of the same size

ala=ikä/inen	under-age
vapaa=miel/inen	liberal-minded
lyhyt=sana/inen	taciturn, curt, brief
moni=mutka/inen	complicated
suomen=kiel/inen	Finnish-speaking
kansan=taju/inen	popular, easily comprehensible
kansain=väli/nen	international
pitkä=aika/inen	long, long-term

The first element of a two-part compound may occasionally differ from the basic form. This is particularly the case with nominals ending in **-nen** (§20.1); in compounds these have the same stem as in the partitive singular, for example:

kokonais=valta/inen	holistic (cf. **kokonainen** 'whole')
nais=suku=puoli	female sex (cf. **nainen** 'woman')
yksityis=kohta/inen	detailed (cf. **yksityinen** 'individual')
yleis=kieli	standard language (cf. **yleinen** 'general')
ihmis=kunta	mankind (cf. **ihminen** 'man')
hevos=paimen	horse herder (cf. **hevonen** 'horse')

Other special cases include:

suur=piirteinen	large-scale; broad-minded (cf. **suuri** 'great')
kolmi=vuot/ias	three-year-old (cf. **kolme** 'three')
neli=vuot/ias	four-year-old (cf. **neljä** 'four')

There are not many compound verbs in Finnish. Note however:

alle=kirjoittaa	sign
kokoon=panna	put together
laimin=lyödä	neglect
läpi=käydä	go through
yllä=pitää	maintain, keep up
jälleen=vakuuttaa	reinsure

22 THE COLLOQUIAL SPOKEN LANGUAGE

- *General*
- *Omission and assimilation of sounds*
- *Differences of form*

§95 GENERAL

This book has so far been primarily concerned with the grammar of standard Finnish, which is predominantly a written form of the language. However, few Finns actually keep strictly to this norm in their speech; it is mostly heard in official, more or less 'solemn' situations in which most Finns rarely, if ever, find themselves (speeches, sermons, radio and TV newsreading, rituals such as the opening of Parliament, often in teaching, etc.).

The norms or rules of this spoken standard language are very close to those of the written language. One often hears the claim that 'Finnish is spoken the same way as it is written'. But this is not literally true. The claim refers to the correspondence between letters and phonemes (§5): one and the same phoneme regularly corresponds to each letter, and vice versa.

In everyday situations not many Finns express themselves in speech exactly as they would in writing. The grammar of colloquial spoken Finnish differs in many ways from that of the written standard and the official spoken form based on this, both in pronunciation and in morphology and syntax.

It is not therefore in any way 'bad Finnish'; it is merely a form of the language used in different situations. In the same way, there have long existed regional dialects which also differ from the (written or spoken) standard language, e.g. the south-western dialects, the Häme dialects, the south-eastern dialects and the northern dialects.

During the past few decades, however, spoken Finnish has been going through a critical transition period caused by rapid changes in society. The most important of these changes have been: the postwar resettlements; changes in the structure of the economy, followed by migration from the countryside and urbanization (particularly the rise of Greater Helsinki); the influence of a uniform, increasingly longer and more thorough education, narrowing not only class differences but also language differences; the nationwide influence of radio and TV; and the linguistically unifying effect of popular light literature.

The birth of Greater Helsinki, the Helsinki-based broadcasting media and the status of the capital city have given rise to a widespread form of free spoken Finnish. Many of the features of this spoken language are nevertheless of older stock, originating e.g. in the western dialects of the province of Uusimaa.

Typical of this colloquial speech are certain omissions and assimilations of sounds (§96) and a number of morphological and syntactic features (§97) which are extremely common, especially in the speech of the younger generation.

§96   OMISSION AND ASSIMILATION OF SOUNDS

There are several omissions and assimilations which are particularly common in the colloquial spoken language. In the examples that follow, the colloquial spoken language is compared with the 'official' pronunciation of the standard language.

(1) The final vowels **-i** and **-a**, **-ä** are dropped (and a preceding long consonant is shortened) in certain endings, of which the most important are the inessive case ending **-ssa** ~ **-ssä**, the elative **-sta** ~ **-stä**, the adessive **-lla** ~ **-llä**, the ablative **-lta** ~ **-ltä**, the translative **-ksi**, the second person singular possessive suffix **-si**, the conditional **-isi** and the past tense **-s/i**.

'Official' pronunciation		*Colloquial pronunciation*
talossa	in the house	**talos**
meressä	in the sea	**meres**
talosta	out of the house	**talost**
merestä	out of the sea	**merest**
autolla	by car	**autol**
häneltä	from him	**hänelt**
vanhaksi	to (become) old	**vanhaks**
autosi	your car	**autos**
hän tulisi	he would come	**hän tulis**
Pekka sanoisi	Pekka would say	**Pekka sanois**
meillä on	we have	**meil on**
Tuula heräsi	Tuula woke	**Tuula heräs**

(2) The final **-i** of diphthongs (e.g. **ai**, **oi**, **ui**, **äi**) is dropped in unstressed syllables. This also often applies to the **-i** of the past tense and the first vowel of the conditional ending **-isi**.

punainen	red	**punanen**
sellainen	such	**sellanen**
semmoinen	such	**semmonen**
tuommoinen	that kind of	**t(u)ommonen**

'Official' pronunciation		Colloquial pronunciation
Kalle sanoi	Kalle said	**Kalle sano**
Pertti kantoi	Pertti carried	**Pertti kanto**
hän kestäisi	he would endure	**hän kestäs**
Keijo antaisi	Keijo would give	**Keijo antas**

(3) When **-a** and **-ä** occur after a vowel they often assimilate to the preceding vowel, producing a long vowel (**ea** and **eä** become **ee**, **oa** becomes **oo**, etc.).

kauhea	terrible	**kauhee**
nopean	fast (genitive)	**nopeen**
tärkeä	important	**tärkee**
kulkea	go	**kulkee**
en rupea	I do/will not begin	**en rupee**
väkeä	people (partitive)	**väkee**
taloa	house (partitive)	**taloo**
varoa	look out	**varoo**

(4) The final **-t** of the past participle **-nut ~ -nyt** is dropped, or assimilates to the following consonant.

olen sanonut	I have said	**olen sanonu**
olen sanonut sen	I have said it	**olen sanonus sen**
Pekka on tullut	Pekka has come	**Pekka on tullu**
Pekka on tullut jo	Pekka has already come	**Pekka on tulluj jo**

(5) In some words **-d-** is dropped or changes to **-j-**.

meidän	our	**meijän**
teidän	your	**teijän**
tehdään	one does	**tehään**

(6) **-n-** and **-l-** are occasionally dropped in the verbs **ole-** 'be', **mene-** 'go', **pane-** 'put', **tule-** 'come'.

olen	I am	**oon**
olemme	we are	**oomme**
menen	I go	**meen**
tulet	you (sing.) come	**tuut**
tulette	you (pl.) come	**tuutte**

§97   DIFFERENCES OF FORM

Some differences of form are closely related to the omissions and assimilations mentioned above (§96).

(1) Many common pronoun forms are shortened in the colloquial spoken language.

'Official' pronunciation		*Colloquial pronunciation*
minä	I	**mä**
minun	my	**mun**
minulla	'at' me	**mul(la)**
minulle	to me	**mulle**
sinä	you	**sä**
sinun	your	**sun**
sinulla	'at' you	**sul(la)**
tämä	this	**tää**
tämän	of this	**tän**
tuo	that	**toi**
tuon	of that	**ton**
tuolla	there	**tuol**
nuo	those	**noi**

(2) Many numerals become much shorter.

yksi	1	**yks**
kaksi	2	**kaks**
viisi	5	**viis**
kuusi	6	**kuus**
seitsemän	7	**seittemän**
kahdeksan	8	**kaheksan**
yhdeksän	9	**yheksän**
yksitoista	11	**ykstoist**
viisitoista	15	**viistoist**
kaksikymmentä	20	**kaksky(n)t**
kuusikymmentäviisi	65	**kuusky(n)tviis**
seitsemänkymmentäkahdeksan	78	**seiskytkaheksan**

(3) First and second person possessive suffixes are often dropped, and the corresponding pronouns are shortened (§36).

(minun) kirja/ni	my book	**mun kirja**
(sinun) kirja/si	your (sing.) book	**sun kirja**
(meidän) kirja/mme	our book	**meijän kirja**
(teidän) kirja/nne	your (pl.) book	**teijän kirja**

(4) The third person plural ending of finite verbs is not used, being replaced by the third person singular ending (§24). In addition, the pronoun **ne** 'those' often replaces **he** 'they', and similarly in the singular **se** 'it' replaces **hän** 'he, she'.

he tule/vat	they come	**ne tulee**

'Official' pronunciation		*Colloquial pronunciation*
he anta/vat	they give	**ne antaa**
he mene/vät	they go	**ne menee**

(5) The passive forms (§69–71) are used instead of the first person plural ending **-mme**.

me sano/mme	we say	**me sanotaan**
me sano/i/mme	we said	**me sanottiin**
me sano/isi/mme	we would say	**me sanottais(iin)**
sano/kaamme	let us say	**sanotaan**
emme sano	we do not say	**me ei sanota**
emme sano/neet	we did not say	**me ei sanottu**
emme sano/isi	we would not say	**me ei sanottais(i)**
me mene/mme	we go	**me mennään**
me men/i/mme	we went	**me mentiin**
me men/isi/mme	we would go	**me mentäis(iin)**
men/käämme	let us go	**mennään**
emme mene	we do not go	**me ei mennä**
emme men/neet	we did not go	**me ei menty**
emme men/isi	we would not go	**me ei mentäis(i)**
emme ol/isi men/neet	we would not have gone	**me ei oltais menty**

(6) The interrogative particle **-ko** ~ **-kö** often takes the form **-ks** (§30.1).

onko(s) teillä	do you have?	**onks teill**
palaako täällä	is it burning here?	**palaaks tääl**
vienkö minä	shall I take?	**vienks mä**

(7) The ending **-ma-** ~ **-mä-** of the third infinitive illative (§77) is often dropped.

mennään nukku/ma/an	let's go to sleep	**mennään nukkuun**
lähden tanssi/ma/an	I'm going dancing	**lähen tanssiin**
tuletkos kävele/mä/än	are you coming for a walk ('to walk')?	**tuuks käveleen**

The case ending **-Vn** then assimilates to the last vowel of the stem, e.g. **nukku/un**.

APPENDIX 1: INFLECTION TABLES

NOMINALS

	Singular	Plural	Singular	Plural
Nom.	talo	talot	kauppa	kaupat
Gen.	talon	talojen	kaupan	kauppojen
Part.	taloa	taloja	kauppaa	kauppoja
Iness.	talossa	taloissa	kaupassa	kaupoissa
Elat.	talosta	taloista	kaupasta	kaupoista
Illat.	taloon	taloihin	kauppaan	kauppoihin
Adess.	talolla	taloilla	kaupalla	kaupoilla
Ablat.	talolta	taloilta	kaupalta	kaupoilta
Allat.	talolle	taloille	kaupalle	kaupoille
Ess.	talona	taloina	kauppana	kauppoina
Transl.	taloksi	taloiksi	kaupaksi	kaupoiksi

	Singular	Plural	Singular	Plural
Nom.	tunti	tunnit	käsi	kädet
Gen.	tunnin	tuntien	käden	käsien
Part.	tuntia	tunteja	kättä	käsiä
Iness.	tunnissa	tunneissa	kädessä	käsissä
Elat.	tunnista	tunneista	kädestä	käsistä
Illat.	tuntiin	tunteihin	käteen	käsiin
Adess.	tunnilla	tunneilla	kädellä	käsillä
Ablat.	tunnilta	tunneilta	kädeltä	käsiltä
Allat.	tunnille	tunneille	kädelle	käsille
Ess.	tuntina	tunteina	kätenä	käsinä
Transl.	tunniksi	tunneiksi	kädeksi	käsiksi

	Singular	Plural	Singular	Plural
Nom.	kieli	kielet	liike	liikkeet
Gen.	kielen	kielten	liikkeen	liikkeiden
Part.	kieltä	kieliä	liikettä	liikkeitä
Iness.	kielessä	kielissä	liikkeessä	liikkeissä
Elat.	kielestä	kielistä	liikkeestä	liikkeistä
Illat.	kieleen	kieliin	liikkeeseen	liikkeisiin
Adess.	kielellä	kielillä	liikkeellä	liikkeillä
Ablat.	kieleltä	kieliltä	liikkeeltä	liikkeiltä
Allat.	kielelle	kielille	liikkeelle	liikkeille
Ess.	kielenä	kielinä	liikkeenä	liikkeinä
Transl.	kieleksi	kieliksi	liikkeeksi	liikkeiksi

	Singular	Plural	Singular	Plural
Nom.	ihminen	ihmiset	ajatus	ajatukset
Gen.	ihmisen	ihmisten	ajatuksen	ajatusten
Part.	ihmistä	ihmisiä	ajatusta	ajatuksia
Iness.	ihmisessä	ihmisissä	ajatuksessa	ajatuksissa
Elat.	ihmisestä	ihmisistä	ajatuksesta	ajatuksista
Illat.	ihmiseen	ihmisiin	ajatukseen	ajatuksiin
Adess.	ihmisellä	ihmisillä	ajatuksella	ajatuksilla
Ablat.	ihmiseltä	ihmisiltä	ajatukselta	ajatuksilta
Allat.	ihmiselle	ihmisille	ajatukselle	ajatuksille
Ess.	ihmisenä	ihmisinä	ajatuksena	ajatuksina
Transl.	ihmiseksi	ihmisiksi	ajatukseksi	ajatuksiksi

	Singular	Plural	Singular	Plural
Nom.	taivas	taivaat	rengas	renkaat
Gen.	taivaan	taivaiden	renkaan	renkaiden
Part.	taivasta	taivaita	rengasta	renkaita
Iness.	taivaassa	taivaissa	renkaassa	renkaissa
Elat.	taivaasta	taivaista	renkaasta	renkaista
Illat.	taivaaseen	taivaisiin	renkaaseen	renkaisiin
Adess.	taivaalla	taivailla	renkaalla	renkailla
Ablat.	taivaalta	taivailta	renkaalta	renkailta
Allat.	taivaalle	taivaille	renkaalle	renkaille
Ess.	taivaana	taivaina	renkaana	renkaina
Transl.	taivaaksi	taivaiksi	renkaaksi	renkaiksi

	Singular	Plural	Singular	Plural
Nom.	hyvyys	hyvyydet	avain	avaimet
Gen.	hyvyyden	hyvyyksien	avaimen	avaimien
Part.	hyvyyttä	hyvyyksiä	avainta	avaimia
Iness.	hyvyydessä	hyvyyksissä	avaimessa	avaimissa
Elat.	hyvyydestä	hyvyyksistä	avaimesta	avaimista
Illat.	hyvyyteen	hyvyyksiin	avaimeen	avaimiin
Adess.	hyvyydellä	hyvyyksillä	avaimella	avaimilla
Ablat.	hyvyydeltä	hyvyyksiltä	avaimelta	avaimilta
Allat.	hyvyydelle	hyvyyksille	avaimelle	avaimille
Ess.	hyvyytenä	hyvyyksinä	avaimena	avaimina
Transl.	hyvyydeksi	hyvyyksiksi	avaimeksi	avaimiksi

	Singular	Plural	Singular	Plural
Nom.	työtön	työttömät	askel	askelet
Gen.	työttömän	työttömien	askelen	askelien
Part.	työtöntä	työttömiä	askelta	askelia
Iness.	työttömässä	työttömissä	askelessa	askelissa
Elat.	työttömästä	työttömistä	askelesta	askelista
Illat.	työttömään	työttömiin	askeleen	askeliin
Adess.	työttömällä	työttömillä	askelella	askelilla
Ablat.	työttömältä	työttömiltä	askelelta	askelilta

	Singular	Plural	Singular	Plural
Allat.	työttömälle	työttömille	askelelle	askelille
Ess.	työttömänä	työttöminä	askelena	askelina
Transl.	työttömäksi	työttömiksi	askeleksi	askeliksi
Nom.	kolmas	kolmannet	suurempi	suuremmat
Gen.	kolmannen	kolmansien	suuremman	suurempien
Part.	kolmatta	kolmansia	suurempaa	suurempia
Iness.	kolmannessa	kolmansissa	suuremmassa	suuremmissa
Elat.	kolmannesta	kolmansista	suuremmasta	suuremmista
Illat.	kolmanteen	kolmansiin	suurempaan	suurempiin
Adess.	kolmannella	kolmansilla	suuremmalla	suuremmilla
Ablat.	kolmannelta	kolmansilta	suuremmalta	suuremmilta
Allat.	kolmannelle	kolmansille	suuremmalle	suuremmille
Ess.	kolmantena	kolmansina	suurempana	suurempina
Transl.	kolmanneksi	kolmansiksi	suuremmaksi	suuremmiksi

	Singular	Plural
Nom.	suurin	suurimmat
Gen.	suurimman	suurimpien
Part.	suurinta	suurimpia
Iness.	suurimmassa	suurimmissa
Elat.	suurimmasta	suurimmista
Illat.	suurimpaan	suurimpiin
Adess.	suurimmalla	suurimmilla
Ablat.	suurimmalta	suurimmilta
Allat.	suurimmalle	suurimmille
Ess.	suurimpana	suurimpina
Transl.	suurimmaksi	suurimmiksi

VERBS

SANO/A VERBS

FINITE FORMS

Indicative

	Affirmative		*Present active* *Negative*	
Singular				
1	sanon	I say	en sano	I do not say
2	sanot	you say	et sano	you do not say
3	sanoo	he/she says	ei sano	he/she does not say

Affirmative		*Negative*	
Plural			
1 sanomme		emme sano	
2 sanotte		ette sano	
3 sanovat		eivät sano	

Passive

sanotaan	one says	ei sanota	

Past active

Singular			
1 sanoin	I said	en sanonut	I did not say
2 sanoit		et sanonut	
3 sanoi		ei sanonut	

Plural			
1 sanoimme		emme sanoneet	
2 sanoitte		ette sanoneet	
3 sanoivat		eivät sanoneet	

Passive

sanottiin		ei sanottu	

Perfect active

Singular			
1 olen sanonut	I have said	en ole sanonut	I have not said
2 olet sanonut		et ole sanonut	
3 on sanonut		ei ole sanonut	

Plural			
1 olemme sanoneet		emme ole sanoneet	
2 olette sanoneet		ette ole sanoneet	
3 ovat sanoneet		eivät ole sanoneet	

Passive

on sanottu		ei ole sanottu	

Pluperfect active

Singular			
1 olin sanonut	I had said	en ollut sanonut	I had not said
2 olit sanonut		et ollut sanonut	
3 oli sanonut		ei ollut sanonut	

Plural			
1 olimme sanoneet		emme olleet sanoneet	
2 olitte sanoneet		ette olleet sanoneet	
3 olivat sanoneet		eivät olleet sanoneet	

Affirmative	*Negative*
Passive	
oli sanottu	ei ollut sanottu

Conditional

Present active

Singular

1 sanoisin	I would say	en sanoisi	I would not say
2 sanoisit		et sanoisi	
3 sanoisi		ei sanoisi	

Plural

1 sanoisimme		emme sanoisi
2 sanoisitte		ette sanoisi
3 sanoisivat		eivät sanoisi

Passive

sanottaisiin	ei sanottaisi

Perfect active

Singular

1 olisin sanonut	I would have said	en olisi sanonut	I would not have said
2 olisit sanonut		et olisi sanonut	
3 olisi sanonut		ei olisi sanonut	

Plural

1 olisimme sanoneet		emme olisi sanoneet
2 olisitte sanoneet		ette olisi sanoneet
3 olisivat sanoneet		eivät olisi sanoneet

Passive

olisi sanottu	ei olisi sanottu

Imperative

Present active

Singular

2 sano	say	älä sano	do not say
3 sanokoon		älköön sanoko	

Plural

1 sanokaamme		älkäämme sanoko
2 sanokaa		älkää sanoko
3 sanokoot		älkööt sanoko

Affirmative		*Negative*	
Passive			
sanottakoon		älköön sanottako	

Potential

Present active

Singular

1	sanonen	I may say	en sanone	I may not say
2	sanonet		et sanone	
3	sanonee		ei sanone	

Plural

1	sanonemme	emme sanone	
2	sanonette	ette sanone	
3	sanonevat	eivät sanone	

Passive

sanottaneen	ei sanottane

Perfect active

Singular

1	lienen sanonut	I may have said	en liene sanonut	I may not have said
2	lienet sanonut		et liene sanonut	
3	lienee sanonut		ei liene sanonut	

Plural

1	lienemme sanoneet	emme liene sanoneet	
2	lienette sanoneet	ette liene sanoneet	
3	lienevät sanoneet	eivät liene sanoneet	

Passive

lienee sanottu	ei liene sanottu

NON-FINITE FORMS

Infinitives

First inf.	sanoa	to say
	sanoakseni	
Second inf.	sanoessa	
	sanoen	
Third inf.	sanomaan	
	sanomassa	
	sanomasta	
	sanomalla	
	sanomatta	

Participles

	Present	
Active	sanova	saying
Passive	sanottava	that must be said

	Past	
Active	sanonut	said
Passive	sanottu	said

HYPÄT/Ä VERBS

FINITE FORMS

Indicative

Present active

Affirmative		*Negative*	
Singular			
1 hyppään	I jump	en hyppää	I do not jump
2 hyppäät		et hyppää	
3 hyppää		ei hyppää	
Plural			
1 hyppäämme		emme hyppää	
2 hyppäätte		ette hyppää	
3 hyppäävät		eivät hyppää	
Passive			
hypätään		ei hypätä	

Past active

Singular			
1 hyppäsin	I jumped	en hypännyt	I did not jump
2 hyppäsit		et hypännyt	
3 hyppäsi		ei hypännyt	
Plural			
1 hyppäsimme		emme hypänneet	
2 hyppäsitte		ette hypänneet	
3 hyppäsivät		eivät hypänneet	
Passive			
hypättiin		ei hypätty	

Perfect active

Singular

1	olen hypännyt	I have jumped	en ole hypännyt	I have not jumped
2	olet hypännyt		et ole hypännyt	
3	on hypännyt		ei ole hypännyt	

Plural

1	olemme hypänneet	emme ole hypänneet
2	olette hypänneet	ette ole hypänneet
3	ovat hypänneet	eivät ole hypänneet

Passive

on hypätty	ei ole hypätty

Pluperfect active

Singular

1	olin hypännyt	I had jumped	en ollut hypännyt	I had not jumped
2	olit hypännyt		et ollut hypännyt	
3	oli hypännyt		ei ollut hypännyt	

Plural

1	olimme hypänneet	emme olleet hypänneet
2	olitte hypänneet	ette olleet hypänneet
3	olivat hypänneet	eivät olleet hypänneet

Passive

oli hypätty	ei ollut hypätty

Conditional

Present active

Singular

1	hyppäisin	I would jump	en hyppäisi	I would not jump
2	hyppäisit		et hyppäisi	
3	hyppäisi		ei hyppäisi	

Plural

1	hyppäisimme	emme hyppäisi
2	hyppäisitte	ette hyppäisi
3	hyppäisivät	eivät hyppäisi

Passive

hypättäisiin	ei hypättäisi

Perfect active

Singular
1 olisin hypännyt   I would have   en olisi hypännyt   I would not have
                     jumped   jumped
2 olisit hypännyt   et olisi hypännyt
3 olisi hypännyt   ei olisi hypännyt

Plural
1 olisimme hypänneet   emme olisi hypänneet
2 olisitte hypänneet   ette olisi hypänneet
3 olisivat hypänneet   eivät olisi hypänneet

Passive
   olisi hypätty   ei olisi hypätty

Imperative

Present active

Singular
2 hyppää   jump   älä hyppää   do not jump
3 hypätköön   älköön hypätkö

Plural
1 hypätkäämme   älkäämme hypätkö
2 hypätkää   älkää hypätkö
3 hypätkööt   älkööt hypätkö

Passive
   hypättäköön   älköön hypättäkö

Potential

Present active

Singular
1 hypännen   I may jump   en hypänne   I may not jump
2 hypännet   et hypänne
3 hypännee   ei hypänne

Plural
1 hypännemme   emme hypänne
2 hypännette   ette hypänne
3 hypännevät   eivät hypänne

Passive
   hypättäneen   ei hypättäne

Perfect active

Singular

1	lienen hypännyt I may have	en liene hypännyt I may not have
	jumped	jumped
2	lienet hypännyt	et liene hypännyt
3	lienee hypännyt	ei liene hypännyt

Plural

1	lienemme hypänneet	emme liene hypänneet
2	lienette hypänneet	ette liene hypänneet
3	lienevät hypänneet	eivät liene hypänneet

Passive

lienee hypätty	ei liene hypätty

NON-FINITE FORMS

Infinitives

First inf.	hypätä	to jump
	hypätäkseni	
Second inf.	hypätessä	
	hypäten	
Third inf.	hyppäämään	
	hyppäämässä	
	hyppäämästä	
	hyppäämällä	
	hyppäämättä	

Participles

		Present
Active	hyppäävä	jumping
Passive	hypättävä	

		Past
Active	hypännyt	
Passive	hypätty	

SAA/DA VERBS

FINITE FORMS

Indicative

Present active

	Affirmative		*Negative*	
Singular				
1	saan	I get	en saa	I do not get
2	saat		et saa	
3	saa		ei saa	
Plural				
1	saamme		emme saa	
2	saatte		ette saa	
3	saavat		eivät saa	
Passive				
	saadaan		ei saada	

Past active

Singular				
1	sain	I got	en saanut	I did not get
2	sait		et saanut	
3	sai		ei saanut	
Plural				
1	saimme		emme saaneet	
2	saitte		ette saaneet	
3	saivat		eivät saaneet	
Passive				
	saatiin		ei saatu	

Perfect active

Singular				
1	olen saanut	I have got	en ole saanut	I have not got
2	olet saanut		et ole saanut	
3	on saanut		ei ole saanut	
Plural				
1	olemme saaneet		emme ole saaneet	
2	olette saaneet		ette ole saaneet	
3	ovat saaneet		eivät ole saaneet	
Passive				
	on saatu		ei ole saatu	

Pluperfect active

Singular

1	olin saanut	I had got	en ollut saanut	I had not got
2	olit saanut		et ollut saanut	
3	oli saanut		ei ollut saanut	

1 olin saanut   I had got   en ollut saanut   I had not got
2 olit saanut   et ollut saanut
3 oli saanut   ei ollut saanut

Plural

1 olimme saaneet   emme olleet saaneet
2 olitte saaneet   ette olleet saaneet
3 olivat saaneet   eivät olleet saaneet

Passive

  oli saatu   ei ollut saatu

Conditional

Present active

Singular

1 saisin   I would get   en saisi   I would not get
2 saisit   et saisi
3 saisi   ei saisi

Plural

1 saisimme   emme saisi
2 saisitte   ette saisi
3 saisivat   eivät saisi

Passive

  saataisiin   ei saataisi

Perfect active

Singular

1 olisin saanut   I would have   en olisi saanut   I would not have
                  got   got
2 olisit saanut   et olisi saanut
3 olisi saanut   ei olisi saanut

Plural

1 olisimme saaneet   emme olisi saaneet
2 olisitte saaneet   ette olisi saaneet
3 olisivat saaneet   eivät olisi saaneet

Passive

  olisi saatu   ei olisi saatu

Imperative

Present active

Singular
2	saa	get	älä saa	do not get
3	saakoon		älköön saako	

Plural
1	saakaamme		älkäämme saako
2	saakaa		älkää saako
3	saakoot		älkööt saako

Passive
saatakoon	älköön saatako

Potential

Present active

Singular
1	saanen	I may get	en saane	I may not get
2	saanet		et saane	
3	saanee		ei saane	

Plural
1	saanemme		emme saane
2	saanette		ette saane
3	saanevat		eivät saane

Passive
saataneen	ei saatane

Perfect active

Singular
1	lienen saanut	I may have got	en liene saanut	I may not have got
2	lienet saanut		et liene saanut	
3	lienee saanut		ei liene saanut	

Plural
1	lienemme saaneet		emme liene saaneet
2	lienette saaneet		ette liene saaneet
3	lienevät saaneet		eivät liene saaneet

Passive
lienee saatu	ei liene saatu

NON-FINITE FORMS

Infinitives

First inf.	saada	to get
	saadakseni	
Second inf.	saadessa	
	saaden	
Third inf.	saamaan	
	saamassa	
	saamasta	
	saamalla	
	saamatta	

Participles

	Present	
Active	saava	getting
Passive	saanut	

	Past	
Active	saatava	
Passive	saatu	

TARVIT/A VERBS

FINITE FORMS

Indicative

Present active

Affirmative		*Negative*	
Singular			
1 tarvitsen	I need	en tarvitse	I do not need
2 tarvitset		et tarvitse	
3 tarvitsee		ei tarvitse	
Plural			
1 tarvitsemme		emme tarvitse	
2 tarvitsette		ette tarvitse	
3 tarvitsevat		eivät tarvitse	
Passive			
tarvitaan		ei tarvita	

Past active

Singular

1 tarvitsin   I needed   en tarvinnut   I did not need
2 tarvitsit   et tarvinnut
3 tarvitsi   ei tarvinnut

Plural

1 tarvitsimme   emme tarvinneet
2 tarvitsitte   ette tarvinneet
3 tarvitsivat   eivät tarvinneet

Passive

  tarvittiin   ei tarvittu

Perfect active

Singular

1 olen tarvinnut   I have needed   en ole tarvinnut   I have not needed
2 olet tarvinnut   et ole tarvinnut
3 on tarvinnut   ei ole tarvinnut

Plural

1 olemme tarvinneet   emme ole tarvinneet
2 olette tarvinneet   ette ole tarvinneet
3 ovat tarvinneet   eivät ole tarvinneet

Passive

  on tarvittu   ei ole tarvittu

Pluperfect active

Singular

1 olin tarvinnut   I had needed   en ollut tarvinnut I had not needed
2 olit tarvinnut   et ollut tarvinnut
3 oli tarvinnut   ei ollut tarvinnut

Plural

1 olimme tarvinneet   emme olleet tarvinneet
2 olitte tarvinneet   ette olleet tarvinneet
3 olivat tarvinneet   eivät olleet tarvinneet

Passive

  oli tarvittu   ei ollut tarvittu

Conditional

Present active

Singular

1 tarvitsisin	I would need	en tarvitsisi	I would not need
2 tarvitsisit		et tarvitsisi	
3 tarvitsisi		ei tarvitsisi	

Plural

1 tarvitsisimme		emme tarvitsisi
2 tarvitsisitte		ette tarvitsisi
3 tarvitsisivat		eivät tarvitsisi

Passive

tarvittaisiin	ei tarvittaisi

Perfect active

Singular

1 olisin tarvinnut	I would have needed	en olisi tarvinnut	I would not have needed
2 olisit tarvinnut		et olisi tarvinnut	
3 olisi tarvinnut		ei olisi tarvinnut	

Plural

1 olisimme tarvinneet		emme olisi tarvinneet
2 olisitte tarvinneet		ette olisi tarvinneet
3 olisivat tarvinneet		eivät olisi tarvinneet

Passive

olisi tarvittu	ei olisi tarvittu

Imperative

Present active

Singular

2 tarvitse	need	älä tarvitse	do not need
3 tarvitkoon		älköön tarvitko	

Plural

1 tarvitkaamme		älkäämme tarvitko
2 tarvitkaa		älkää tarvitko
3 tarvitkoot		älkööt tarvitko

Passive

tarvittakoon	älköön tarvittako

Potential

Present active

Singular

1 tarvinnen	I may need	en tarvinne	I may not need
2 tarvinnet		et tarvinne	
3 tarvinnee		ei tarvinne	

Plural

1 tarvinnemme		emme tarvinne	
2 tarvinnette		ette tarvinne	
3 tarvinnevat		eivät tarvinne	

Passive

tarvittaneen   ei tarvittane

Perfect active

Singular

1 lienen tarvinnut	I may have needed	en liene tarvinnut	I may not have needed
2 lienet tarvinnut		et liene tarvinnut	
3 lienee tarvinnut		ei liene tarvinnut	

Plural

1 lienemme tarvinneet		emme liene tarvinneet	
2 lienette tarvinneet		ette liene tarvinneet	
3 lienevät tarvinneet		eivät liene tarvinneet	

Passive

lienee tarvittu   ei liene tarvittu

NON-FINITE FORMS

Infinitives

First inf.	tarvita
	tarvitakseni
Second inf.	tarvitessa
	tarviten
Third inf.	tarvitsemaan
	tarvitsemassa
	tarvitsemasta
	tarvitsemalla
	tarvitsematta

Participles

		Present
Active	tarvitseva	needing
Passive	tarvinnut	

		Past
Active	tarvittava	
Passive	tarvittu	

APPENDIX 2: LITERATURE

Aaltio, Maija-Hellikki. *Finnish for Foreigners.* I (twelfth edition), II (fourth edition). Otava, Helsinki 1999. (Elementary Finnish for beginners (I) and more advanced students (II).)

Abondolo, Daniel. *Colloquial Finnish: The Complete Course for Beginners.* Routledge, London & New York 1998.

Branch, Michael, Antero Niemikorpi and Pauli Saukkonen. *A Student's Glossary of Finnish.* WSOY, Helsinki 1980. (The central vocabulary of Finnish in the light of frequency-based studies.)

Hakulinen, Auli and Fred Karlsson. *Nykysuomen lauseoppia.* Third edition. Suomalaisen Kirjallisuuden Seura, Helsinki 1995. (Comprehensive scholarly description of the syntax of modern Finnish.)

Hämäläinen, Eila. *Aletaan! Suomen kielen oppikirja vasta-alkajille.* Fifteenth edition. Helsingin yliopiston suomen kielen laitos, Helsinki 2000. (Elementary Finnish for beginners.)

Hämäläinen, Eila. *Jatketaan! Suomen kielen oppikirja alkeet osaaville.* Ninth edition. Helsingin yliopiston suomen kielen laitos, Helsinki 1998. (Finnish for advanced students.)

Karlsson, Fred. *Suomen kielen äänne-ja muotorakenne.* WSOY, Helsinki 1983. (Comprehensive scholarly description of the phonology and morphology of modern Finnish.)

Lepäsmaa, Anna-Liisa and Leena Silfverberg. *Suomen kielen alkeisoppikirja.* Seventh edition. Finn Lectura, Helsinki 1999. (Elementary Finnish for beginners.)

Nuutinen, Olli. *Suomea suomeksi.* I (twelfth edition), II (eighth edition). Suomalaisen Kirjallisuuden Seura, Helsinki 2000, 1997. (Elementary Finnish for beginners (I) and more advanced students (II).)

Saukkonen, Pauli, Marjatta Haipus, Antero Niemikorpi and Helena Sulkala. *Suomen kielen taajuussanasto.* WSOY, Helsinki 1979. (Frequency dictionary of Finnish.)

Silfverberg, Leena. *Harjoituskirja suomen kielen perusopetusta varten.* Fifth edition. Finn Lectura, Helsinki 1998. (Practice-based book for beginners.)

Silfverberg, Leena. *Harjoituskirja suomen kielen jatko-opetusta varten.* Fifth edition. Finn Lectura, Helsinki 2000. (Practice-based book for advanced students.)

Silfverberg, Leena. *Suomen kielen jatko-oppikirja.* Fifth edition. Finn Lectura, Helsinki 2000. (Finnish for advanced students.)

White, Leila. *From Start to Finnish: A Short Course in Finnish.* Finn Lectura, Helsinki 2000. (Elementary Finnish for beginners.)

White, Leila. *Suomen kielioppia ulkomaalaisille.* Finn Lectura, Helsinki 1997. (Practice-based Finnish grammar.)

APPENDIX 3: SOME RELEVANT INTERNET ADDRESSES (AS OF JUNE, 2000)

Note: you find an operational up-to-date version of these links under my home page at:
http://www.ling.helsinki.fi/~fkarlsso/finlinks.htm

http://www.helsinki.fi/~tasalmin/fu.html
  Tapani Salminen: Names and classification of Finno-Ugrian languages
http://www.helsinki.fi/hum/sugl/kulonen/Finf13uk.htm
  Ulla-Maija Kulonen: The origin of Finnish and related languages
http://www.finland.org/finbks.html
  Books about Finnish as a foreign language
http://www.hut.fi/~jkorpela/Finnish.html
  Jukka Korpela: Information concerning Finnish
http://eunuch.ddg.com/LIS/InfoDesignF97/paivir/finnish/sitemap.html
  Päivi Rentz: Introduction to Finnish
http://www.ling.helsinki.fi/~fkarlsso/genkau2.html
  A Finnish noun has more than 2,000 forms, want to see an example?
http://www.lingsoft.fi/cgi-pub/fintwol
  Lingsoft's automatic morphological analyzer FINTWOL (here you can get an analysis of any Finnish word-form!)
http://dictionaries.travlang.com/FinnishEnglish/
  Travlang's small Finnish-English online dictionary
http://www.freedict.com/onldict/fin.html
  On-line English to Finnish dictionary
http://finland.cimo.fi/studyingfinnish/index.htm
  Studying Finnish in Finland and abroad
http://www.domlang.fi
  Research Center for the Languages of Finland
http://www.helsinki.fi/hum/skl/
  Department of Finnish, University of Helsinki
http://www.helsinki.fi/~jolaakso/sgrlinkit.html#skl
  Other departments of Finnish

http://www.helsinki.fi/hum/sugl/
Department of Finno-Ugrian Studies, University of Helsinki
http://www.edu.fi/koulut/yliopistot.html
Finnish universities
http://www.finlit.fi/
Finnish Literature Society
http://hul.helsinki.fi/tilke/indexeng.html
Front Page of Finnish Research Libraries
http://www.publiclibraries.fi/
Front Page of Finnish Public Libaries
http://www.stat.fi/index.html
Statistics Finland
http://www.ling.helsinki.fi/~fkarlsso/links-5.html
A selection of archives and databases in Finland
http://www.ling.helsinki.fi/~fkarlsso/kuvatietokanta.htm
Some picture databases in Finland
http://www.ling.helsinki.fi/~fkarlsso/links-8.html
Science-related organizations in Finland
http://www.lingsoft.fi/
Lingsoft: language technology for Finnish
http://www.lysator.liu.se/nordic/scn/faq41.html#index
Finland: Basic facts
http://www.vn.fi/vn/english/index.htm
The Finnish Council of State
http://ky.hkkk.fi/~k21206/finhist.html#rus
Pasi Kuoppamäki: A web history of Finland
http://www.utu.fi/agricola/e/
Agricola - The Finnish History Network
http://www.kaapeli.fi/flf/index.html
Finnish Literature Forum
http://virtual.finland.fi/finfo/english/kirjaeng.html
Esko Häkli: the birth of Finnish literature
http://www.fng.fi/
Finnish National Gallery
http://www.fimic.fi/
Finnish Music Information Centre
http://www.yle.fi/aanilevysto/firs/index.htm
Finnish Institute of Recorded Sound
http://www.mek.fi/
Finnish Tourist Board
http://personal.inet.fi/private/hovi.pages/sa-int/
The Finnish army in World War II
http://www.sauna.fi/pages/index.htm
The Finnish Sauna Society
http://www.lysator.liu.se/nordic/scn/faq46.html#top
Finnish Sauna
http://www.ling.helsinki.fi/~fkarlsso/
Home page of the author

SUBJECT INDEX

(Numbers refer to sections: §)